The Disenchantment of the World

NEW FRENCH THOUGHT

SERIES EDITORS
Thomas Pavel and Mark Lilla

TITLES IN THE SERIES

Mark Lilla, ed., *New French Thought: Political Philosophy*

Gilles Lipovetsky, *The Empire of Fashion: Dressing Modern Democracy*

Pierre Manent, *An Intellectual History of Liberalism*

Jacques Bouveresse, *Wittgenstein Reads Freud: The Myth of the Unconscious*

Blandine Kriegel, *The State and the Rule of Law*

Alain Renault, *The Era of the Individual: A Contribution to a History of Subjectivity*

Marcel Gauchet, *The Disenchantment of the World: A Political History of Religion*

Marcel Gauchet

The Disenchantment of the World

A POLITICAL HISTORY OF RELIGION

Translated by Oscar Burge

With a Foreword by Charles Taylor

 NEW FRENCH THOUGHT

PRINCETON UNIVERSITY PRESS · PRINCETON, NEW JERSEY

Copyright © 1997 by Princeton University Press
Published by Princeton University Press, 41 William Street,
Princeton, New Jersey 08540
In the United Kingdom: Princeton University Press, Chichester, West Sussex

Translated from the French edition of Marcel Gauchet, Le desenchantement du monde
(Paris: © Editions Gallimard, 1985)

Library of Congress Cataloging-in-Publication Data

Gauchet, Marcel, 1938–
[Désenchantement du monde. English]
The disenchantment of the world : a political history of religion / Marcel Gauchet ;
translated by Oscar Burge ; with a foreword by Charles Taylor.
p. cm.—(New French thought)
Includes bibliographical references and index.
ISBN 0-691-04406-6 (alk. paper)
1. Religion. 2. Religions. 3. Religion and politics. 4. Civilizations, Secular.
I. Title. II. Series.
BL48.G3413 1997
200--dc21   97-20046 CIP

Published with the assistance of the French Ministry of Culture

This book has been composed in Adobe Bauer Bodoni

Princeton University Press books are printed on acid-free paper and meet the guidelines
for permanence and durability of the Committee on Production Guidelines for Book
Longevity of the Council on Library Resources

Printed in the United States of America

10 9 8 7 6 5 4 3 2 1

Contents

Part Two: THE APOGEE AND DEATH OF GOD

CHRISTIANITY AND WESTERN DEVELOPMENT

CHAPTER 5

CHAPTER 6

Foreword

BY CHARLES TAYLOR

1.

Tʜɪꜱ ʙᴏᴏᴋ ʙᴇʟᴏɴɢꜱ to a type that is all too rare these days. By setting out a global theory of religion, of its history and transformations, Marcel Gauchet has attempted something that forebears once dared, but that today seems nearly impossible in face of the immense accumulation of historical and social scientific scholarship. The author knows full well the risks he is running. But he argues, rightly I believe, that by never spelling out the big picture we have become unconscious of our ultimate assumptions, and in the end confused about them. While recognizing how fragile these large theories are and himself drawing on an immense range of specialized research (of which the footnotes give only a partial idea), Marcel Gauchet embarks on his ambitious project, convinced that we need theory on this scale, if only to define precisely our views. Otherwise we will be like "dwarfs who have forgotten to climb on the shoulders of giants." For having undertaken this courageous enterprise, the community of thinkers and scholars is greatly in his debt.

This book is about religion, but it is also about what people often call "secularization." In other words, Gauchet tries to understand religion in terms of "the exit from religion," to grasp the phenomenon from the standpoint of those who have lived through its demise. There is a clear debt to Weber here, as the title implies. But when people talk about 'secularization,' they can mean a host of different things. In one sense, the word designates the decline of religious belief and practice in the modern world, the declining numbers who enter church, or who declare themselves believers. In another, it can mean the retreat of religion from the public space, the steady transformation of our institutions toward religious and ideological neutrality, their shedding of a religious identity.

There are two ranges of phenomena here, distinct but in some ways linked; and that obviously has suggested two kinds of theories. One makes the decline in personal belief the motor, and explains the secularization of public space as a consequence of it; the other reverses the relation, and sees the changing place of religion in social life as the crucial factor, and the retreat of individual belief as flowing from it. The first

kind of theory, focusing as it does on beliefs, has given an important role
to the rise of science. Science, it has been said, has displaced religion,
made the old creeds incredible, and that is what has transformed public
life. The crisis felt by many believing Christians in the nineteenth century after the publication of Darwin's theories is taken as a paradigm expression of the process at work. But this kind of view has tended to give
way in the twentieth century to theories of the second sort. The influence
of Durkheim was important here. On this view, religion is more than just
a set of beliefs. It is a pattern of practices that gives a certain shape to
our social imaginary. Religion—or, as Durkheim liked to put it, the
sense of the sacred—is the way we experience or belong to the larger social whole. Explicit religious doctrines offer an understanding of our
place in the universe and among other human beings, because they reflect what it is like to live in this place. Religion, for Durkheim, was the
very basis of society. Only by studying how society hangs together, and
the changing modes of its cohesion in history, will we discover the dynamic of secularization.

Gauchet's theory is situated in this Durkheiman tradition, but he has
very considerably transformed it. The earlier, belief-centered theories, he
seems to argue, understated the difference between the ages of faith and
the secular present. Durkheim allows for a fundamental transformation
between societies with different principles of cohesion, but he stresses the
continuity of belief, treating modern secular societies as having their own
"religion," e.g., that of the rights of man. For Gauchet, the transformation was much more fundamental. Living in a religious society involved
a very different way of being than we know in our secular age. The failure to see this comes, he believes, from the mistaken way we think of this
development as "development." That is, we tend to think of religion itself as unfolding its potentialities when it moves from being "primitive"
and mutates into one of the "higher religions."

Gauchet proposes that we reverse this story. As he understands religion, it was at its most perfect, its most consistent and complete, precisely in its "primitive" stage. The move to higher forms during what
Jasper calls the "Axial period"—for instance, to Confucianism, Buddhism, Upanishadic doctrines, prophetic Judaism, and Platonic theoriz-
ing—introduced a break, an inner inconsistency, in the religious world.
They opened a breech through which the eventual exit from religion
came to be made. This exit was not inevitable (Gauchet is very much
aware of the extraordinary contingency evident time and again in this
history), but it can be said that the original breech was the necessary
condition of our world.

So Gauchet's story is not one of a development, moving to higher and
higher stages. Rather, it is a story of the breakdown of religion, a kind
of break-up through stages, which eventually gave us a social reality

quite opposite to the one that existed at the outset. This means that the rise of the secular age can be understood only to a limited degree as a linear unfolding of a previously existing potential, and that it is much more important to understand the unpredictable and unwanted byproducts of religious thought and practice that later arose.

2.

So what is Gauchet's basic idea of "religion"? He starts with reflections on what is specific to the human animal. A human being is one that reflects on itself and its situation, that does not simply take up a predetermined place but redefines it. The human being is not only reflective, he is also an agent. His crucial capacity is working on and transforming the world.

In relation to this distinctive potentiality, the original religious mode of being consisted in a sort of radical "dispossession." It projected us into a world in which the order was already irrevocably fixed in an earlier time of foundation, and each of us had an assigned place in this order that we could not repudiate. In this world, our defining potentialities were in a sense preemptively abandoned. There was no question of reflecting on who we were and how we fit in; no question of transforming the order of things. This is the sense of Gauchet's notion of "dispossession," a sort of renunciation of our potential, unconsciously carried through—presumably in order to foreclose the endless search for meaning, and to establish firmly the sense of reality.

To fill out this schema, Gauchet picks up on a number of features that recur in many early religious forms. There the world order is seen as established in a past "time of origins" (in Eliade's term) that is inaccessible to us except through ritual renewal. A crucial feature of our religious consciousness is in our relation to this unrecoverable past. By this very token, however, we are all on the same footing as members of human society. No one stands closer to this origin point than others; each has his or her role. Societies under this rule partake of a basic equality contained within a coherent whole. Each part, each role, has its meaning in relation to that totality.

For Gauchet, the rest of human history, what we normally call history, is the story of the breakup of this unity. This goes through several stages, the first of which seems to be the growth of the state. Early societies, those of unbreeched religion, have often been described as "stateless." Their basic equality took the form of a diffusion of power among different roles, held together by unchallengeable custom. Once something like state power arose—with Pharaohs in Egypt, say, or Stewards of the God in Mesopotamia—the equilibrium was broken. States concentrate power and exercise control; by nature they cannot be entirely guided by preexisting law or custom. State power cannot be innovative, especially when war between states leads to conquest and empire. The sacred web of order now mutates into a hierarchy. There are now people, or strata, that are closer to the invisible order than others. The Steward of the God, or the divine king, is the link by which the higher power of the Gods makes connection with society, and this power trickles down, as it were, through the hierarchical levels, to its lower levels.

In this sense, the dynamic of change for Gauchet seems to be political. Indeed, the drama of the actual exit from religion is largely recounted in terms of the development of the late-medieval and post-medieval European state. Where the primacy of the political seems harder to credit, however, is in between. The aforementioned "higher" religions of the Axial period all took the diffuse and variegated order of earlier religion tried to unify it under a transcendent supreme principle. This could be a supreme creator God, or some unified principles of order, like the Tao; or the endless cycle of Samsara, offering an escape beyond into Nirvana, or an order of Ideas unified by the Good. This meant that there was something beyond the order we live in. And this in turn changed the whole structure of religion, in several connected ways.

First of all, the order was no longer self-explanatory, but depended on a higher reality, or principle. Growth toward this higher reality then became possible, either through devotion or understanding. This in turn brought with it individuation, a turn toward the subject called as an individual to understand the Ideas, or approach God, or attain Enlightenment. This in turn meant that the holy was no longer in an irrecoverable past, and that there were ways of making contact with it, whether in receiving the revelation of God, or in grasping the Ideas. The relation to the past was no longer the all-important one.

Thus the religious order mutated. But it still seemed to have the crucial property of its original form. Humans were still dispossessed, in that the meanings of things was fixed in a given order, but now we could change our relation to it by becoming the servants of God, seeking Enlightenment, or grasping through reason the Ideas. And this is not without importance.

3.

The rest of the story essentially explains how certain forms arose, in which the favored way of approaching the highest reality (in this case, God) eventually wrought a destruction of the whole idea of sacred order. This is the story of the "religions that bring about the exit from religion," i.e., Judaism and then Christianity. In some aspects, this story—of how Judaism and later Christianity brought about disenchantment by attacking the notion of a sacred power in things and emptying the cosmos in order to confine the holy to God alone—has already been explored. But the way in which Gauchet sets it out in the second part of the book is highly original, and introduces some strikingly new and interesting ideas. I find particularly fascinating his account of the development of the modern state, which I mentioned above.

Following this, the second chapter of this second part gives an account of what it is to live in a postreligious age. The old Feuerbachian (and Marxist) idea, that humans return out of their religious and material alienations into a full possession of themselves, a kind of limpid self-understanding in freedom, is condemned by Gauchet as illusion. Our self-understanding and sense of agency still relate us to something "other," to something we do not understand and cannot transparently control. His attempt to work this idea out in relation to modern democratic self-rule is tremendously suggestive and interesting. Here in modern secular society is a form of life in which the key temporal dimension is the future, seen as something that we must shape. We are indeed at the antipodes of the original religious society, which was rivetted to the past. And yet the very nature of this controlling activity renders this future less and less definitely conceivable. Instead of being captured in a definite plan, it becomes "pure future."

Does this mean that religion is a thing of the past? Here a tension seems to emerge in Gauchet's conception. Throughout most of the book, 'religion' has meant the original socially embedded understanding of the universe as sacred order, in which humans are contained. But obviously, something has survived into the present that people also call 'religion,' namely personal faith and the collective practices it inspires. (Of course, once you move outside of the Atlantic zone, religion survives in a much more robust and traditional form. Gauchet is not at all unaware of this. Indeed, it is part of his central point that Christianity was the religion that first produced exit from religion, and so the postreligious world exists only in ex-Christendom.) Gauchet in no way wants to deny this survival of faith. He toys with the idea that it, too, might disappear, but avoids committing himself to this perilous prediction. But this issue raises the question of just what is meant by 'religion' in his discussion.

Throughout the book, 'religion' means a certain kind of shared way of life. Religion, we might say, is a form of culture. Obviously a functioning culture requires belief on the part of its members, so culture includes faith. When the culture dies, faith can be left as a residue in certain individuals. Is this the relationship Gauchet is assuming? In that case, one would predict the withering away of faith.

But the discussion in the very last section ("Le religieux apres la religion") seems to suggest another answer. Religion (the culture) preempted all those difficult questions about who we are and what is the meaning of things. With the end of this culture, these questions now cannot be avoided; and each individual is faced with them. This makes for a great unease. There are no easy answers to these questions, and so it is natural that people will search everywhere, quarrying, among other places, the religious ideas of the past. This suggests a picture, which in some ways meets contemporary experience, of a more and more fragmented and individual search for spirituality, in which the searchers are ever more mobile, not only in taking up exotic traditions, but also in altering their positions as time and experience dictate. On this view, personal religion or faith would be the attempt to answer the troubling questions that were preempted by religious culture, by picking fragments shored against the ruins of that culture, or other similar elements.

It is clear that we are dealing here with an atheist view of the matter. This is not to criticize Gauchet's approach, because it is impossible to address this whole matter while leaving the crucial question of the existence of God, or Nirvana, or whatever, totally in suspension. But it is here that I find his approach less than fully convincing, even—indeed, especially—in relation to the story he tells.

Some of the most crucial transformations in the forms of religious culture he records are due to the concerted actions of people moved by faith. The rise of Christianity is a striking example. The question must arise how these mutations in faith can be explained. Gauchet's approach seems to be that we can find the explanatory light we seek in the tensions that have arisen in the structures of religion: we saw, for instance, how the higher religions of the Axial period virtually pushed us toward an interiorized, reflective attempt to understand the single principle at the source of everything. But the nature of this push has to be further described. The tensions in the structure can only be understood in light of what the structures are doing for us, what the depth motivation was underlying the whole dispossessive move into religion. Otherwise put, we can only define the tensions in light of what we see as the point of the enterprise. For Gauchet, the point seems to have been to give meaning an absolutely firm and unchallengeable standing in our world. The tension that arose with the higher religions therefore came from the fact that they reintroduced questions that were meant to be closed.

But can the new departures in faith, of Buddha, of Jesus, or for that matter of St. Francis or St. Teresa, be understood simply in terms of the hunger for meaning? If the basic aim is just to make sense of it all, why is it that karuna or agape are so central to these traditions? Can the evolution at this level of detail be accounted for simply in terms of the structural tensions of "religion"? If so, then the explanatory primacy of these structures would indeed be vindicated. Faith would be merely a "dependent variable," flotsam on the sea of a postreligious age. But perhaps these mutations can only be explained by supposing that something like what they relate to—God, Nirvana—really exists. In that case, a purely cultural account of religion would be like Hamlet without the Prince.

While I opt for this second view, and hence cannot accept Gauchet's fundamental characterization of religion, this book is the living proof—if we still needed one—that you do not have to be ultimately right to make clear some truly profound and important features of our religious history, nor to open tremendously fruitful and exciting vistas for further exploration. No one interested in clarifying our thought about religion and the secular can afford to ignore this remarkable and original book.

The Disenchantment of the World

Introduction

Tʜɪs ʙᴏᴏᴋ is the sketch of a project. It does not claim to exhaust its topic, *the political history of religion*, but tries rather to determine its principles, scope and prospects.

The book's structure has been determined by the dual nature of its thesis. The first part claims that if we look beyond the still existing Churches and the abiding faith, we will see that the religious has reached the end of its life in the modern world. The second part claims that the modern Western world's radical originality lies wholly in its reincorporation, into the very heart of human relationships and activities, of the sacral element, which previously shaped this world from outside. Religion's demise is not to be ascertained by declining belief, but by the extent of the human-social universe's restructuring. Though this restructuring originated within religion, it escaped from and reversed its original religious orientation, and this reversal of the age-old organizing influence of the religious will be the book's main focus.

The current twilight of the gods highlights religion's former role in two ways: first, it shows how abandoning religion has distanced us from it; second, it shows how the metamorphosis still binds us to it. We cannot understand religion's origins and major developments unless we try to understand the enormous transformation which has shaped us and which came about through the *disenchantment of the world.* For Weber this expression specifically meant "the elimination of magic as a salvation technique." I do not believe that broadening it to mean the impoverishment of the reign of the invisible distorts this meaning. For as I will try to show, the disappearance of enchanters and powerful supernatural beings is only the superficial sign of a much deeper revolution in relations between heaven and earth, which decisively reconstructed the human abode separate from the divine. The true significance of the link between Protestantism and capitalism lies not in the influence of spiritual norms on worldly behavior, but in our interaction with the beyond and our investment in the here-below. Entrepreneurial asceticism is thus more an early indication of this movement than its exclusive expression. This perspective takes us far beyond capitalism and leads us to recognize Christianity's specificity as a major factor in our relations with nature, our forms of thought, mode of human coexistence and political organization. If our social order differs so radically from previous ones by hav-

ing successfully reversed heteronomy on every level, the seeds of this development are to be found in the unusual dynamic potentialities of the
spirit of Christianity. They provide a coherent focal point that allows us
to grasp the fundamental interdependence of such seemingly unrelated
phenomena as the rise of technology and the development of democracy.
Christianity proves to have been *a religion for departing from religion*.

For this reason, Christianity remains the most relevant religion in a
postreligious society, especially in Catholicism in Europe where, as distinct from America, Christianity has taken a stand against the world that
issued from it. Let me be quite clear: I am not proclaiming yet again the
death of the gods and the disappearance of their devotees. It is evident
that the City-State, including those who still believe in the gods, continues to exist without them. The gods have survived, but their power is
fading. However untroubled and prosperous they may appear, their real
source has irretrievably dried up. The functional necessity that from the
outset defined the content, determined the forms, and accelerated the development of religions, has been absorbed into the very mechanisms of
civilization. This process allows for the survival, in the personal sphere,
of a residue handed down as the legacy and influence of a rich tradition,
a residue that perhaps will never disappear and is by no means nonsen-
sical. It is a subjective link with the spirit of religion, which could be
used to contest my right to speak of an "end" of religion. My reply is that
there is no other suitable word for describing the disentanglement of
contemporary religious phenomena from their original reason for existence and from what has sustained their life, activity, and imagination
over thousands of years. What is currently alive in the Christian faith has
no connection with the circumstances surrounding its birth, the conditions that allowed it to assert itself and develop, or the role through
which its major themes and variations have been played out. Again, this
does not mean that its survival is in jeopardy. It does, however, mean
that we can only understand the phenomenon of the religious if we begin
by taking note of the irrevocable division separating its past from its
present. If we were to imagine an imminent miracle freeing the Polish
people from Soviet oppression, we could also imagine that Catholicism,
due to its role in safeguarding national identity, playing a spiritually
dominant part within the framework of a free government. The hopes
placed by the West in such reserves of religious fervor, and this model of
possible reconciliation between faith and democracy, are understandable.
We would nevertheless still be dealing with an *atheistic society*, made up
of and governed by a *believing majority*. Refusal to acknowledge the independence of faith and democracy results in serious misunderstandings,
which usually hinder the treatment of the subject. These misunderstandings are caused by retrospectively projecting *our own* extremely

psychological or sociological categorizations onto the history of religion, encouraging us to see a religious "sentiment" at work. Thus we may read into religion an existential response to the unavoidable horizon of death, while at the other extreme we may make religion an influencing force in social life, a retrospective "legitimating" factor, acting as guarantor for a clearly defined independent order. This is analogous both to the way in which our own avowals and beliefs are influential within a framework determined by other constraints, and to the way in which the private need to believe persists, even when collective belief is on the wane. All this is partly true, but is totally misleading if it is meant to account for the main thrust of the religious achievement, its place in the structure of previous societies, and its historical paths. Such interpretations are more pertinent to understanding its loss of status, and amount to mistaking its decline for its golden age. By taking religion to be what it is at the end of its reign, they prevent us from grasping it in its natural state, when it thoroughly informed how humans inhabited and organized the world.

To understand what used to be, we must give an accurate account of what no longer exists. There can be no agreement on what was once significant without a clear awareness of its current insignificance. Though I must emphasize the departure from religion, I do not wish to minimize retrospectively its importance, but rather to deal with it in such a way as to recognize its substantial constitutive influence in previous societies. It is worth pointing out that in this area skeptics have created as many barriers to understanding as believers. Believers are obliged to consider only the continuity of experience linking them to their tradition, and to ignore the social-historical circumstances of their common belief in favor of its timeless validity. Of course they admit that the faith previously carried more weight than it does now, but then add that this is a superficial phenomenon which has no bearing on its form and content. However, nonbelievers' uninvolvement does not equip them any better to deal with the problem. It can even lead them in similar fashion to deny any significance to the superstitious veils interposed between the human mind and its true nature. For such people, these veils are simply a sign of impotence revealing the limits of a development whose positive side must be sought elsewhere. Thus, the diametrically opposed standpoints of aloofness and passion, involvement and uninvolvement, hostility and partisanship conspire to deny the historical role of the religious.

We need look no further to understand the almost complete abandonment of the subject since Durkheim's and Weber's major but short-lived attempts. Hence the dual nature of my hypothesis. It is not enough to dispute the validity of the apologists' reconstruction dictated by faith, which tries to salvage the transhistorical perpetuity of *homo religiosus*, by relativizing its historical connections. We must also free ourselves from the atheist's illusion that religion may tell us something about the underlying psychology of the human race or about the workings of the savage mind, but tells us very little about the nature of the social bond and the real driving force behind history. The picture created by this groundless assumption is no less distorted than the first. It may even more effectively conceal what a society structured by religion is, and what religion itself is. I have tried to avoid both extremes. If this book was written by a nonbeliever convinced that it is possible to go beyond the age of religion, it was also written with the equally firm intention of maintaining a distance from the obtuse naivete of the lay tradition, by systematically attempting to empathize as much as possible with the seminal mystery of the religious outlook. Not without good reason has this outlook preoccupied our forefathers and dominated practically all of history. It is the expression of a fundamental option that even today resonates in our innermost being and whose imprint can be found in the very dispositions that have separated us from it. We have broken away from religion only by finding substitutes for it at every level. My primary concern is to recover the significance and coherence of this basic human option.

The difficulty with such an undertaking is that it sets us against our most entrenched notion and precomprehension of history. This notion, if I may put it in a crude form, identifies development with growth and, at a deeper level, with progression from an order to which we are *subjected* to one which we increasingly *will*. In this view, "naked man," completely powerless in the face of overwhelming natural forces, gradually secured, increased, and expanded the range of possible relations to his surroundings. As humanity multiplied, it saw its institutions develop to the point where slackening constraints, whether in our relations with objects or humans, seem to have been consciously planned. We once had nothing and were compelled to adapt to scarcity; but we have increasingly become the creators of our living conditions. We used to submit to the domination of our peers; now we recognize each other as free and equal contributors to the collective rule. In this scenario, religion would seem almost inevitably to be the intellectual correlate of our former natural powerlessness, while it is simultaneously acknowledged to be a means of indirectly surmounting a situation of extreme impoverishment. Man submitted to forces beyond him whose mysteriousness he overestimated, but by explaining them he somehow overcame what he submitted to.

The body of ideas I have just described is very deep-seated. It derives its legitimacy from many sources and simultaneously satisfies several requirements, not least that of common sense. And however outmoded it may appear, it still continues tacitly to influence discussions that claim to have freed themselves from it. But if we want to understand the religious, we must confront this body of ideas head on and not just dismiss it or denounce its one-sidedness. There is clearly conflict at the heart of human history between what is passively accepted and what is willed. But this is only half the picture. The part played by the willed is from the outset considerably greater than current paradigms would indicate. This is true to such an extent that we actually know only societies regulated by an overall comprehensive (unconscious) design in which all their segments and mechanisms meaningfully interact. We simply must learn to accept that this design may be diametrically opposed to the one we have been persuaded to regard as universal. An alternative paradigm is necessary here—one that does not exclude the previous one but allows us to recognize that the traits of civilization which we equate with the absence of development might *also* have completely different ends than development.

In other words, humanity is not oriented in only one direction. The human race undoubtedly has a stubborn tendency to increase its power and objectify its freedom, demonstrated as much by the way it dominates its environment as by its collective organization. But hidden in the depths of time is another humanity whose secret has been lost, and needs to be rediscovered, one that found a way to be at one with itself in its accepted dependency and its passive relation with the world. This is a complete reversal: we passively accept situations where our ancestors took the initiative; and we try to take the initiative where they were happy to submit. For if it is true that we initiate our world by creating it, we conversely submit to the changes thus unleashed. Consider, for instance, our attitude toward the mobility arising from the reign of freedom. There is complete reverence toward an order of things we take to be radically beyond our grasp, but in return for this we are assured of an absolutely stable position inside a universe whose structure is determined elsewhere— the guarantee of an inviolable accord with a Law. The order that has been presented as being passively accepted is at the same time one that we can immediately and willingly identify with, whereas the order we create is one where it is initially difficult to recognize ourselves and requires some effort to decipher—an order, moreover, whose effects we endure while having no control over them. This fundamental paradox contains the key to our entire history, for the essence of religion is both to gain self-possession by consenting to dispossession, by turning away from the goal of dominating nature and to legislate on our own behalf in favor of another goal, namely that of securing an identity defined and controlled at every step.

The study of "nonliterate" peoples provided the main challenge to the naive evolutionist model of history driven by growth. The disclosure of the existence of extremely sophisticated modes of social organization and of highly elaborate conceptual systems in populations with a "rudimentary" level of technical development has forced us to develop a more comprehensive schema. Nevertheless, our notion of history has remained largely influenced by the idea of a beginning. Levi-Strauss's approach provides the most striking example: though his masterly elucidation of procedural rules forces us to acknowledge mythical thought as fully fledged, he equates this thought with the "savage frame of mind," grasped in its natural state, before teleological considerations harnessed its activities. The religious viewpoint lets us radically revise this perspective. If we take primitive societies to be those organized almost entirely by submissive adaptation to external constraints, then such societies do not exist. There are, *a fortiori*, no primitive societies revealing humans in their pristine nakedness, as if they had just sprung into existence, prior to any cumulative civilizing effect on them and their surroundings by labor. Nothing in the pattern of living communities, either our own or others accessible to us, can give us the slightest idea of humans becoming human, of the "elementary forms" of their social and psychological life. We can never have any direct knowledge of this inaugural state either from near or afar.

A chasm separates us from our origins, one that science only serves to widen by making increasingly absurd conjectures about them. In fact, the most archaic human remains we possess come from fully civilized societies that clearly share a common history with us, and which undoubtedly share the same set of options as us. If I retain such terms as "savage" or "primitive" for understanding them, this is because there are no suitable alternatives, and because I feel it is better to adopt consciously a tradition that is open to criticism than to attempt to surpass it by conjuring up a new term. The main point, however, is that though I want to include these societies in my analysis, I also want to preserve the very sense of difference which, until recently, was responsible for their exclusion from history. We must be conscious of our similarity to them, but preserve the decisive discontinuity separating them from us which has for such a long time branded them as "other"—the most obvious difference being their lack of a State, while the main similarity lies in the role of religion. If we start from the point where the religious occupies the entire social space, including whatever will be subsequently taken over by the State, we can determine the source of these societies' differences from, and similarities to, our won. They are similar, in that their deepest organizational level arises from a distribution of the same elements

and dimensions as ours. They are radically different, in that this distribution is determined by goals completely opposed to ours.

From this angle, the emergence of the State clearly appears as the
main event in human history. It is not simply a stage in the progressive
differentiation of social functions and the stratification of status. Nor
does it represent an inexplicable phenomenon that suddenly appeared
and unfortunately destroyed a more natural and just order. It corresponds to a massive revision of the articulation of the human situation,
to a transformation in the strict sense of the word—all the elements in
the earlier arrangement will be found in the later one, but differently
connected and distributed. This logical redistribution had enormous
practical consequences. Though the systems on both sides of the "cata-
clysmic" rift may be formally equivalent, their embodiments in the real
world have nothing in common. This major shift resulted in an upheaval
that brought turmoil into the new world at both the material and spiritual level. This is where our five thousand years of "history-as-growth"
really began, a period that was ridiculously brief and amazingly swift
compared to the unimaginably long *duree* from which it arose. After
dozens of millennia with religion dominating politics, followed by five
millennia with politics dominating religion, we are at the point where religion has been systematically exhausted and its legacy has gradually disappeared. This should give some idea of the extent of the wrench we
have experienced, one from which we have barely begun to recover.

This entire process has usually been interpreted the wrong way
around. Many have wanted to see it as an evolutionary process by which
vague or rudimentary religious ideas have become more precise, profound, and systematic, a notion clearly the result of an optical illusion.
By looking at areas where religion has survived, from America to New
Guinea, we can form a concrete image of religion as it was in the beginning, in its purest and most systematic form, in the world prior to the
State. Though this image may not be totally reliable, burdened as it is
with unresolvable uncertainties, it presents in all its fragility a permanent challenge to our comfortable notions of what it means to be civilized. As soon as we enter the sphere of institutionalized domination, we
are inside a universe where religion's original radical core comes under
attack by being exposed to the action of mechanisms that alter the
prospects for life, thought, and action and whose impetus will continue
to shake and loosen its hold. The so-called "major religions" or "universal religions," far from being the quintessential embodiment of religion,
are in fact just so many stages of its abatement and disintegration. The
greatest and most universal of them, our own, the rational religion of the
one god, is precisely the one that allows a departure from religion. So we

must change our perspective. When dealing with religion, what appears to be an advance is actually a retreat. Fully developed religion existed before the bifurcation which, somewhere around 3000 BC in Mesopotamia and Egypt, plunged us into another religious world, one capable of existing without religion—our own.

So when I use the term "savages" to refer to those races with a primeval religion, I am using it with the original strong connotations that it would have had in the mouth of an official of the pharaohs or the Incas, referring to those troublemakers outside their borders who had "neither king nor law," a connotation adopted by Europeans from the sixteenth century onward. In this book primitive society is strictly understood not only as a society without a State, but as one *prior* to the State. It is important to be clear about this because of the hopelessly confused misunderstanding that the notion of "nonliterate peoples" conveys, owing to an unfortunate combination of academic compartmentalization with the legacy of a tradition that identifies the other by its deficiencies—in this case societies lacking our defining traits. Since they cannot write, we need a particular discipline, with its own methods of observation, to reconstruct what is inaccessible to us through normal archival methods. However, we must be careful: a society with a State may well be nonliterate, so this term may be applied to extremely diverse civilizations. This might appear to be a semantic quarrel, were it not that the deep-seated influence of this inherited classificatory framework has lead people to place societies arising from deeply differing historical strata on the same level. So, for the sake of a primitiveness they openly reject, people persist in lumping together realities where their basic divergence is what is instructive. This misunderstanding is usually accompanied by an interest in Africa, a continent shaped over a long period almost entirely by the State in a highly peculiar manner, even where its influence was indirect. African peoples are considered to be the touchstone for "precapitalist social formations" or for some sort of "mode of lineal production." To grasp the full extent of the confusion, we must note the contribution of Marxism, the last stage of ethnocentrism, which has a strong interest in enlisting these fateful recalcitrant beginnings into the ranks of the righteous cause of the forces of production. A salutary warning against the new obscurantism the social "sciences" are capable of producing.

·　·　·

If we want to discover the most fundamental matrix of choices underlying the religious option—and here I can do no more than offer a few suggestions—we would probably have to look for it in the constituting ambiguity of the experience of time, in the way in which our perception is divided between an "always already there," which reduces us to nothing, and a "yet to be realized," which throws us into the wide open space of action. On the one hand, if I may put a primal natural phenomenon in more readily accessible psychological terms, we always arrive on the scene *after* things have been determined, so we have no grasp of them and have no choice but to comply with their rules in order to become part of and lose ourselves in them. On the other hand, we find ourselves thrown into the world as originating beings for whom there is no before, which is why we are beings of *action* who cannot avoid changing ourselves and our surroundings, even when we try desperately not to, as we have done for the greatest part of our history. Starting from this primeval double-sidedness, everything takes place as if the human species has chosen to favor in turn one or the other of these temporal dispositions: either a bias in favor of the priority of the world and the law of things; or one in favor of the priority of humans and their creative activity: either submission to an order received in toto, determined before and outside our will; or responsibility for an order accepted as originating in the will of individuals who themselves are supposed to exist prior to the bond holding them together.

When I use the word choice, it should be understood that I am not talking about arbitrary decisions made in a vacuum. What I have in mind are some possibilities for coming to grips with a well-defined number of determining constraints. We are forced to classify them as choices, not because they are based on rational grounds or testify to the astonishing power of our instituting imagination, but because their very nature prevents us from relating them to the causes which determine their success. They neither fall from the sky nor arise from nothing, but are deeply embedded in a limited body of primordial conditions whose predetermined potentialities they cultivate—conditions affecting the definition of the overall collective structure. Take the choice for the absolute past mentioned above, a classic example of the appropriation and systematic use of a founding dimension which is still deeply meaningful for us, even if it no longer informs our societies' legitimation system. If we accept that things are as they are and should be, because they have been handed down from their origins as legacy of an unchanging tradition to be dutifully preserved, then the entire social organization makes its appearance along with this concrete self-determination in its relation to the *duree*. The result is a type of inscription in the natural world, a way of grouping beings, and a form of political bond and social relationship, including the conceptual structure. We are dealing with a core of basic possibilities regarding humans' relations with their equals, themselves and the world. My classification of time into two separate configurations is only one component of this core viewed from a certain angle, as part of a coherent whole, within a global self-understanding.

To put it bluntly another way: there is a transcendent element in history regulating a reflexive relation through which the human race actually chooses from a number of possible ways of being. When we deal with these few invariable axes that come to light through the major successive shapings of collective-being, we are touching on the very conditions of possibility for a human-social space, for a personal and collective identity. There are a range of factors that give us both our individual and social selves and which, for example, ensure that we are primally tied to others and concomitantly, that we are able to see ourselves from the other's viewpoint. They also give us the capacity to oppose ourselves, to impose our own rules, and they ensure that we exist within the compass of a power, inside communities whose constitution allows them to grasp themselves by separating out one of their members or a section of them. These examples are only simple illustrations. There is also another level, that of humans' relation to what enables them to exist in this way, where these founding dimensions and the different combinations they allow become the subject of a far-reaching choice controlling one or other of the major social forms history offers us. Such are the assumptions that ultimately justify both the procedure and object of this book. They justify the procedure, in that they legitimate a specific enquiry which goes behind the endless variety and extremely fluid nature of societies and cultures to the underlying organizing schemas, which have by turns defined the foundations and orientations of the human enterprise. They justify the object, because religions provide the obligatory entry point for an enquiry of this nature. They stretch across time to give us the key to the disposition of remote societies, and only through them can we access the logic of different configurations that has transformed the collective relation to those articulations, which in turn create a collective.

So despite the differences in customs and ways of being, the divergent mythologies and different modes of subsistence, we can reconstruct a coherent system of societies prior to the State, where religion does indeed play the central role—a role that in turn sheds light on its content and expressions. As I have already said, this system entails the radical anteriority of every ordering principle, and is thus a system of dispossession, inheritance, and immutability. Nothing we hold or do in everyday life derives from us but rather from beings who are other to us, from a different species that established it in earlier times. Our only function is to preserve their inviolable legacy and to repeat their sacred teaching. It is vital to understand that we are not dealing here with a variation of the religious phenomenon in a general sense, in the sense of reverence toward an external higher foundation, a variation that anecdotal and capricious mythical accounts of origins could lead us to consider naive. We are dealing with the logic of religion as seen in its extreme form and its most systematic structural embodiment. The only absolutely rigid and irreversible separation is that of the foundation's temporal separation, its relegation to a primordial past. The founding events and acts had already taken place, but they were at the same time destined to be endlessly perpetuated, both through rituals to revive them, and through filial piety demanding that the legacy be reproduced in every detail. Absolute separation from the original model is the vector of its absolute dictatorship. Only through the division between a seminal past and a derivative present was this dictatorship truly outside society and consequently able to command complete obedience. Once this religious exteriority occupied a space as a god-subject governing the world in the present, it was relativized rather than deepened. Such a god could be communicated with, his decrees interpreted, and the application of his laws negotiated. We were no longer within the framework of an order handed down unchanged in its original entirety. The power of some humans over others now removed part of religion's exclusive rule. Similarly we can see how, in a system where the legislative past is beyond reach, there was no place for politics, in the sense of society's active control over itself through a separated power, because that space was occupied by the reign of the original and the customary. No one among the living could justifiably claim a privileged connection with the invisible foundation as it did not need anyone to gain universal acceptance. This does not annul the role of the political but rather confines it to strict limits. Furthermore, this process of organizing submission through dispossession, rather than imposition, accounts for the manner in which origins are to be conceived and narrated. This is extremely difficult for us to fathom, contradicting as it does our habitual thought patterns, because it is an *explanation* that precludes us from getting close to what is being explained, i.e., from what we call *comprehension*. For us, to think something is to appropriate and identify with it. In the world of myth, on the other hand, the very act of thinking assumes we are separated from the cause of what we are thinking. Here the entire social order is gradually arranged according to this central articulation placing the present under the control of the absolute past. How then was religious dependence maximized? Primitive religion provides the answer: by distinguishing the present from an original state of affairs, which in turn justifies the present.

If I speak about religion *as such*, it is because I believe that all known religions can be understood in relation to the absolute nature of this primal disposition, whether they derive directly from that disposition or are a transformation of it. The bulk of this book is devoted to analyzing the origins and modes of this process. Its axial vector is in the first instance the action of the State, whose emergence can be regarded as the first religious revolution in history. This *de facto* revolution contains another strictly spiritual one, which redistributed the terms of the initial arrangement by incarnating amongst humans what had been separated from them. What was originally excluded became embodied within society, where the founding law now had its representatives, administrators, and interpreters. From now on, the linchpin of collective organization would be found in those representatives who were, on the one hand, in league with the invisible legislator and, on the other, at odds with the main part of humanity whose commandments and law they enforce. This will result in the systematic subversion of religious life: henceforth, political action and the notion of the divine will interact. All subsequent major spiritual and intellectual developments will arise from the contradictions between the inherited representations of the foundation, in whose name sovereignty is wielded, and the historical forms clothing its practice. The implicit thrust of the subjugating relationship, whether internal or external (conquest), is incompatible with the image of a legitimacy embedded in the past and borne by tradition. Fledgling States will profoundly remodel for their own purposes this image from previous societies. If domination was to be underpinned by religion, then deities with personal features had to be installed in the present, deities powerful enough to sustain the universal encompassing action that domination automatically takes as its natural outlook. On this basis, we can divide the history of religions into two main periods: one where the political order, by virtue of its spiritual potentialities, precedes the systems of sacred rites supposed to justify it. And a second one where, after these potentialities have come to fruition, religious organization, by virtue of its embryonic vision of the terrestrial city, precedes the established state of affairs it is supposed to legitimate. I believe that this crystallization of new possibilities brought about by the State's dynamics is the reason for the sudden appearance in the first millennium BC—in China, Greece, India, Iran and Israel—of the new conceptual instruments, divine figures, and feelings about the human condition that we still base our lives on. It adopted different expressions: philosophy's path is quite different from that of monotheistic faith and there is a great distance between Confucianism and Buddhism, Taoism and Zoroastrianism. Nevertheless, the fundamental elements, which were combined and used in different ways to produce an original configuration in each instance, remained essentially the same. Furthermore, implementing this process produced widely differing outcomes. There are two major paths: one compromised between maintaining the original religious structure and integrating new material—the path of oriental religions with the notion of being as a void; the other, directly opposed to it, was the radical path of subjectivizing the divine and structurally separating the physical from the spiritual. Though destined to turn the world upside down, this latter path, Jewish mono-

theism, was with good reason born in a tiny sliver of land situated between major civilizations and was initially extremely marginal. My major
concern in this book will be first to reconstruct Jewish monotheism from
the circumstances surrounding its first appearance to the deployment of
its long-term consequences; and then, to follow its development from
where Christianity takes over to the point where the seeds of terrestrial
autonomy contained within it come to fruition. This is the point where,
thanks to religion, a society with no further need for religion arises.

.   .   .

A few words on the idea of history accompanying my reconstruction of
the stages and transformations of the religious. Any originality it may
have lies in the way it combines two perspectives normally regarded as
incompatible: the uniformity of human development and the existence of
radical discontinuities within it. The word "uniformity" does not mean
continuity and does not mean that the same imperatives and ends have
always prevailed everywhere. Conversely, discontinuity does not necessarily involve an irreducible plurality of instances and configurations,
each one uniquely and impenetrably closed in on itself and the result of
the world's unpredictable vagaries.

When I single out some basic forms of collective establishment I am
not simply itemizing a number of highly speculative and unique "aspects
of being," whose disappearance and replacement is brought about by
spontaneous leaps that preclude our understanding them. These forms
are not random: they remain within a narrow circle of possibilities defined by necessity and have a universal significance allowing us to sym-
pathize and communicate with them from afar. For example, once we
become aware of the benefits of acquiring an identity and take into account the dispossessive effect of the power of change, submission to the
unchangeable becomes comprehensible. From a strictly logical point of
view all these forms are identical, in that the articulations and distribu-
tions of the basic terms of the collective-being created by them are formally interchangeable. But at the same time they have no "why or
wherefore." Though they are contained within each other there is no internal necessary transition from one to the other. Though they are all
highly motivated, all consistently controlled by entirely meaningful
choices, there is no determinist chain of ideas that could explain why one
rather than another of these ways of being was installed, or why it was
abandoned. Nothing compelled the human race to enter history by
denying its capacity to create history; nothing obliged it to partially tear
itself away from history through the arrival of the State; nor was there
anything which, once it has taken this step, would forcibly drag humans
to the stage where they had to change completely to a voluntary and

reflexive historical production. Just as nothing prevented their return to obeying the past and submitting to something higher than themselves.

This does not mean we should treat these transitions as products of pure human inventiveness to be accepted as inexplicable lest we distort them. We can most certainly follow them and illuminate their realization. I will give two, at this stage sketchy, attempts to elucidate the birth of monotheism, and the bifurcation in western societies, which point toward uncoupling the here-below from the beyond. We will see how it is possible to relate these two major upheavals to historical processes whose course can be understood by traditional methods—in other words, *essentially* indeterminable processes. In reconstructing them, we must take seriously the possibility that they might never have occurred. These historical changes are part of an enigmatic freedom at work in the midst of becoming; a freedom through which humans may unconsciously determine themselves and their self-consciousness; a freedom all the more enigmatic in that it makes us what we are through its primary function of applying constraints. If, as I believe, indetermination exists at the deepest level of history, its location has been quite clearly defined and can only be grasped from within its close association with the determinate.

.   .   .

Owing to the nature of its object, my programmatic account can hardly be anything more than a hybrid, halfway between an abstract delineation of the logic of major historical forms and a more detailed consideration of their historical embodiments. It tries both to establish a general framework of analysis and to illustrate how an approach mindful of the religious phenomenon's deep structure can advance our knowledge on some hitherto intractable issues. This approach will unavoidably produce imbalances and precariously interwoven perspectives: too little detail may be given to some major issues and too much attention to some minor ones. I openly acknowledge that this also lends a certain arbitrariness to my references, which have not been arranged systematically, but determined by the constraints of a selective probing necessitated by the encyclopedic scope of the enquiry. What I have brought together in these pages, as best I could, will subsequently have to be separated and investigated in two contrasting ways: on the one hand, by adopting a broader more abstract perspective; and on the other, by making closer contact with the complex thickness of the data of actual history. On one side lies the pure theory of the conditions of possibility for being-a-self and collective-being; on the other, there should be a more extensive investigation of some particularly representative instances of the manifestation and operation of the transcendental in the empirical realm, whether it concerns the watershed of Western Christianity's reformations,

the specific matrix of the Eastern spiritualities or savage peoples' reflexive and religious system.[1]

Let me assure the reader that I recognize the dangers of this enterprise
and the uncertainties involved in any superficial version of universal history. I am fully aware that things are "more complicated" than I have
presented them. I understand mistrust toward the genre "philosophy of
history" and I am aware of the damage caused by "ideas of totality." My
sole excuse for deliberately taking these risks is the need to understand
and my conviction these risks must be taken. This does not mean we
should yield to the lures of speculation, but that we should respond critically to the need for meaning whose main victims are those who naively
believe they have freed themselves from that need.

It is time to conduct a twofold reexamination: one relating to those
philosophers who claim to have freed us from the delusions of history,
the snares of reason, and the illusions of totality; another relating to the
current practice of the human sciences, and the constrictive intellectual
aporias resulting from their reaction to the ideal of a positive knowledge.
Though these two trends started out from opposed principles, their end
result has been the same: discrediting any attempt at a global orientation
on behalf of smallness, plurality, and marginality, accompanied by the
proliferation of specializations and the bureaucratic explosion of scholarship. These two dead ends have, in their various forms, greatly restricted our understanding. As far as "freeing" up thought is concerned,
it is easy to see that justifying the abyss, the deep mysteries of indeterminacy, of difference, of heterogeneity and similar nonsense, all depend
on a dogma mirroring the one they claim to free us from, except the new
dogma has the additional inconvenience of an extremely impoverished
heuristic. Moreover, a certain shortsighted confinement to the routine of
an increasingly narrowly defined domain clearly produces a situation
where results proliferate in inverse proportion to their interest, not to
mention significance. There can be no question of turning our backs on
the investigative methods developed over the last century by the new social disciplines. But it is no longer possible to dispense with the type of
theoretical and philosophical questioning they tried to avoid and believed they had broken with. We must preserve what they have taught us
about content and method while renewing ties with the "speculative"
and "totalizing" tradition they in fact failed to extinguish—to proscribe
and censure (Durkheim or Freud) here is a sham; Montesquieu or
Rousseau, Tocqueville or Marx still tell us more about society than all of
sociology combined. We can no longer be granted the luxury of peacefully cultivating our tiny gardens within the framework of a well-orga-
nized division of labor where our overall understanding of things is supposed to increase by systematically accumulating minutiae. We have all

PART ONE

The Metamorphoses of the Divine

THE ORIGIN, MEANING, AND DEVELOPMENT

OF THE RELIGIOUS

The Historicity of the Religious

Is THERE such a thing as a *religious function*, a subdivision of the *symbolic function*, which, along with speech and tools, organizes our relation to reality, and makes humanity's detour through the invisible the pivot of its activity? Is there a broad common bond between the religious sphere and social reality, whereby sacral otherness allows the group to found itself or expresses and institutes the essential superiority of collective-being over that of its individual members? The question of the relation between religion and society can essentially be stated in those terms.

Surely even raising these questions implies an affirmative answer. It is commonly admitted that the religious factor in history has a constant, if not invariable, quality making it a necessary precondition for the existence of a human society, whatever role we assign it in the primordial structuring of the collective sphere. It is a primordial phenomenon insofar as it can be found as far back as we go in human history; it is universal in that we do not know of any society which has escaped it; and it is recurrent, as can be seen by its influence in recent times in movements with thoroughly antireligious motives, such as the various totalitarian enterprises. All of which would indicate that we are faced here with one of those ultimate constraints inherent in collective-being, which will always remain and whose singular necessity we should try to discern behind its increasingly diverse manifestations.

I have adopted an interrogative approach because I believe the time has come to question widely accepted theories and to reinterpret the irrefutable data behind them. Without doubt the religious has been a constant factor in human societies up to now. I believe, however, that it must still be regarded as a *historical* phenomenon, that is, one with a definite beginning and end, falling within a specified period followed by another. As far as we know, religion has without exception existed at all times and in all places: yet I will attempt to show that religion is organized not as a constraint but as an *instituting action*, not as an obligation but a choice. Finally, if we can detect signs of basic religious schemas in social processes where we would least expect them, this is because religion is the millennia-old veil of a deeper anthropological structure, which continues to operate in another guise after the veil has disappeared.

Religion substantially means the translation and embodiment of social man's negative relation to himself into social forms. Its relative disintegration over the last two centuries allows us to glimpse the general pat-

tern behind the particular expression to which it has so long given substance. To say that religion is a way of institutionalizing *humans against
themselves* simply states what is most specific to the organization of
human beings: a confrontational posture toward things as they are, making it structurally impossible for humans to entrench themselves and set-
tle down, and steadfastly condemning them to a transformative nonac-
ceptance of things—whether dealing with nature, which they cannot
leave alone; with their fellow beings, who they perceive as potential objects for annihilation; with their culture, which they can only relate to by
changing it; or, finally, with their own inner reality, which they must similarly deny or modify. The central noteworthy feature of the religious is
precisely that this constitutive power of negation has been given the task
of disguising itself, has been assigned and has accepted the function of
denying itself—especially in its relation to the instituted social order,
which is my main concern. The underlying force defining humans is one
of refusal, which they express by rejecting their own ability to transform
the organization of their world.

The essence of religion lies in this process of establishing a dispossessive relationship between the world of visible living beings and its
foundation. Moreover, it is important to recognize that man's religious
rejection of himself and reliance on the past, which might be called the
"indebtedness of meaning" (*dette du sens*), are only secondary formations, socially effective transcriptions of a powerful underlying movement which is neutralized and diverted by this peculiar instituting
process. The religious is the principle of mobility placed in the service of
inertia, it is the principle of transformation mobilized to protect the inviolability of things, it is the power of negation wholly redirected toward
accepting and renewing the established law. The entire mystery of our
history lies in the fact that in his conflictual relationship with himself,
man began by denying precisely this unsettling truth about himself, this
uncertainty about his place in the world, and the productive instability
of his being in motion. In this sense, religion represents the enigma of our
backwards entrance into history.

CHAPTER 1

Primeval Religion or the Reign
of the Absolute Past

THE MOST noteworthy feature of this backward entrance is that it began by being radical, was relativized, opened up, and then to a certain extent overthrown. The idea of religious development has a long and venerable tradition. It is generally governed by the notion that our conception of the divine developed (monotheism being its highest stage of development) while religious activity was correlatively differentiated within the totality of collective activities, as part of an increasingly complex social structure. As soon as we make the relation to the social foundation the center of gravity of the religious, we are led to radically invert our perspective. We now see religion's most complete and systematic form is its initial one; later transformations, which we thought corresponded to more advanced stages, progressively call the religious into question. Its origins lay in radical dispossession, where the foundation was considered to be wholly other. Later formulations of the divine image, which reinforced its power and, one would think, human dependence on it, actually corresponded to a reduction of the religious other as the world's ultimate organizing principle, in favor of agents here-below. The path from primitive religions to modern Christianity was largely an attempt to reappropriate the source of meaning and law initially transferred beyond the grasp of human actors.

. . .

I admit there is difficulty involved in reconciling the idea of choosing the instituting principle with the absolute radical uniformity of its adoption. We can best observe the same twofold affirmation, as varied in expressions as it is unvaried in content, in the remnants of societies existing prior to the State. We can see in all of them both a radical dispossession of humans in relation to what determines their existence and an inviolable permanence in the order bringing them together. The underlying belief is that we owe everything we have, our way of living, our rules, our customs, and what we know, to beings of a different nature—to Ancestors, Heroes, or Gods. All we can do is follow, imitate, and repeat what they have taught us. In other words, everything governing our "works and days" was *handed down to us*. Major obligations and petty exploits, the whole framework encompassing the practices of the living, had their origins in a founding past that ritual both revitalizes as an inexhaustible source and reaffirms in its sacred otherness. Such a regularly recurring, thoroughly consistent device, obviously countenances a primordial, universal and above all relentless determinism. One is strongly tempted to believe that more than just a powerful motive or a strong obligation must be involved for such a consistent set of attitudes to have won out, for thousands of years, among the infinitely fragmented groups and cultures throughout the world. This is no doubt one of those areas that strongly confirms the unity of the human race and its history—and consequently one where we can most readily identify the relevant determining factors.

Some might include among these factors the limited development of technical resources and means of controlling nature in general—making religious dependence an expression of the inferiority experienced by humans in the face of overwhelmingly nonhuman forces. This viewpoint can be countered by pointing out the relatively strong autonomy of this conceptual and attitudinal system in relation to its material substratum, and its systematic organization of factual experience. Let us take an established historical fact, namely, that a change as fundamental to the means of production and subsistence as the "neolithic revolution," one of two major transformations in societies' material basis, was able to occur without bringing about any systematic cultural and religious change. The majority of primitive or savage societies known to us are neolithic and their adoption of agriculture in particular did not lead to any substantial modification in the belief system. Rather, this adoption was translated into the language of dispossession and indebtedness, and this momentous human achievement of agriculture became a gift from the gods, introduced in ancient times through a hero whose example was thereafter dutifully followed. The independence of this structure, which can lay down laws capable of denying the most obvious facts, is confirmed elsewhere by the analysis of economic behavior, itself dictated by global norms of sufficiency and stability diametrically opposed to any intention to produce a surplus—an example being where a gain in productivity brought about by a superior set of implements is offset by a reduction in working hours. So even if we were to accept that this symbolic organization of indebtedness toward a founding past reflected humanity's greatly reduced status in the face of natural forces, we would still have to account for its systematic bias toward immobility, which, instead of provoking attempts to overcome it, has tended on the contrary to prevent any such attempts and to perpetuate the existing weakness. Moreover, not only were major events absorbed, obliterated, and denied by a conceptual system that recognizes only the primal and the immutable. This system also denies the obviousness of daily change, of the alteration of things, of the transforming activity that individuals continually and unintentionally bring to bear on their social relations and the surrounding culture, not to mention the adaptations caused by external factors. Of course, societies must be historical since pure repetition is absolutely impossible for humans. Yet human societies have continually spent most of their time methodically and successfully repressing this indisputable fact. For if this system has not prevented them from continuously changing, often against their agents' wishes, it has nonetheless condemned them to a cycle of slow change. The essence of the religious act lies wholly in this antihistorical frame of mind. Religion in its pure state is drawn into a temporal division that puts the present in a position of absolute dependence on the mythical past, and guarantees the irrevocable allegiance of all human activities to their inaugural truth. At the same time it ratifies the non-appealable dispossession of human actors from what gives substance and meaning to their actions and gestures. The key to the inter-relationship between religion and society, as well as the secret of the nature of the religious, lies in its radical conservatism which structurally combines co-presence to the origin with disjunction from the originary moment, combining unstinting conformity to what has been definitively founded with a separated foundation.

. . .

We are therefore dealing with an *a priori* organization of the conceptual framework, which cannot be related to any external determinism. If we want to understand why it exists we must conduct an internal analysis. Only when we consider this organization as the central component of a broader mechanism can we clearly see its contents in terms of its results. For this systematic denial, and the accompanying preservation of what exists, proves to be loaded with crucial implications. For example, *political ones*: the rigid separation of existing individuals from the instaurating age controlling them is an ironclad guarantee that no one can claim to speak in the name of the sacred norm, can claim special relations with the divine foundation in order to enact its law or appropriate the principle of collective order. Radical dispossession is thus a means toward ultimate political equality which, although it does not prevent differences in social status or prestige, does prohibit the secession of unified power. There can be no privileged status among the living in an inviolable received order. Everyone is placed on the same level, the role of the leader being restricted to extolling the wisdom of ancestors and recalling the unalterable and necessary permanence of things. The notion introduced by Pierre Clastres of *society against the State* thus derives its entire significance from the political viewpoint inherent in primitive religion.

By the expression "society against the State," I mean a society where the religious removal of the founding principle prohibits a separate legitimating and coercive authority. On the other hand, it also means that such societies contain the structural potential for a similar political division—and this potential is at the root of the impersonal reflexivity at work in the religious choice which first neutralizes and then conceals it. I make this point to counter the charge that could be laid if the phrase *"choice against"* were interpreted as a kind of finalism. How, one might ask, can there be a negative view of something that has not yet occurred? The problem cannot be resolved from an external or hypothetical perspective, but must be related to an internal factor mistakenly regarded as one of the conditions for social existence. If we wish to understand the sociological action that wards off political domination through religious dispossession, we must remain within the framework of a fundamental anthropology and return to the primary structures which cause society to be. Society's implementation is a meaningful choice only insofar as its social space is originally organized and identified by an internal opposition establishing the universal potentiality for power to separate itself. This choice does not negate the polarization of power and society, as seen in the analysis of functions attached to leadership confined to the bounds of speech and reputation. Rather it neutralizes this polarization by partitioning off the heroic past. The remarkable enigma is the stubborn human bias toward self-negation, the unconscious and systematic refusal to assume the constituting dimensions of human-social reality. It is as if whatever caused man to be what he is was so unbearable that he had no choice but to repress it immediately.

This transferal of foundations and causes to *the other* (i.e., to others, to the origins) responds not just to the problem of political division, but to structural questions raised by the bond between humans or their stance toward nature. It is not possible here to examine each of these articulations, which would require me to show how they help constitute human-social space, and to describe their arrangement in detail. Let me just say that in every case there is a similar neutralization of a structurally antagonistic relation. Thus the temporal disposition, which makes the present completely dependent on the primordial, cannot be separated from a spatial one that makes the world of the living a continuous part of the natural order. Taken to extremes, religious dispossession means becoming part of the living universe, being physically integrated into the heavenly cycles and into the supposedly permanent organization of the elements and the species. The potential antagonism embedded in hu-mans' relation to nature is neutralized by substituting a symbolic atti-tude of belonging for one of confrontation. Something in their organiza-tion—something inherent to tools and language—removes humans from nature. Religion, in its original pure state, is the desire to merge with na-ture. This also involves deploying the extraordinary structuring activity of the savage mind, so well highlighted by Claude Levi-Strauss, where we can recognize the vestiges of this confrontation with the domesticated world—just as we can recognize the primordial necessity of power in the savage chief's role.

Shifting the causes of the instauration elsewhere neutralizes the radical antagonism of beings that is inscribed in the bond holding them together. This disposition is closely related to previous ones: if the customary modes of human coexistence are accepted as wholly predefined, then no conflict arises between social actors about the content and forms of collective re-lations. All possible conflict between individuals and groups is given pre-cise predetermined limits as to its prospects and possible outcomes.

This highlights what is undoubtedly the most general characteristic of the religious in its relation to the social: when we talk about religion we are ultimately talking about a well-defined type of society based on the priority of the principle of collective organization over the will of the in-dividuals it brings together. The reader will recognize here the model of society that Louis Dumont calls "holistic," due to the primacy of the whole over the part organizing it, as opposed to our own individualist model, which assumes first the dispersion of independent atoms, then the creation of structure through the citizen's free expression. The holistic model coincides historically with the age of what might be called reli-gious societies, not in terms of their members' beliefs but in the way these beliefs are actually articulated around a religious hegemony, that is, around the absolute predominance of a founding past, of a sovereign tradition, which predates personal preferences. On the other hand, en-tering the age of individualism means leaving the age of the religious, where both *dependency on the whole* and *indebtedness to the other* are simultaneously relinquished.

In its most highly developed form, the received order's logic can an-ticipate and halt the development of any intrasocial conflict: it is tacitly assumed that you cannot disagree on fundamentals, on what binds you to your fellow humans. You can certainly risk your life, but you cannot question the very principle of coexistence. If there is a place for war, there is none for destroying meaning. If we are to explain how effective forms of collective-being are arranged to neutralize the structural antag-onism linking humans together, we must revise the *rule of reciprocity*. This rule tells us nothing about logical necessity in savage societies or

about the social bond reduced to its most elementary expression of reciprocity, i.e., the established fact that there are others. On the contrary,
this rule is wholly instituted and is an active participant in the general
structure of religious refusal. It expresses the priority of the relationship
between individuals over those involved in it, and thus the priority of the
established norm, and it begins with the radical direct encounter of mutual recognition. This presents the permanent possibility of starting from
the bottom, of systematically redefining and reestablishing human relations by rethinking their foundations. In other words, it is the instauration of a social relation that excludes questioning its own terms and conditions. At the heart of what attaches humans to their fellow beings lies
the turmoil of unresolved conflict. In both peacefully negotiated exchange and the restitutive chain of vengeance, the law of reciprocity is
the nonquestionable religious aspect of the foundation which shapes social relations. It is the uncontested predominance of ultimate causes, a
predominance insured against what brings people into contact, whether
it be free choice or mortal opposition.

.   .   .

Everything is thus related back to the core elements of customary *permanence* and sacral *dependence*, which is the primordial essence of the
religious. What gives meaning to our existence, what drives our actions,
what sustains our customs comes not from us but from those *before us*,
not from humans like us, but totally different beings, whose difference
and sacrality lies in the fact that they were creators, while everyone since
is an epigone. There is nothing currently existing whose place and desti-
nation were not set down in earlier times and followed by our age of repetition; and hence everything established is to be traced back through
successive generations. In short, historically speaking, the real kernel of
religious attitudes and thought lies in accepting the *external as the originating source and the unchangeable as law.* This is not just a body of
representations and beliefs: over the longest *duree* of human societies we
find that discourse, beliefs, and ritual practices only show the tip of a
global articulation of the social body in religious terms, while the heart
of the collective organization controls both society's political form and its
place in nature, as well as the form of its agents' relations. This is a col-
lection of attitudes and a conceptual system so coherent and entrenched
that they have endured to our day, despite political upheavals, technological revolutions, spiritual and cultural transformations, as well as the
collapse of the type of social organization most closely corresponding to
them. Something of this pagan sense of habitual dispossession survived
in our peasant societies, at least to the end of the last century, in the
midst of a world which, taken as a whole, no longer has anything in

common with its birthplace. It is as if history, the advent of States, economic changes, religious upheavals, were all made above and beyond
this primordial stratum, and have managed only very slowly to absorb
the final tenacious residue of a primal choice into its creative processes.

The word *choice* is the only one capable of indicating the tenor either
of this instituting operation, which at a stroke neutralizes all destabilizing factors, or of the dynamic tension promoting the group's essential
unity, the *inviolability* of its rule and the *exteriority* of its foundation. It
ultimately comes down to a manner of accepting the primary structures
through which the social as such comes to be, one that has the quite remarkable characteristic of using methods of systematic denial and
masking. The constitutive dimensions are always at work in the form of
opposing the role of power, becoming antagonistic to the world, and
separating while co-belonging; they are simply reintroduced and rearranged in such a way that their effects are neutralized. The forces of
change are put completely in the service of preserving and giving unwa-
vering assent to what exists. This initial act which for such an enormous
duree determined that societies be organized in terms of denying and ex-
orcizing themselves, is the deepest enigma of human history. It is an unconscious act, and to understand its execution would require an explanation of the mystery of the "subjectless subject" form of the collective.
It is free in that we cannot attribute it to an external determinism. But
this does not mean it is arbitrary, since we can understand humans' natural inclination to establish the feeling of dependence on the other, just
as we can understand the gains that might result from this immobility
and dispossession. We see how act creates meaning as soon as we consider the major landmarks in the development and control of the psyche,
which may not fully explain dispossession, but does indicate the best way
to shed light on these origins. There is no doubt that the essential secret
of this inaugural excision of the self is contained wholly within the an-
thropogenetic operation itself. We can best understand the universal denial that initially greeted these instaurating structures by elucidating the
basic processes through which humans are given to themselves by being
bound to others, through which the collective bond is established at the
same time as the conscious division. In other words, whatever causes division might just as easily prevent its occurrence. Here we see in its main
historical expression the full mystery of the discord inscribed from the
beginning in man's relation to himself.

.   .   .

If we want to analyze the religious phenomenon and reconstitute the significant stages in its development, the lesson from primitive societies is
quite clear: we must consider the content of religious ideas according to

their *implementation point* and not according to the apparent internal complexity of their composition or organization. There has been a strong tendency to read the history of beliefs within a general history of growth, seeing it as a progressive rationalization of dogma and a deepening of notions of the divine. Although this is in keeping with the facts, it completely obscures the significance and true nature of the evolution thus observed. In practice, despite the fluidity of their mythical discourse and their barely perceptible images of divinity, primitive religions adopt an absolute and radical form. Only after certain practices and representations have been relocated within the social apparatus does it become clear that they were its keystone, which then allows us to understand them. These practices and representations show no sign of even a rudimentary spontaneous form of intelligence, or of an elementary understanding of things—in short, no sign of a primitive stage of development. The instituting law's demand for otherness, which systematically prevents social division, determines both their content and modalities. Only when we take this basic necessity into account can we see the religious system articulated in all its detail. This is how the mythical past achieves its hegemony. In order to understand its precise meaning, we must recognize that it is the only way to establish a clean break between the instituting and the instituted, the single adequate means for founding an order accepted in its entirety and completely removed from man's grasp. But it is accompanied by a paradox, insofar as its very extremity transforms distance into proximity, absence into presence, division into coalescence. And that other age, the sacred moment of origins, regularly returns through ritual to restore our world, by appearing to bring about a recurrence of what has already definitively taken place. This constant return to and tapping into the inaugurating moment is a result of the drastic distance separating us from it. Furthermore, as far as origins are concerned, there can be no creation in the sense of a unique global event attributable to the sovereign will of a subject or group of subjects. There are beginnings, arrivals, changes in the world and the creatures who populate it; there are partial and successive instaurations which seem accidental and are attributed less to the gods' decision than to heroic ancestors, through whose intercession humans can grasp the creative design of things. The greater the gods, the more extensive their power, the more they can be held directly accountable for the creation of the world, and the more humans can gain practical access through them to the rational necessity of the origin. This is the fundamental paradox of religion's history: the growth in the gods' power, which might reasonably be expected to be detrimental to humans, proves to be to their ultimate advantage, even though it may in the short term have increased their subjugation. This growth in the gods' power proves to be the very means for recovering the grounds that gave rise to them. The feebleness of primitive deities who do not even instaurate, let alone control, the destiny of their world, are a measure of how the living are dispossessed and made dependent on what separates them from the origin. They bear no relation to the instituting operation other than through ritual and its repetition. A more general application of the present analysis would have to show how the union of the abstract with the concrete, of endless new beginnings with countless fragmented paths, are specifically *countersubjective* modes of mythical thought, which all have their origins in the same logic of withdrawal. This way of thinking was totally instituted, and is diametrically opposed to any of the savage mind's supposed natural operations. It wants to reconcile the possibly "natural" need for an understanding of the whole with the social and religious imperative to safeguard an order. It is thus a way of thinking which, unlike ours, does not aim to understand the world with an eye to its global control (from either the human subject's or the divine subject's viewpoint), but rather wants to establish the present, past, and future absence of any guiding principle presiding over the general course of things.

These cursory remarks are very general and by no means exhaustive. However, I would like to touch briefly on two other features for the comparisons they allow: the first concerns the form that dealings with the invisible are likely to take in such a system; the second concerns the way in which the received code is applied and experienced.

Shamanism is a good example of the way in which manifest realities and occult forces, visible resources and invisible powers, are structurally linked in primitive religions. Here we have specialists who initiate communication with the spirit world and manipulate its representatives, but who, despite the considerable prestige and fears they inspire, are steadfastly confined to the common lot of their society. This is because, in reality, the visible and the invisible are entwined in a single world. When these shamans temporarily go beyond the everyday world into another by using appropriate skills and trances, this does not mean that they acquire a different nature cutting them off from their fellow humans. The shaman remains a *technician* endowed with a special ability to move between the living and the dead, between spirits and magical forces. He is in no way an *incarnating force* creating a permanent union between the human world and its creator and ruler. In other words, the shaman confirms that even if it were possible to travel beyond tangible reality within such a system in the present, one cannot cross over to the side of the founding past and the instaurating law, whose impersonal perpetuation is guaranteed by its ritual recurrence. Faced with this decisive gap, everyone, including the leader and the shaman, is equal.

This means that within such a framework the code of life is one with the group's law, which in turn is in principle immanent to collective practice. There is no divergence between norm and being which can be institutionalized. There is no place for an ethics which can independently define the correct way to behave, nor for a social imperative that would have to gain acceptance over its agents' spontaneous inclinations. The two major cultural characteristics inherent in primitive religion are: adherence to what exists, and the supposed conformity of collective experience to its ancestral law. All subsequent religious evolution will challenge these characteristics.

CHAPTER 2

The State as Sacral Transforming Agent

IN THIS CHAPTER I will schematically highlight the consistent tendencies that justify going beyond pure chronology and speaking about a *primeval religion*. It is essential to begin with the religious organization of savage tribes, since they contain the key to the entire history of the relationship between religion and society. The radical nature of this organization allows us to get a proper perspective on what we are accustomed to call the "major religions," and forces us to seriously reconsider their significance. We have normally assumed, on the basis of their richer symbolism and more profound speculations, that these religions represent the true beginnings of a religious history leading to a more sophisticated representation of the divine, and we consider the diffuse paganism of primitive peoples to be simply a useful testimony to the universal nature of religious feelings in a rudimentary or undifferentiated state. This totally misleading perspective is due to an equally complete failure to recognize the role played by the earliest religious understanding of things in societies prior to the State and the factors shaping it. The mythologies of the earliest major despotic developments clearly appear more stable and better organized, perhaps more imbued with a properly spiritual sense, than the unstable creations embedded in the sensory world of the savage mind. *A fortiori*, so do the first metaphysical formulations of transcendent religions, which suddenly emerged in the last 500 years BC. Nevertheless, among savages, barbarians, and civilized peoples, the deepest, most unmistakable religious factors are not what they might seem. The main developments in the theological and cultural spheres within higher cultures actually represent, under the theological guises of affirming the deities' person and power, so many stages along the path to *reducing the foundation's practical otherness*, an otherness most fully realized in primitive societies. If we believe that at the core of the religious lies an implicit assumption that whatever causes and justifies the visible human sphere lies outside this sphere, then we must acknowledge that this assumption has received its fullest expression and its most detailed interpretation and application in primitive societies. Once we relate subsequent events back to this primordial dispossession, it becomes apparent that they are best interpreted in terms of reappropriation. What looked like a continual deepening of the experience and conception of the *Other*, proves to have been a progressive reappropriation of what was initially removed. The gods withdraw and simultaneously the nonquestionable becomes questionable, being affirmed by the hold humans have on the organization of their own world. Emphasizing divine difference proves to go hand-in-hand with broadening the power humans have over themselves and the order they comply with. The more God is thought of and venerated as the Wholly Other, the less his creatures' existence is perceived and treated by them as being controlled by something other. The major religions are major stages in challenging the religious, if not major steps toward departing from religion.

This is by no means a one-dimensional, one-way process. Quite the contrary, since in this case advances and retreats are closely entwined, owing to the stubborn persistence of primordial reverence toward the unchangeable, and are also linked with the concern to preserve stability— making any sort of historical necessity impossible. The fact remains that through a series of massive upheavals everything proceeds as if human destiny, law, and the form of collective-being, were coming into question, not so much in the minds of the participants as within the social mechanism and its dynamics. It is as if challenging the instituting principle, which was previously excluded from collective practice, slowly became more central. I do not intend to re-create and follow this development in its entirety,[2] but will concentrate on three major upheavals that I consider crucial. The first corresponds to the State's emergence. Another is brought about by the appearance of a divinity from beyond this world and of a religious rejection of this world during what Jaspers has appropriately called the "axial age." The final one is that represented by Western Christianity's internal trajectory. Three crucial transformations of the religious *Other*. Three fundamentally important shifts of the *interaction* between the invisible and the visible. Three reformulations of humans' indebtedness toward what goes beyond them, each one a decisive step toward recovering themselves.

.   .   .

The most important of these upheavals is undoubtedly the first one, the birth of the State. This event severs history in two and brings human societies into an entirely new age—brings them decisively *into history*, not in the sense that it pushes them from a state of inertia into one of motion, but rather that it modifies in every way their *de facto* relation to change and hence their actual rate of change. At first there is no fundamental change: we remain within a religious logic of indebtedness and the inviolable nature of things as laid down, and hence in a frame of mind which is theoretically antihistorical. But whatever the agents' attitudes and beliefs, whatever they think and intend doing, the very articulation of the social relation condemns them henceforth to question the collective organization's validity right down to its sacred foundation. As much as they want things to remain the same, humans cannot help creating and sustaining change. Admittedly, it was always to some extent like this. The conservatism of primitive societies, however rigid, has not prevented them from continually changing, any more than it has completely restrained their members' inventiveness, as we see from the great achievements of the neolithic age. What is different here is not that there is inexorable change, despite attempts to safeguard and perpetuate identity. It is rather that where those neutralizing mechanisms aimed at sheltering the social framework from the dynamics of group relations are at work, the advent of political domination acts contrariwise by objectively setting up, at the heart of the collective process, a debate about the meaning and legitimacy of the whole. So political domination not only produces or generates greater instability and more effective transformations, it also reshapes both the intra- and inter-social relations in such a way that the interplay of their most substantial forces tends to loosen the previously unchallengeable human bonds. Hence the far-reaching transformative consequences of the emergence of the political division, which historically speaking is quite recent, roughly five thousand years ago, as against probable scores of millennia when the world was organized so as to exactly replicate things and to deny collective division. It is as if the human action had initiated an unstoppable trend, putting them permanently at odds with what their beliefs continue to assert is out of reach, while their new existential framework forced them to question the social bond determined from outside. Once begun, there can be no turning back.

With the State's appearance, the religious Other actually returns to the human sphere. While it of course retains its exteriority relative to the State, the religious penetrates and is embodied in the State. In short, the religious severance separates humans from their origins beforehand in order to forestall the sudden appearance of a division between them. Once a mechanism for domination appears, the severance occurs inside human society and separates humans from each other. The dominant ones are on the side of the gods while the dominated are not. There are many versions of this phenomenon, from the god as living despot where the Other that humans depend on openly adopts a human form, through to the temple where the god is actually present without being properly incarnated in human form, but with servants and human mediators. In any case, the crucial point is that divine otherness, whatever its shape, has been transported into the social space and the nonhuman has been incorporated into the structure of human ties. The main thing is that from now on the instituting force is made visible and accessible, whether in the guise of a place and an institution or an individual nature. These will be humans completely different from their fellow beings insofar as they participate directly or indirectly in the invisible sacred center fuelling collective existence. They are the ones who speak and organize in the name of the gods, who have control of rituals where the original meaning of things is revived and through whose flesh one is literally in contact with the higher principle governing the world. This coercive presence, this bringing power into the midst of human affairs, gives rise to a critically important corollary, namely, that the same gods are brought back within reach and, in practice, become socially questionable, caught up as they are in the mechanism they theoretically created. Here we see the gods increasingly dependent on what is supposed to depend on them, that is, on the actions of an ever-changing system they are supposed to keep intact.

This political severance introduces a dynamic, a principle of change, into the heart of collective practices on the physical, spiritual, and symbolic levels. This is due not only to the tension that goes with exercising domination, but also to the structural imperative encouraging every separated power, however conservative, to actually bring about social transformation. *Imposing* an order, even in the name of its inviolable legitimacy, means *changing* it, however quietly or surreptitiously. This makes the order pass imperceptibly from the level of the received to that of the *willed*—which has considerable repercussions on how its authors and its foundations are portrayed. But the transformation with potentially the most far-reaching consequences is the change in relations with the outside. Domination contains within itself the prospect of being extended: as soon as the ruling power becomes separate, it broadens the horizons of its dominion and shows its distance from its subjects, and hence its authority over them, by expanding its sphere of influence. In other words, the imperial ambition to dominate the world comes with the State. We can foresee the upheavals this will bring about in the representation of man's position in the world. The order of each particular community preserves its stability by being designated as a received order, yet the support for the system's absolute validity is shaken to its foundations by the sudden appearance of imperial universalism. For this reason wars of expansion could no doubt be justifiably considered one of the greatest spiritual and intellectual forces to have ever operated in history. This social apparatus articulated by political division shows it cannot operate on any level without surreptitiously undermining the immutable sacred foundations which are supposed to impose their law on it. The power of a few individuals to act in the name of the gods is the barely perceptible, yet irreversible step toward everyone having an influence on the gods' decrees—the imperceptible yet definite beginning of a collective grasp on the previously sacrosanct order. The State ushers in the age of opposition between the social structure and the essence of the religious. Political domination, which decisively entangles the gods in history, will prove to be the invisible hoist lifting us out of the religious.

. . .

We can schematically describe the situation at the religious level as the extremely diverse outcome of an interactive compromise between maintaining the fundamental structure of primitive religions and undergoing three major transformations: one relating to hierarchy, another to the power relationship, and the third to the dynamics of conquest.

Hierarchy

During this stage, the mode of representing dependence on the nonhuman, remained essentially unchanged, especially regarding the rearranged orders of reality: the Natural and the Supernatural, visible diversity and invisible plurality continued to blend harmoniously within one and the same cosmic biological totality, linked by a close network of differences and correspondences nourished by myth. Nevertheless, the articulation of a hierarchical structure, as much among humans as between humans and their gods, provided the first major new factor that would profoundly modify our relation to supernatural powers. It is easy to see external signs in the dawning of the cult as such, of formally conducted sacrifice, and regulated worship. But the decisive aspect of the change, which took place at a much deeper level, neither appeared in lived experience nor could be deduced from it as an increased awareness of difference from gods who were now more clearly identifiable. The main point was the definitive destabilization of the relation between the instituting invisible and the instituted norm, a structural consequence of redesigned social relations, due precisely to the founding other's materialization in the human sphere.

Hierarchy means incorporating the foundation's otherness into the very substance of the social tie, and redistributing it at every level. Seen in this light it was not really a new creation, but resulted from reshaping and redistributing the archetypal religious dimension, namely, the one in which the established collective order has complete authority and seniority over the will of particular individuals. In the savage world, the community of living beings is both separate from and dependent on those who define origins;[3] in the world of political division a perceptible framework developed that both distinguished and physically welded together the humans involved, and gave immediate meaning to the ties between them. At stake in the relation between the higher and the lower is the encounter of individuals with the law, this principle which is "other," which distinguished individuals but also gave rise to the *sameness* holding them together. We can perceive in this unifying difference—the very essence of the hierarchical structure—an echo of the exteriority that ensured the full and accurate conformity of human groups to their instituting principle. In other words, hierarchy replicated at every level of the social relation the seminal relation between society and its foundation, as a function of the main interaction between the visible and the invisible. The instaurating power was mediated through the sacred "other" thus embodied in the "other" of power at the top of the visible hierarchy. This power then trickled down into its actual sphere of application, permeating and nourishing it.

Hierarchy actually ensures this very union of the social body with its reason for existence, its cause and its norm which, prior to the State, were all preserved in ritual acts—in particular those revolving around initiation, branding, and identity. But although they may have the same functions, substituting one for the other does have ramifications; it involved a basic change in the mutual arrangement of the terms to be united. In primitive societies, a radical separation from the founding period was evenly counterbalanced by a complete union with the legacy of its origins. The strict separation of the instituting principle was precisely what guaranteed the unchanging conformity of collective existence to its primordial reasons. The seamless interweaving of the present and the past, the bringing together of the invisible and the visible, of what is present and what is absent, of the totally familiar and the totally concealed, led to such an intimate reconciliation between the two orders of reality that it no longer made sense to treat them separately, as if each had its own autonomous substantiality. The two orders now occupied the same sphere and each one existed for and through the other. On the other hand, once the visible and the invisible intersect, there is a problem with the structural interconnection between this sacral presence and the absence from which it arose, a problem that could neither be resolved nor ignored. To be more precise, if we look at the newly formed relation between the visible and invisible in regard to the hiatus created by incarnating the beyond here-below, it becomes problematical in a way that is felt throughout the entire hierarchical apparatus. Once the division of reality was inscribed into the general process of reconciling the social with its own foundation, and long before it entered people's awareness, this division raised questions. The attempt to identify with the instaurating other could not but highlight its ultimate difference, the extent to which it went beyond its concrete manifestations. And the more humans felt the presence of something superior to them, the more they were struck by its absence. The social structure's internal workings engendered the potential space for a theology, that is, a speculation on the absent, on what previously managed to evade both mythical status and human understanding. The seeds of the breakdown in the unity of the cosmos, of the separation of a here-below from a beyond, can all be found in the deployment of State order. To all intents and purposes, the other would not materialize into a separate power without being transformed: it carried something that would make its transcendence conceivable. Here again, there were social consequences, for this primordial knot between the here and the beyond had repercussions for the entire range of human ties. And we will see how the division between the visible and the invisible order can tell us a great deal about subjection. Breaking the previous continuity between a here-below and a beyond would decisively transform the forms of subordination and the tie between the individual and the collective. Independently of what could take place in the minds of those who either lead or obey, the State, by its very existence, inevitably affected the spiritual dimension. As it unfolded, the State clandestinely brought about symbolic transformation and determined what could be conceived; subsequent religious revolutions would reveal the hidden symbolic significations generated by this social process.

Domination

The second major factor contributing to a transformation of the divine figure was the subjective dimension inherent in the power relationship. As distinct from hierarchical gradation, this dimension was at odds with the perpetuated representation of an inviolable cosmic order owing everything to the founding past, within which order the sovereign function remained a cog just as predetermined, objectively defined, and precisely located as the rest of the vast structure it was slotted into.

Because of its strategic position at the interface of the visible and the invisible, power's role in this framework was in principle wholly one of preserving the general cohesion of the world through magic and symbols, in accordance with a code that had always been handed down and did

not come from any individual. But in reality, the structure forced the organizing sovereign to go beyond the theoretical limits of his role, and
this deeply affected the organization of the system he is central to. This
occurs insofar as the sovereign's action is controlled by a coercive relationship with the beings and groups beneath him. Through coercion he
keeps the rest of society faithful to his laws and in harmony with the
forces of the universe. The internal workings of this relationship are capable of producing a subjective dynamic that profoundly challenges
what was established as unchangeable, from the viewpoint of either the
institutionalized power or its supernatural guarantor. This can occur
when the situation has reached the stage of providing a direct outlet for
opposition, and when the sovereign head is led, seemingly naturally, to
mobilize the alleged will of the invisible forces above him, and to present his own action as a guiding will that must be consciously embraced
to prevent the collapse of the human and cosmic edifice. In other words,
both the substance of the social order and its sacred support depend on
the direct effectiveness of conscious control. Put another way, both the
intra-social relation and the relation to the extra-social tend to be *subjectivized*. We can see how this involves a two-stage shift in relation to
the rigid framework of a received order: the first is a shift from the past
toward the present; the next is a shift away from the essentially impersonal nature of ancestral law and the contingent actions of instaurating
mythical heroes, toward personalizing both the instituting law's content
and application, which in turn redefines its necessity. And when these
two shifts are combined we can detect the new nature of the supernatural powers likely to result from it, by how they are fixed and identified,
and by how they are connected to our affairs. These powers no longer
simply occupy a parallel world that can be detected through its magical
influences. They embrace this world, which they partially control, and
are responsible for its institution. These forces provide an immediate
guarantor for the foundation of things, whose intentions can thus be
speculated on.

I am simply sketching a matrix of logical possibilities, which clears the
way for later developments, but says nothing about the infinitely varied
ways in which each specific context shapes the outcome of possibilities
that are basically the same everywhere. Religious upheaval is inscribed
in the State's action, contained within its necessities as dictated by the
political division. Broadening the State's influence subjectivizes supernatural forces, which can only further broaden its practical scope for
domination by making it an intermediary for an instituting will that it
administers. We see how the dialectic between the visible force and its
invisible guarantor, between the actual and the presumed power, slowly
draws the religious into history.

Conquest

Of all the State's actions, war has the most serious consequences from the viewpoint of social representations. The advent of the State, which of course did not invent war, modifies war's form and meaning, and literally reverses its role. Because of the way each primitive social unit maintains its identity, war between them follows a pattern of differentiation or proliferation. The ceaseless interplay between alliance and discord, the permanent state of hostilities in one form or another, sustains and extends the multiplicity and dispersion of groups that are regularly threatened by internal splits. Each community maintains its identity by remaining in a potential state of conflict with all the others, and the dynamics of war always serve to widen the gaps. Should the opportunity arise, one group may expel or eliminate another, but it never absorbs the other group. However, once the State becomes a separate entity, part of its function is to expand and assimilate. The prospect of conquest is inscribed in the chain of subordination and is an active integral part of the political division. In practice, the power relationship precludes a state of equilibrium. Those above the common run of mortals are obliged to assert that they are increasingly higher, different, and removed from the others. Power continually strives to increase itself. This internal distance between the ruling authority and its subjects is what makes the unlimited absorption of the external world both conceivable and feasible. In the eyes of the system of domination, those dominated are all the same. In comparison to the overwhelming splendor of the despot, the appendages pale into insignificance. Likewise, there are and must be a limitless number of dependent and obedient subjects. In the same way, every other sovereign formation can only be grasped as something to be reduced: every subordinating power must itself be subordinated. The true king is the "king of kings," according to the obsessive formula of imperial titleholders. In other words, universal domination, the ultimate unification of the known world under the authority of the most powerful of the powerful is latent in the narrower form of domination.

I should not need to point out that historically the major attempts at conquest failed, owing to compromise between the logic of expansion and the logic of ethnic or cultural affiliation, and often reverted to unifying a relatively homogeneous area of civilization. This does not in any way detract from the symbolically unrestricted nature of the aim prefigured in the outbreak of martial activity. Once we have a State with its logic of expansion, however limited its concrete realization, the universal bursts upon the scene of human experience with all its ramifications. This is a major trauma producing what is perhaps the most profound spiritual shock wave in history, clearly seen in the aftereffects resulting from the revised scope of the human enterprise, when the center of the collective self is forcibly relocated; these aftereffects include the breakdown of mental patterns and disruptive forces, which will radically revise the image of the world. An entirely new religious order and conceptual framework is concealed in the crucible of violent conquest driven by a policy of unification.

How can the divine avoid undergoing a radical reassessment when the terrestrial monarch aspires to reconstitute the arrangement of the entire visible sphere? When the despot succeeds in passing himself off as the master of the universe, where can the gods, who give rise to the world and legitimate its course, be placed in relation to it? And what status should they be given? How can humans not look to the gods to justify him to whom the rest must submit? These are questions that again do not need to be explicitly raised in order to have an effect on the established social significations, as they are imposed by the very motion of the collective body.

However the most decisive factor is the questioning of the partition between real humans living in conformity with the real law, and the others, a questioning that inevitably ushers us into the reign of the universal. As we saw, what is at stake in the primitive logic of potential group conflict is not only the permanent reassurance of the group's indivisible identity but also its socially incarnated certainty that it occupies the center of the world. Radical ethnocentricity is an integral part of the system: ours is the only proper way to exist and we are the only ones worthy of being called human. This is the obligatory correlate of the definitive materialization of the union between the collective practice and the time-honored norm that founds it, and is constantly reaffirmed by bloody conflict. Moreover, each social unit has no recourse but to exist along traditional lines, since it cannot question and transcend its own particular confines. On the other hand, the imperial goal of global unification opens up a yawning chasm between daily compliance to ancestral laws within a well-defined group, and the viewpoint of the universal in action. When defining the proper life, there is now an irresistible lever, anchored in the social bond, for decentering the customary lifestyle and redefining its validity, its completeness or its self-sufficiency. Where previously there was a code for every aspect of life, there is now a tendency to surreptitiously *duplicate* levels of experience: on one level the inherited unquestioned norms, which are specific to the narrow original community and determine its contours, continue to exist; but on the other level there is the ultimate law of the universe or the universal being, demanding that all those living be encompassed, without distinction, by the terrestrial Master of the Universe. At the center of the development of so-called "historical" religions, we will find a break between the narrow circle of

the familiar and the vast orbit of the limitless, a hiatus between immediate realities and ultimate truth, and a departure from the internal constraint resulting from social localization and the internal voice instilled
by the common human perspective. When the nearby is disengaged and
torn away from the remote, and the contingent from the essential, we see
the appearance of an unresolvable tension, which will create something
that will subsequently develop into "spiritual life."

. . .

I must emphasize yet again that this has nothing to do with positing an
underlying determinism affecting the religious transformations whose
horizon I have sketched. It is not as if the unfolding political division
necessarily had to create a new world of representations and beliefs from
nothing. The process is deep and complex, but in another way. Effective
power makes new mental horizons possible. It brings symbolic and unconscious effects in a whole range of spheres which break, all in their
own way, with the original framework of the order received in its entirety. But this is where its creativity stops short: it works in the dark and
does not bring anything to light. There is nothing in this process to suggest a guiding influence which must make the contents of the thought it
carries more explicit. The transition from creating the possibility to exploiting it is wholly contingent. In any case, these two states fall under
two socially distinct logical forms. Besides, the new configurations of religious experience could have remained latent within the mechanism that
produced them. In actual fact, we do see them spread imperceptibly,
penetrating the architecture of time-honored beliefs and incorporating
themselves antagonistically into the structure of the natural Supernatural
and the founding era, sometimes by authoritarian directives from above,
sometimes by developments from below. Hence the incredibly complex
and diverse hybrid character of these "archaic" religions (to use the current terminology), both in their cultural formations and their intellectual
orientations. This character is due to juggling and compromising deeply
contradictory orders, one inherited from the age where the control of
human existence was beyond the human sphere, and the other arising in
and through the dynamics of the interhuman split.

The Axial Age

So there is no unidirectional process allowing us to explain religious innovation solely in terms of a constantly applied irresistible force. Rather,
there is a gap between the explicit belief system and the lines of force underlying the thinkable, a space in which circumstances and structural
pressures can cause inventiveness and change to flourish. But we still

cannot comprehend the enormous groundswell, which over several centuries (from approximately 800 to 200 BC) swept from Persia to China, from India to Greece, including Palestine. This period divides religions into pre and post, those coming before and those coming after it (which is why Karl Jaspers has called it the "axial age" of universal history[4]), and the two groups cannot be conceptually reunited without referring to the enormous spiritual activity inscribed deep within the political division and to its expansion. So deep is the discontinuity established by this revolutionary reorientation, this total radical transformation of the religious, this transvaluation of the rules of life, that it appears to come from nowhere. Yet in reality they are all intimately connected with the secret symbolic metamorphosis brought about from within the State order. This does not mean that the State order had an intrinsic capacity to impose these changes; their sudden appearance remains a mystery. But from the point of view of their content and remarkable consistency, their sudden appearance would remain completely unintelligible if not for their connection to the shadowy figure of the despot.

The gap between the here-below and the beyond, subjectivation of the divine principle, and universalization of life values: these are the three main outcomes of the religious subversion embedded in the innermost depths of the collective articulation and they break into social discourse during the spiritual upsurge of the axial age. Everything set up as signs of the religious—signs we instinctually identify with the religious—as a means of relating to or thinking about reality, had for a very long time been imperceptibly delineated in the social bond. This lets us understand the enormous reaction provoked by the spiritual reformers, and why new beliefs have regularly spread under the guise of a social movement—as if in response to a long silent, but deeply felt expectation. The reception of doctrines needs to be explained along with their appearance. The uncompromising demands concerning humanity's destiny and the calling to go beyond immediate boundaries strike an immediate chord whose conjunction can only be explained by going back to the common origin of conceiving a belief and adhering to it, namely, the hidden logic of the State as an intrinsically religion-producing enterprise. But it also creates the conditions for a dissenting reception and a disruptive discourse. That which bears and sustains inspired discourse or the founding word simultaneously distances minds from prevailing beliefs, and spreads the vague expectation of something new.

Of course, this does not explain everything. We must acknowledge the part played in each specific context by factors that accelerated the quest for a spiritual solution. Behind these, however, lies the mysterious operation of a broader and less direct causal factor: the effect of symbolic projection inscribed in the structure and running of societies, which indirectly made the new figure of the Other in this world universally perceptible. The personality of the instigators or founders of religion is important: indeed it is worth noting that from Lao-Tzu to Zarathustra, from the prophets of Israel to Buddha, we see the *principle of individuality* burst into history, much more so than with the great monarchs whose person and function can scarcely be separated. But we must keep in mind that they acted primarily to reveal a version of the sacred which, though tacitly perceived, was at the same time concealed so as to be unthinkable. Hence the restorative capacity of these various ways of structurally linking estrangement from the world and the split between appearance and truth. Hence too, the capacity of these teachings to spread rapidly by mobilizing, no doubt for the first time in history, individuality understood as *inwardness*. Behind and despite the apparent maintenance of ancient values and forms, a space had been inexorably carved out, and made available in the hearts of individuals, for a different understanding of life. This gaping invisible distance lets us glimpse, for example, how the empire considered most secure because of its power and longevity, could be undermined from within by moral and religious disintegration, namely because its shadow pointed relentlessly beyond itself, its official cults and a rigid image of the world, toward the inconceivable yet inevitable figure of *something else*.

If we confine ourselves exclusively to their doctrinal content, it is extremely difficult to grasp the "axial" unity of this series of unexpected occurrences. This is due not only to their differing contexts, their remoteness from flourishing traditions, and language barriers, but much more deeply to the *uneven development*, if I may venture the expression, of the various outcomes of the time. The norm remains a compromise between the new message and time-honored structures, along with all this implies about variations in the relation of force and the extent to which the new is liberated from established beliefs. The formal criteria relating to this single mode of thought scarcely convey what I believe to be the common inspiration behind these numerous moral codes or theologies, and it is difficult to find any categories capable of properly expressing this. This is much more a result of the interaction of discontinuity and continuity than of the problems of translation that every comparative approach runs up against. In this case the new conceptual form cannot be separated from the content to be thought—and one of my main concerns is to explain the spiritual origins of what we consider the rational, while explaining the general conditions for departing from the world of myth. Now it would be an enormous task to go beyond the manifold expressions and show that we are dealing with a unique process involving the severance of the here-below and the beyond. These dimensions, particularly those in an oriental framework, are simply confined there, held back by the previous unified organization of the cosmos and only allowed to freely show themselves elsewhere. At any rate, in the vast majority of cases, the two types of order, namely immanence and transcendence, counter-subjective plurality and subjectifying unification, come together and coexist. Neither one is completely obliterated by the other, nor is the original monism completely replaced by a dualist vision. There is rather a very uneven breakthrough of a vision of the Supernatural in terms of separation, within or based on this primordial structure, which accommodates visible and invisible within the same sphere. As the persistence of magic attests, this is an extraordinarily significant structure which will continue almost up to our own time, even after transcendence has unfolded to its full extent. It should be pointed out that the religious formations of an age always arise after these conflicting tendencies have been resolved, either openly or tacitly, by establishing a new equilibrium around such points as the *reinterpretation of the primordial*, the *structural link between the one and the many*, or finally the transition from illusion to truth. However, a thorough analysis and comparison lies beyond this schematic account, so I can only offer a few broad remarks.

While it is extremely difficult to establish a common source of inspiration by looking at the constructed theologies, cosmologies, and soteriologies, this is not so difficult to do so for religious attitudes and experience. It is commonly agreed that, although there are no closely related categories and directly comparable intellectual organizations, there does exist a common body of human sentiments about existence and related conduct, such as rejecting this world and aspiring to another, belittling this life and seeking another, imposing imperatives on oneself. Here again any general notions covering the entire spectrum of rules and beliefs are highly problematical. The approximate nature of these terms does not, however, prevent us from clearly discerning the new relation to reality—both the self's reality and the reality surrounding it—which lies at the heart of these various ascetic attitudes and sustains them. And it is through this crucial disposition, this experiential core, that we can best grasp the *metamorphosis of otherness* which constitutes the basis of the axial age. So my task in regard to these problems and their possible solutions is twofold: first, disregarding any specific doctrine, I will attempt to reconstruct the ideal model of this transformation of how the Other is conceived and perceived; I will then investigate in more detail the particular logical train of events that has given this same revolution in transcendence its most radical expression.

CHAPTER 3

The Dynamics of Transcendence

INITIALLY, the religious division ran between the human order and its foundation. We have just seen how it shifted to run between humans and we can now discuss a further shift, this time *within humans*. At the heart of the self lies the possibility of discovering or mobilizing another self, of looking at one's own normal self, and hence immediate reality, from an outsider's viewpoint. The experience of an inner split is more than just a gap. It opens up a *fracture in being*, which allows an illuminating access, from within, to more truth than is given by communal existence. The revelation originating from within this difference is the beginning of contact with a completely different and higher order of reality.

Herein lies the crucial point of the change, in this bifurcation and juxtaposition whereby religious division was transposed into individuals and installed at the heart of universal being. It was not only the nature of the religious experience that was radically transformed (into what it has remained right down to us); at the same time the underlying ontological structure was inverted in every detail. Despite its revolutionary repercussions regarding the position of the founding Other, the State's sudden appearance did not substantially modify the original organization. In terms of hierarchical subjugation, the outcome was the same as that which ensured primitive equality: everyone fell into his or her preallocated position, everything corresponded to its appropriate definition, the tangible order fitted into its sacred base. In a word, the visible and the invisible coalesce into *a single unified reality*. But there is a readjustment of the interconnection between the visible and the invisible, turning unity into disunity, complementarity into difference, harmony into disharmony. Meaning was no longer given by a destiny allocated to you but could now be found here-below in a voyage of inner discovery. It was no longer to be found in the human and cosmic hierarchical chain but now lay beyond it.

This organizing gap created various possibilities, especially at the interpretive level. Once the experience of this duality was admitted, it was perfectly logical to seek to overcome it by dispelling the illusion of the subject's and the world's substantiality, and returning to the impersonal and impenetrable unity of the primordial nothing. An opposite, and equally logical, approach was to expand this duality into separation, by splitting off this world's passive objectivity from a source of subjective omniscience. This fundamental divergence would decide the fate of the relation between inheritance and innovation: either the new spiritual experience would be ultimately absorbed into the previous structure, in which case maintaining the absolute unity of this world and its other involved the radical impersonality of this other; or this experience would be translated into an original structure based on duality, where the other became the absolutely other to this world, as the personified infinite.

In both cases, the change in thinking was similar. Paradoxical though it may seem, the proliferation characteristic of mythical thought's union of the visible and the invisible was reversed. In a universe presented as *united*, thought corresponds to a logic of the *many*; in a universe divided between presence and absence, there suddenly appears a way of thinking the "One." This is how the axial turning point, both in its social inscription and its religious expression, came to pass in human thought. Even if the foundation and what it founds end up being ultimately reunited, the difference between them allowed the possibility of *thinking totality as such*, of generally attributing what was to either an intrinsic or extrinsic single principle, through whose mill everything had to pass. This means thought is compelled to go behind the multiplicity of sensory perceptions to return to the underlying One. Hence the unending attempts to dissociate the singular from the universal, the abstract from the concrete. Such were the operating conditions for establishing a properly *speculative* way of thinking opposed to mythical thought.

Once these formal characteristics have been fully isolated, the next step of my analysis is to show how a division was established within this philosophical type of reflection that emerged everywhere—in China and Greece, India and the Middle East—in conjunction with the change in the religious axis. This dividing line followed the fundamental fracture between immanent impersonality and transcendent subjectivism, between underlying identity and separated otherness. More particularly I will show how the birth of what we call rationality depended on a specific mode of subjectivation and separation from the creating Other. More on that later. For now, I want to establish the direct link between the change in the conceptual system and the transformation of the ontological structure. Conceiving things through universals was the identical twin of the two-way restructured connection between the given and what justified it, just as apprehending life through the universal was its practical counterpart.

Reshaping the rules of existence corresponded precisely with the same schema as the reform of the understanding. On one side was the law of belonging, the immediate and characteristic requirements of the group; but opposite this lay the call of the Other, the demand for the essential and the worthy, indifferent to circumstances, united and unchanging. Dividing norms instead of reconciling them meant that the gap between the levels of being became a split within the ought-to-be. This raised, at the deepest level, the problem as to whether one should be faithful to the city's law or should conform to the divine law. Not that they were in principle opposed or contradicted each other. Quite the contrary. However you look at it, the city's law is also an expression of the divine, since it must have some sort of relation to the supernatural will; to submit to it is to communicate with the highest source of meaning. The fact remains that from now on there is something else, which cannot exhaust human obligation. Even if there is a high degree of harmony between the rule of this world and the necessities of the other, their uncoupling and the insurmountable distance between them raise the constant possibility of conflict between them. It is always conceivable to appeal above the terrestrial powers to the beyond, and this excludes anyone from successfully assuming the latter's sovereign representation here-below. It is always possible to discover within the self a secure base for acting properly, in the name of a universal obligation, and even for opposing established custom if need be. The articulation of collective constraint and of obligations toward the invisible, however institutionally stabilized, remains intrinsically problematic, and potentially open to question.

All this relates to the social actor's behavior. But on a more general level, the relation between orders of reality became problematical the moment the union between the instituted visible and the instituting invisible was dissolved. What is the value of this world compared to its Other? From now on, it will be structurally impossible to stop asking this question. At one extreme lay gnosticism's great rejection, the irrevocable devaluation of this world in favor of the unimaginably other to which the soul aspires. This position was difficult to maintain, given the problem of accounting for the origin and status of the "evil" here-below. At the other extreme, we see an attempt to reintegrate the order here-below with its source in the beyond, the theocratic attempt to put worldly life on the same footing as life directed toward the beyond. Between these two extremes was a wide variety of intermediate solutions, including some interesting compromises based on a division of duties. On the one hand, a minority of what we might call "professionals," namely monks and hermits, lived separately from their fellow beings and exclusively for the other world; on the other, the vast majority benefited from the light of these virtuosi dedicating themselves to the things of this world and finding spiritual self-realization, by respecting earthly necessities. In this way, the value placed on life here-below could be both decreased or increased in a system that basically had a stabilizing function, since it could lead to either of two different outcomes: either an ascetic individualism or an integrating holism. Yet whichever path was taken, unorthodox or heretical choices would remain open, and herein lay the major innovation. In a world faithful to the past and its established forms, the weight of power and the force of tradition provided such stability that they concealed the break with the bygone nonquestioning age. The existence of a possibility is one thing, its exploitation is another. The actual reign of orthodoxy tells us nothing about its foundation or the prospects of heterodoxy—the decisive factor being the establishment of heterodoxy as a possibility within orthodoxy itself. However stable it may be at any given time, the religious vision of human destiny will henceforth be essentially unstable. Belief in what really matters—the status of our present works in terms of ultimate justification—now creates the space for another interpretation alongside it. The ultimate content of belief can no longer be socially controlled by any regulatory body.

We must completely discard the widely accepted view of religion as an "instrument of legitimation," a view that assumes an unvarying religious function behind its variable content, and consequently assumes that through the ages both rulers and subjects hold an identical position with regard to the sacredly established order. This view is to some extent correct. But because it is abstract and general, it obscures religion's true position in the social apparatus. It accordingly obscures the significance of the changes in religion's mode of application to the collective organization, accompanying the changes in content. This view prevents us from understanding the nature and scope of the fracture which, while it certainly allows legitimation, nonetheless radically transforms the relation between religion and society. We were previously in an instituted system of the unchallengeable, where the embodied union of the invisible and the living prevailed, and beings were linked in a unique hierarchical chain joining humans to the Supernatural. This gap between terrestrial powers and the divine principle underpinning their superior status, broadens inexorably and cannot be completely controlled by any power. Through it, we enter into the age of potentially unlimited, even if unrecognized, questioning. There is now something permanently beyond the reach of power: what sustains power will soon be able to be used against it. Inherent to the new understanding of the divine is an irreducible autonomy of belief, actions, or development that opens onto the true face of reality. In the extreme case, the rule of faith opposes the rule of law. The religious, going against its time-honored commitment to the original and unchangeable, now becomes movement, invention, history. The main practical effect of transcendence as a doctrine is to expose the belief system to dissidence, thus installing instability at its center. It condemns to change a system that passionately desires to remain the same.

Distancing God and Understanding the World

From the religious actor's viewpoint, this transformation may be described as a twofold process of *reducing otherness* and *promoting interiority*. At first glance, the idea of reducing otherness may seem somewhat strange, since we are trying to account for the transition from experiencing proximity to that of experiencing difference—to speak schematically, from a system of cohabitation with several minor deities to one of being separated from a single all-pervasive divine principle. In this case, should we not speak of both a conceptual and a perceived deepening of otherness? The paradox is that an increase in a figurative or experienced otherness corresponds to a decrease in an actually implemented otherness; strengthening the image of the Other involves an actual decline in dependence on it. I have already mentioned this inverse relation between the explicit ordering of experience and the silent but effective ordering of the structure. One could almost devise a law to apply to this situation, a law of human emancipation through divine affirmation. It could be summed up as follows: the greater the gods, the freer humans are. The degree of human obligation toward the law given to them from outside is, contrary to appearances, inversely related to the degree of concentration of, and separation from, the divine. And if we assume that such a law exists, the sudden appearance of transcendence supplies the unique occasion for its application. The entire significance of religious history may be condensed into this moment. There is a strong temptation to see in this unifying removal of the divine a rise in the external determination of the human order, as compared with the immediate and abundant presence of the previous polytheistic Supernatural. Nothing could be further from the truth. Immanence presupposes severance from the foundation, while transcendence brings it nearer and makes it accessible.[5]

To understand this we must look at the temporal dimension. During the transition from immanence to transcendence there is also a leap from the *past* to the *present*. We can speak here of an elemental change from temporal to "spatial" exteriority. Temporal exteriority, the symbolic exteriority of the past, is absolute, while "spatial" exteriority, "real" exteriority in the present, is relative. Immanence is the result of distance from the instituting period, since which time nothing has happened; thanks to its remoteness, it is actually present in a world that replicates and revitalizes it. Supernatural beings and the gods themselves inhabit a completely formed world, within which they regularly exert an influence, without dictating its course. The sudden appearance of transcendence goes hand in hand with a reunification of two dimensions that were initially separate: the *original* and the *actual*, the inaugural institution and the actually present forces of the invisible—a reunification that completely alters the nature of supernatural power, by conceiving it as both our world's source and its driving force.

Two ideas follow logically from this: the idea of *creation* as copenetration of past and present, of the originary principle and the actual organization of reality; and the idea of being as a unique and separate principle. In this dual perspective, the idea of creation is essential to crystallizing transcendence. It completes the break with the mythic-magic age by reworking its central theme of the origin, in order to completely revise its significance by reversing the deity's relation to the world. The commencement used to be precisely what living beings were cut off from and hence dependent on. The old deities remained within the world without being able to act on it as a totality, whatever mysterious ability they had to influence the changing cycle of life and events. On the other hand, the God who creates from outside his creation has a grasp on the totality of things, which he controls both in its everyday aspects as well as in its deepest articulations. These two representations are poles apart: in the first case, there is disjunction from and conjunction with the origin; and in the second, separation from a god who has been defined by his ability to make the world wholly present. The gulf between them appears to originate not so much from a new creative religious vision as from the orderly transformation of a previous organization.

This transformation's mode of expression is absolutely revolutionary because it makes *the foundation accessible*. There is no doubt that human dependence ends up being much more pronounced, while the chasm between the creatures' impotence and their creator's omnipotence increases to the point of becoming unbridgeable. But this immense deity holding us in its hand is still out there. The order of things is determined by the action of a single will, which remains as it was, something with which we can *communicate*, yet must be *deciphered* and *interpreted*. What took place in the beginning is continually repeated, but the beginning as such remains inaccessible. There is no path leading to it. We can only consolidate and renew the legacy it has left us, which is both purely external and completely incorporated into our acts and gestures. Instead of a separate deity in whom everything originates, there is first an *internal* deity whose entrenchment is structurally guaranteed by the perceived distance between him and the world, a deity with whom we might possibly have an intimate connection and with whom we can communicate, whose wisdom and intentions are to be restored, grasped, and experienced within the self. But he is also a *problematic* deity whose absence from this world, which is his creation yet self-sufficient, provides the basis for an open interrogation about his enigmatic designs. Ours is a world intended to be as it is by a supreme intelligence who guarantees its substantiality, yet also a world capable of operating on its own, in the absence of a god. Meaning has now ceased to be given and is instead something emergent or reconstructed. God's intentions are inscrutable yet essentially knowable.

The certainty of God and the mystery of the world, the objective autonomy of this selfsame world and its dependence on God's total subjectivity for meaning, all indicate one thing: transcendence not only separates reason and faith, it also divides subject and object. The world's objectivity is the result of a radical separation from God, which moreover frees and institutes the cognitive subject in humans by making it autonomous in relation to divine understanding and withdrawing it from the hierarchy of beings. There is no intellectual access to a God radically separated from the world, so humans are now on their own, with only the light of their investigative faculties to assist them before this silent totality that resists their aspiration for meaning. We are dealing not with two outcomes but three. The distinction between the bearer of knowledge and the objective phenomena cannot be made without the deity's complete withdrawal from the world. This distinction presupposes and accompanies the withdrawal. At the heart of the modern revolution in the conditions for knowledge lies the religious affirmation of transcendence, and the successful transition away from the ontological One uniting God with the world. Once divine exteriority has completely unfolded, the transformation of the mode and status of the intelligible reaches its logical conclusion. We see the dissolution of any residual unity between things, between the source of that meaning and human understanding, alongside the emergence of the constitutive opposition between stark reality and the pure self. On the one hand we find the strongest possible affirmation of God's splendor; on the other, the autonomy of human reason. Not only does the separation of the deity allow humans to begin understanding the beyond, it also provides the initial foundations for making the world intelligible, independent of God.

The history of civilized forms of thinking, of philosophy working its way from myth, through theological speculation, to practical science, has its origins here in this activity of making the divine different. We begin with the order of *accepting* and pass into that of *understanding*, from what is presented as *given* to something capable of being *reappropriated*. This is not the same as now treating something that had to be repeated as something transitional. There is a simultaneous transformation of the *na-*

ture of causes and the *relations* they foster, of what is to be thought and thought's presumed capabilities. I have spoken above about the re-union of what had been radically separated in the original primitive pattern—that is, the founding past and the magical present—to characterize the opening up of transcendence. This operation is all the more significant since this division in time is also the division of the savage mind's functional axes. One is the counter-subjective organization ensuing from the complete union between the instituted present and the instituting past, which shows itself in manifold dynamic actions that fragment, classify, and distinguish. The other is the savage mind's basic tendency to subjectivize the surrounding world, what has been called its anthropomorphism, its spontaneous understanding of phenomena in intentional and personifying terms. The savage mind takes will to be the essential cause of things (a will that another will can accelerate, influence, or counterbalance through magic). Reversing transcendence, turning union with the foundation into separation from it and consequently reabsorbing creation into the divine present, means simultaneously unifying and condensing the subjective dimension within the invisible source of being. The spirits who used to be the driving force behind nature flow back outside it to dissolve and be gathered up into the full self-presence of a mundane subject. Others have pointed out the slowness with which these occult forces are purged from the natural world and reabsorbed into the absolute of the other world. The division of the one into two, the dissociation of subjective and objective, was a difficult one and took place almost imperceptibly over more than a thousand years. Nevertheless this division was from the beginning inscribed in the structural transformation brought about by doctrines of transcendence.

The viewpoint of unity immediately and totally alters the prospects for thought by merging what had previously been divided up (the actual and the original) and distinguishing what had previously been intermingled (the Natural and the Supernatural). There is an all-encompassing viewpoint from which the totality of what has a reason for existence is held together and kept coherent and self-present. The basis of things is dependent not on something arbitrary to which we must submit, but on an overall internally defined and wholly self-congruent structure. In a word, God does not and cannot do whatever he wants. He acts according to necessity, that is, in compliance with the absolute self-presence characterizing him. What exists through him is inevitably integrated into a totality which in the last resort contains its own sufficient reason. This notion will be the main cause of divisions among the faithful.

If God is indeed all-powerful, his intelligence must go far beyond ours. There must be an abyss separating us from the wisdom of his creation. Besides translating inaccessible truths into our language, revelation is there to remind us precisely of this abyss. This theme of revelation recalls the very phenomenon of reversal summarized above in terms of the notion of creation. Creation recovers the origin's mythical dimension while revelation extends the dimension of the given to which we must humbly submit. However, there is a decisive difference regarding the continuity which, in the world of myth, ties the present to the past. The difference is that revelation implies a clear historical break, between before and after, between the age of confusion and the age of truth. As far as the world of revelation is concerned, humans have never lived in strict conformity with the proper norms. Now the beginning of the human era is separated from us by a clearly measurable distance. If revelation follows the notion of mythical foundation in presupposing that humans are given life by supernatural beings, it also radically differentiates the intervening deity from the ghosts of the world of myth. Instead of having acted definitively at the beginning of time, the god of revelation also operates in a present. He is normally absent from this world and his own creatures continually fail to recognize him; yet he is still concerned with the fate of humans whose destinies he monitors. In other words, he is the all-embracing subject of a world separated from him. Revelation, as much as it testifies to the infinite superiority of divine intelligence, simultaneously opens onto something intrinsically intelligible, not something to be received passively. There is no doubt that, given its extremely hierarchical nature, dogma has been able to operate historically as an invitation to submission, if not renunciation, in a much stronger and deeper way than we can possibly understand. Yet beyond the social use made of it, revealed truth also implies the premise that God has made the ultimate foundation's inner core at least partly accessible to the human mind.

The most crucial difference brought about by revelation is this: what supposedly imposes itself on human understanding proves to be something that humans can actually appropriate or renounce, something whose meaning they can penetrate and whose repercussions they can independently experience from within. Of course, no one can ever attain the height of divine wisdom; but wisdom's goals and acts, insofar as we can grasp them, are dependent on what we ourselves can inwardly reconstruct. When the need arises, our intelligence is capable of operating on the same level as divine intelligence whose extent otherwise infinitely surpasses our own. Hence, there is an interminable oscillation between doctrines, and an open-ended controversy between those inclined to emphasize the power of human reason to identity with divine reason, and those who emphasize the irreversible difference separating us from divine reason. At the same time, there is a tendency to re-establish the barrier between us and the unknowable.

I have already mentioned the difficulties inherent in a consistent gnostic position of this sort and the nature of the knowledge which allows us to escape it.[6] There are two possibilities. The first is that this fallen world testifies to the limits of the true God's power in his struggle against contrary principles, and that our misfortunes are the result of a dangerous mishap in this cosmic war, rather than the result of some sort of intelligent design. In this case we abandon the framework of transcendence to return to the image of a deity located within the cosmos (of which our world is only one part), a cosmos where this deity grapples with forces of evil capable of challenging it. The relative equality of the opposing parties, in their claim to represent the supreme powers of the invisible, forces us to situate their confrontation within a fundamentally *united* universe.

At the opposite extreme is the second possibility, namely that this lower world declines because the separate wholly other has deliberately delivered us to destructive powers in his control, yet for some reason has given us the means to see the light of his saving truth. In this case, it is impossible to push the radical entrenchment of the unknowable to its logical conclusion. Even if this is all we know about God, it is enough for us to gain access to his reasons. All this shows how difficult it is, once we have accepted the premise of a transcendent personal god, to halt his development into an intelligible god, whether in the name of orthodox revelation, or in the name of a radical rejection of this world, and a radical humility. The view that best preserves the inner logic of the idea of God's difference is the one that concludes we can rationally understand God's actions on the grounds that he is fulfilled in both his own and the world's subjective self-congruence. This view has prevailed in history, and for once the paths of the real and the actual coincide.

I will return later to this theme—the dual process of realizing the divine and affirming the powers of the human mind. For the moment, it is important to investigate the link between the development in religion's content and transformations in ways of thinking. On the one hand, we have the complete unfolding of transcendence to the point where a subject outside the world is fully developed. We have a god increasingly depaganized, increasingly liberated from any perceptible ties to this world and increasingly reunited solely with himself—a god who, by becoming fully present, allows the world's order to be imagined in terms of objectivity and internal necessity. On the other, we have a rational being, detached from the world by God's difference, finding itself in a position to understand independently what God has willed, as seen in the course of phenomena and their immanent laws. God's will is thus accountable to an independent understanding, self-contained in the same way as the world it confronts is internally regulated.[7] We do not look for God in things, we look for their internal law which, insofar as it testifies to the full rational self-sufficiency of this world's order, refers to the ultimate self-coincidence of the world's divine subject. God is ultimately attested by his absence, through the confluence of the order of reasons and the order of things, at the heart of this mysterious harmony between the free exercise of thought, guided only by deep necessities, and the constrictive organization of reality, which appears increasingly as the deployment of an ever-deepening necessity—a fragment of the deepest necessity, of the most complete self-adequation that could be imagined. So the development of the divine absolute not only drives and mirrors the progress of human reason, but ultimately motivates its path to autonomy. God's greatness, taken to the highest level, puts humans on an equal footing with the mystery of creation and validates their independence as cognitive subjects.[8]

Divine Greatness, Human Liberty

But there is *political* as well as intellectual emancipation. The god who is no longer present in nature also stops revealing himself in the hierarchies organizing the collective bond. The absolute separation that constitutes the deity as the world's absolute subject dissolves any superior will imposed on humans, abolishes any mediating power, and cancels any explicit direct dependence on the beyond. The theoretical revolution in the world's objectivity goes hand in hand with a practical revolution in the human-social sphere's autonomy. The new ability to access the social order through action corresponds to the ability to access the natural order through thought, both orders being completely distinct.

The sovereign now ceases to be the living incarnation of the bond between heaven and earth, the personified union of the visible order with its invisible foundation, which is what sovereigns had been from time immemorial. He may plead his "divine right" but his role has changed, despite the apparent terminological continuity. He no longer makes the visible carnally present but symbolizes its absence. He no longer welds this world to the other but testifies to their separation. In actual fact he attests that God's difference leaves the human community completely to itself. This is how the political body's ontological independence, and its ability to set its own laws, comes to be embodied in the development of sovereign power. The State's logic becomes one of restoration. By increasing its influence, the State contributes to placing the source and causes of collective-being back within reach of the social actors. We will see that the absolutist monarchies' entire activity can be thus interpreted as participating in a process that is both deeply "secular" and democratic, hence profoundly self-demoting. In terms of its new religious structure, power acting from above as an expression of what radically transcends human will is here working against itself, by constituting power from below into legitimate power, which means expressing individuals' metaphysical freedom. The symbolic structure of democratic power takes shape in the mirror of monarchical power.

Significantly, modern individualist theories of the social contract appeared as soon as so-called absolute power was actually installed. The reality of the sovereign State permits the new conception of a society carrying its constitutive principle within itself. This State assumes for itself the general right to administer inherent in the terrestrial sphere's self-sufficiency, along with the active principle of collective cohesion. Once humans can imagine the social bond originating in a primal instaurating act, and once it is assumed political authority makes society what it is, a dynamic process is set in motion. This process guarantees the eventual interpenetration of the two dimensions, bringing the contemporary social mechanism into line with the norm of the founding past. When a collective foundation, supposedly brought about for terrestrial reasons, is condensed into the State, the hierarchical principle is subverted and ruined. The power that sets out to represent the collective body's internal identity, instead of being merely the incarnation of the other in society, challenges the ultimate symbolic and religious legitimacy of the system's hierarchy much more than its legal or social manifestations. This power destroys the hierarchy's ability to transpose instituting exteriority into the bond between the lower and the higher. In these conditions, the more the sovereign increases his control of and responsibility for social life, the more he dismantles the image of superiority organizing the social order. And as a result, the social order begins to appear the outcome of the will of individuals who *de jure* precede it and who consequently have to be conceived in the abstract as equals. In other words, the more administrative authority develops and the more any imposition from above loses legitimacy, the more the logic of representation perceptibly gains credibility. The legitimate organization of the collective body can only result in the explicit cooperation and instituting operation of its members. This idea and its practical development are given credence and disseminated by the action of a State which, while attempting to renew previous forms of hierarchical constraint, definitively undermines them. This State, in an almost suicidal manner, creates individual independence while continuing to presuppose the primacy of the social order.

The democratic inversion of sovereignty was from its very beginning inscribed in sovereignty understood as an idea of the modern State, as an expression of the new relation between power and society resulting from the completed revolution in transcendence. Once the split between this world and the beyond has caused political authority to take responsibility for representing and organizing collective-being, then individuals will soon exercize sovereignty, whatever royal trappings of authority remain. The State colossus is first strengthened, only to open itself up later to its subjects. By deepening the separation from its subjects, the State ends up being identified with them, in that those who submit to power will eventually claim the right to constitute it. The end result of ontological duality is the restoration of the social bond to human control, an achievement unique to western history. This history is religious to the core. It is the crowning achievement of a two-thousand-year process of surreptitiously reducing otherness by the dynamic process of making God different. Human actors now gain access to the mastery of their collective destiny through the realization of the divine infinite—mastery, it should be pointed out, that does not in any way free them from a preoccupation with God in their social activity. However, now they have to testify their faithfulness to his law from within their instituting freedom, individually, instead of having to express it collectively through external submission to coercive superior beings who are supposed to make God's presence concrete. We have gone from being within religion to being outside it, by God's greatness creating human freedom. Hence the strange way religion is neutralized within the universe it has decisively contributed to shaping. If we have surpassed the religious, it has not left us, and perhaps never will, even though its historical effectiveness is finished.

. . .

The perspective I have adopted does not lead, as some may object, to underestimating the recurrent and merciless conflicts characterizing this history. It simply gives them a different meaning. Of course, the right to free thought was obtained only after a hard struggle against the obligation to believe; and the objective understanding of things had to be painstakingly weaned from their superstitious, magical, or metaphysical understanding. So clearly individuals' political autonomy was only affirmed by waging a merciless struggle against the logic of collective subjugation. But should we conclude that this struggle was basically a confrontation between religion and its other? According to this scenario, religion is dogmatic in form and its essence is dependence, while reason and the project of freedom, though initially intermingled with belief, were destined both to turn against and destroy it, and thus embody a space wholly outside the religious, with only a contingent bond or obligation toward it. I, however, maintain that this "secular" understanding of reality and of the social bond is essentially constituted from within the religious field, whether it was nurtured by religion's substance or deployed as an expression of one of its fundamental potentialities. The secular mind is a concrete expression of a changing transcendence and used

religious truth to form itself, as much as did the official cult or the ecclesiastical discourse. Furthermore, the conflicts that constantly pit
emerging secular expressions against orthodoxy or dogma should really
be seen as so many internal conflicts which set opposing interpretative
options of divine difference against each other.

This all results from the extremely unusual situation created within
the framework of transcendent religion, by the enormous initial gap between structural possibility and actual content. It can also be seen to result from the initial contradiction between the potential logic of the new
scheme in regulating the conjunction/disjunction between the visible and
the invisible and the practical and experiential content of belief. We have
seen how, by changing from a unifying system linking the human to the
divine, and the visible to the invisible, to a system of duality based on
the separation of their respective spheres within a single world, God's
sudden appearance as a universal and distinct subject puts the potential
radical overthrow of religious organization at stake. However, this revolution in order and structure will for a long time and for very good reason, remain unexpressed. The ancient principle of cosmic-theological
unity, the crushing burden of an age-old heritage, will continue to prevail and to inform religious experience. There is a god from another
place but present inside the world. There is a beyond separated from us
by an unbridgeable chasm, but through the grace of a sovereign mediator there is complete union between the order here below and its source
in the beyond. There is in principle the autonomy of a natural desacral-
ized sphere, but in practice we find the unity of being affirmed through
magic, analogy, or mysticism. Hence there is from the outset an irreversible split between two tendencies reflecting dogma's inner tensions:
on the one hand, there is a tendency to continually reinvent God's difference; and opposed to this, an unshakable conservative tendency to
safeguard a living bond between heaven and earth. Giving infinite depth
to the other versus the restoration of being's ultimate identity. From a
certain viewpoint, it is always possible to turn God's greatness against instituted religion, which can be systematically accused of offering only a
restricted vision. But it makes just as much sense to maintain the opposite viewpoint, which has always been the unconscious cornerstone of
human social and spiritual life. Christian Europe's entire religious and intellectual history will revolve around this unique central point: it is biased
in favor of God's omnipotent exteriority and requires a certain effort to
block or reverse its effects. This is the Archimedean point for understanding the extraordinarily complicated successive disputes and battles.

If we wish to gauge the precise nature of the opposing positions, and
the consequences of their antagonism, we must carefully disentangle appearance and reality in each instance. The protagonists are regularly
portrayed in misleading fashion. Genuine innovation takes place in con-

ditions brought about by a restorative return to a primeval authenticity or integrity (as in Augustinism or Jansenism, for example), as does the conservative tendency, though for reactionary purposes. The latter concentrates on defending the mediating Church and, through it, the personified solidarity between the here-below and the beyond. But by so doing, it disentangles the visible world from its invisible principle. This occurred in late medieval mysticism which rediscovered God's immediacy at a moment of political and ecclesiastical crisis, and in Romanticism, which tried to restore the general cohesion of a universe splintered by objective knowledge. But we must not be misled by all these shifts if we are to grasp the underlying processes at work here.

I will return later to the very special historical conditions that first allowed these deep oppositions to operate openly in the West and then secured the victory of the party for change. What concerns me here now is the ultimate identity of the antagonists in the quarrel between the old and the new. We usually misjudge this conflict because we judge it according to its recent past when, after the process has been essentially completed, the churches waged a futile rear-guard action against the spirit of the times. If we judge the quarrel by this final episode, the entire course of events assumes misleading clarity: a principle of tradition and orthodoxy is identified with the essence of religion; opposed to this is a principle of freedom and criticism seen to be independent of religion. Mistaking a late skirmish for the main battle obviously closes us off from the tensions of prior history, just as it prevents us from perceiving the religious roots of secular thought and action. It prevents us from grasping the nature, possibilities, and stakes of transcendent religion by reducing it to its institutional heritage, to the impoverished extension of what was always only one of its constituent elements. Not only do faith's official expressions represent only one aspect of western religion, they are the heritage, especially in Catholicism, of its conservative side, of its long-term attempt to contain divine exteriority within extremely narrowly defined limits. But transcendent religion's basic characteristic is to be found rather in its innovative attempt to provide increasingly sophisticated versions of God's difference and to display their consequences. The reality of the process initiated by the advent of the Christian concept of the deity should not be sought in something that appeals to an explicit continuity with tradition. We must rather look for it in what broke with institutional repression in the Church—that is, the Reformation—in response to the structural split contained in the notion of a unique creator god. This response became autonomous in the guise of rational divine purposes accessible to the human subject, and finally attained such self-sufficiency that it could do away with any reference to God. It is misleading to see a conflict between being inside or outside religion, between the God of faith and godless reason; we must grasp how reason progresses through god. So powerful is this process in laying foundations that we can say there is at least as much, if not more, religious inspiration behind what has flourished since the sixteenth century outside established dogma, than in what has been preserved inside it. This, in any case, brings us nearer to the full truth of transcendence understood as a dynamic process with an in-built capacity to unfold beyond its rigid doctrinal formulation. In other words, religious history extends beyond a narrowly conceived history of religion. Its generative principle is the progressive expression of the totality of possibilities latent within the schema of divine oneness. The unity of its dual approach becomes clear as a function of this organizing center: it is a metamorphosis of the other world and, correlatively, a remodeling of being-in-this-world in all its aspects.

The evolution of the religious content goes inextricably with changes in human activity. Once the central issue has been clarified, we have to define properly the second part of the process, namely, the close intermeshing uniting this transformation of the divine with the enormous intellectual, political, and material change from which our secular civilization has emerged. The complete materialization of transcendence as structure also establishes a new order of worldly practice, a new way of thinking, an original relation to nature, a new form of self-orientation and a new bond with others. Rationality, individual freedom, and appropriation of the natural world: these three axes mark the concrete shift from unity to duality that is at the heart of western religion. All three are incipient in the new articulation of the visible and the invisible presupposed by the Christian deity. They come to fruition in line with the complete dissociation of the visible sphere from its invisible principle.

From Myth to Reason

We have now seen how the development of our modern understanding of the world in terms of objective necessity is closely related to the affirmation-propagation of the divine absolute. Deepening God's subjective plenitude destroys the vestiges of the ancient hierarchical cosmic vision, expels any residual occult forces from the material essence of things, and ultimately leads us to conceive a series of phenomena rigidly determined by sufficient reason. At the end of this development lies a mind-set diametrically opposed to the mythical one—just as the conjunction/disjunction of the visible and the invisible, which organizes transcendent religion, is the counterpart to the religion of the founding past. Deep down, the "intellectual equipment" remains the same from one system to an-

other—despite its different cultural functions the human mind has a
"natural" consistency. The basic operative possibilities are identical but
are arranged in completely different ways, depending on how they are
functionally integrated into two diametrically opposed religious and social devices.

We cannot clearly distinguish the spontaneously acting savage mind
from the domesticated mind oriented toward effective action. There are
two main ways of organizing the conceptual framework whose modes depend on *how they are instituted*, since they ultimately depend on the
type of bond that relates society to its foundation. These two ways of organizing correspond to two extreme forms the collective foundation's exteriority may theoretically adopt. In both cases present reality is determined by a principle completely external to it: in the first, by the origin
and the founding past; in the second, by the divine subject and its unlimited self-presence. The only difference is that this transition from absolute past to absolute presence amounts to reversing what can be conceived about the foundation, as well as being a complete turnaround in
man's relation to the ultimate source of meaning in his universe. Since
the origin has already occurred, it cannot be determined but only recited
and repeated, while God's mind, though clearly unfathomable in its
depths, is still accessible through its effects, because of his work's perfection and necessity. The deity culminates in absolute self-unity sig-
nalling its ultimate separation from us, and leaves the world to us to understand, to penetrate and change in every way.

There can be no truly internal history of thought that does not take
into account what holds together the horizon of the thinkable and the
tools for thinking it. A genuine history of western reason can only be
written in terms of structure and structural transformation which simultaneously modifies both the ideal content and the conceptual form. As
far as western reason's birth and its departure from the mythical mold
are concerned, the structural upheaval occurs with the sudden appearance of the viewpoint of the One. This ideally attributes all being to a
unique regulative principle in opposition to myth's multifaceted logic. It
also initiates unlimited self-questioning, governed by recurrent irrecon-
cilable oppositions: the one/the many, the sensible/the intelligible,
form/content, etc. These oppositions replace the consubstantiality of
their counterparts in the savage mind. In this process, the world's objectivity emerges through the dissolution of being's unity, through uncoupling the Natural from the Supernatural within one cosmic-biological totality allowing each to extend completely independently. At the same
time, the well-ordered network of correspondences and affinities holding
the universe together is replaced by a clearly defined causal sequence.
This means that the previous requirement to integrate individual things

into the whole, by analogy or by affinity, is projected onto the connection between things, which now becomes completely a matter of necessity. From this we can see that the scientific spirit already exists in magical speculation, just as the modern idea of causality exists in the notion of occult influence. Moving from one level to the other directly and internally transforms the general conditions for representing reality, as determined by the evolution of the human/divine relation. In short, the mind is not free of its contents—or at least it is only so within a circle secretly defined by an organizing principle. It adjusts to them and both are transmuted by a structure intimately connected with the collective organization.

From Dependence to Autonomy

The sudden appearance of the personal god carried with it a radical transformation of human beings' status by making them all distinctive and turning them back on themselves. The relation with the supreme powers now became both *direct* and completely *internal*, whereas previously contact with the foundational principle took place through hierarchically subordinating the parts to the whole. The relation to the supreme power ceased to be transmitted through the bond between beings so it could be focused within each one of them. Moreover, in this as in other matters, the Christian faith only represented the cutting edge of a much broader movement. From the moment the alliance of the visible order and its invisible roots began to break down, from the moment we began postulating the existence of a unique principle secretly controlling all of life, there was an internal separation corresponding to the fracture in being. The hiatus between appearances and reality resulted in the emergence of an ethics of withdrawal and mobilization giving us access, within the self, to the true good concealed by human intercourse. The Christian imperative to convert, instigated by the revelation of the creator's interest in his creatures, was simply an extreme version of this. From now on, an inner being existed alongside or rather beneath the social being, an inner being ultimately completely independent of God. In every believer there coexists one actor fettered by the world and another unfettered through commitment to the other world.

There is no need to elaborate on the possible destabilizing effects of legitimating the innermost core separately from the collective norm. These effects remained largely dormant, insofar as divine exteriority still had to maintain a direct link between the terrestrial and celestial orders— and to the extent that the mediating church in particular remained the obligatory sacramental intermediary between God and the faithful, with all the consequential obligations of membership and submission. As transcendence unfolded and the two kingdoms slowly drifted apart, interiority gradually gained enough momentum to begin contesting the hierarchical principle. The more God was separated from us by his infinite nature, the more the relationship with him tended to become purely personal, to the point of excluding any institutional mediation. By becoming absolute, the divine subject could only find a legitimate terrestrial guarantor within inner presence. So initial interiority directly turned into religious individuality.

We are still a long way from the individual as a social and political category. We could, it is true, imagine a community of believers both thoroughly individualized in their relation to God and oriented exclusively toward spiritual ends. The transition from extra-worldly religious individualism to intra-worldly social individualism could thus have been achieved by fusing the spiritual and the temporal. The simplicity of such a direct transfer makes this a tempting but, to my mind, completely misleading model, as it does not help us understand the inverted priority in the relationship between the social constituent and the social whole, an inversion fundamental to our world. Calvin's City-Church was still a long way from the modern conception of a society of independent and self-sufficient equals. The City-Church demanded communal homogeneity and collective pressure and, starting out from a thoroughgoing holism, the progress of the city allowed a corresponding individualized quest for salvation through worldly activity. The individual actors' final emancipation from the collective totality occurred in a more roundabout way. The determining factor was not the believer's unique relation to God, but the much broader relation of power to the creator's supreme will—insofar as it would control the form of the relation between the social members. The State's intermediary role and its religious transformation allowed the individualization of the faithful to be carried out in the public arena. So God's full realization meant a purely personal faith, in both a legal and factual sense, as well as a regulated transformation of sovereign power. Sovereign power stopped being a mediatory living realization of the instituting invisible among visible creatures. As a result it ceased to function as the keystone of a truly hierarchical order, reflecting at every level this physical intermeshing with a higher order. Sovereign power withdrew from its previous role of embodying the need for submission to the outside, and was entrusted with a new one of guaranteeing the human sphere's ultimate self-sufficiency and autonomy. From then on, not only was the political instance no longer in a position to animate the previous unifying arrangement of higher beings, but all its actions moved imperceptibly toward undermining its own basis and underlying principle. The State, acting independently of its operators' wills, but in accordance with the schema of the community's self-congruence, would from now on control and justify its deepening hold, and the very nature of its intervention would work inexorably to release its subjects by undoing the priority, and thus the prescriptive nature, of the law holding them together in relation to their will. The bond no longer came first but second in relation to what it bound together, arising from an amalgamation of their free wills and receiving its legitimate authority from a special delegation of sovereign individuals. The democratic upheaval occurred after the growth of power resulting from the divine's withdrawal, when the responsibility for collective cohesion had been placed entirely in the hands of political authority. Even though he was wholly "absolute" and had "divine right," the sovereign who became a terrestrial stand-in for an absent god was condemned to transfer sovereignty downward. Only after power had been produced by society was he in a position to exercize the totality of functions and prerogatives that the separation of the terrestrial and celestial kingdom opened up and allocated to him.

Thus, any continuity between the believer freed from the world and our community-independent citizen, would be provided on the collective level by the additional path opened up by the final unfolding of transcendence and the change in the social bond's structure, brought about by what made every Christian completely free before God. Modifying the whole freed the individual from any obligatory membership by transferring the entire collective dimension into the State's domain, and only through this process did internally autonomous human beings gain control of themselves. We should avoid two extremes: the first, starting from an increasingly exclusive personalization of faith, proposes a purely religious origin for the individual without sufficiently taking into account the enormous gap between the register of inner freedom and the order of social constraint as a whole; the second is satisfied with seeing a purely social origin for the primacy of individuality, in the transformed power relationship, without seeing the religious source of this mutation of the sovereign principle, without grasping the continuity which in the long-term linked the city of equals with God's people. The history of the principle of individuality thus merged with the process of expressing transcendence: the first emerged tentatively with the second. The believer was completely alone before a god completely outside the world, and the citizen was alone and free before human autonomy incarnated in the sovereign State, both of them expressing the changed relationship to the other world and the revolutionized relationship between the inhabitants of this world, and both being the complementary ultimate logical outcomes of western religion.

CHAPTER 4

From Immersion in Nature to Transforming Nature

THERE WAS yet a third side to this enormous revision of the field of human experience, one I have until now only briefly alluded to. This was a transformation of our practical relation to the world, a transformation that took place by actively turning the religious otherness, that previously guaranteed the world's inviolable order, against the world's reality. Once the split appeared between the here-below and the beyond, between appearance and truth, we changed from a basic acceptance of the order of things and of the law of destiny, both organized by the primordial religion of the past, into a fundamental religious rejection of this world in the name of the other world. At this point, the salvation imperative and access to the true life gave meaning and direction to this life. Widening the split affected activity oriented toward the other life thus: whereas this life used to involve maintaining stringent self-control and an inner distance from the world's vanities (while at the same time maintaining an external distance from the unchangeable necessities of its order by continually adhering and submitting to them), it now turned to the things in this world and tried to transform them. All the power once directed toward maintaining a self-identical human-natural universe, all the energy deployed to neutralize change, was now turned against nature and put in the service of universal change.

In other words, everything that humans had turned against themselves in favor of being's unshakable identity now became the driving force behind an unrestrained action against everything surrounding them. We cannot understand the extraordinary alterations accompanying the emergence of modern societies unless we see them as a series of major reorientations of religious rejection. This third and last change completed the cycle by transferring what used to belong to the invisible back into something visible and correlatively transmuting a passion for the immovable into a source for change. The history of the other reaches its conclusion once we move from humans totally under the control of the other to humans radically other to every *given* in general, where the neighboring universe is a product of their activity. Understanding our obligation to challenge, or at least not blindly accept, *received* reality, allows us also to understand the high value our predecessors placed on the *received* order of things. Our orientation in being is diametrically opposite theirs; we are just as much in tune with what determined them and just as close to it, but our distance from them allows us to understand them. The term "lord and master of nature" does not simply represent a certain level of scientific, technical, and economic development, but much rather expresses a symbolic organization of experience, where material abilities and intellectual attitudes cannot be separated. These abilities and attitudes are complementary expressions of orientation within reality, and can be illuminated by comparing them with earlier religious orientations.

Indebtedness to the Gods, the Inter-Human Bond,

and the Relation to Things

The religion of the absolute past and its absolute repetition implied a certain disposition both within the natural world and in relation to it. Transposing the founding patterns into another time, which the present simply revived and copied, had the effect of submerging the human order in nature's order, making them practically inseparable. If the origins belonged totally to a previous era, this applied equally to day and night, the succession of seasons, the course of the stars, the distribution of animals and plants, or the divisions between humans. The unqualified respect shown time-honored practices was to be paid equally to the organization of the surrounding universe. We could no more have grasped the rules that definitively established the proper way of living than we could have changed the course of nature. A scrupulous renewal of custom went hand in hand with a concern to leave the state of things as it was. Given the system's logic, we could not but feel ourselves fully and profoundly at one with this state of affairs. Not only could we not for a moment imagine ourselves opposing it, but the feeling of co-belonging to it was so powerful that any aggressive or debilitating action in turn called for a ritual compensation and a formal restoration of the balance. In other words, in such a framework the relation to nature was totally conditioned by the relation to the social bond. This relation did not exist as an autonomous sector of activity: it was completely determined from within the inter-human relation.

This state of affairs continued while the ontological structure of the One prevailed, the most accurate model for this being the conjunction/

disjunction of the visible and the invisible within the framework of primitive religion. Whenever we talk about the co-presence of the Natural and the Supernatural within a single world we are talking about humans' association with this Natural/Supernatural, the impossibility of directly confronting it, and the restricted access to the forms of interhuman relations. We will not learn anything about the human attitude to nature over such a long period by retrospectively projecting onto it an attitude it adopted somewhere in the seventeenth century. To do so would certainly prevent us from understanding both the transformation itself as well as the real reasons for earlier "underdevelopment"—according to my criteria—and the extremely slow rate of progress previously achieved regarding the exploitation of natural resources. It is totally misleading to treat the period before and after the transformation as a continuity. Earlier dispositions were not just the same as ours, lacking only our self-assertiveness and effectiveness. They were completely different and had a tendency to reject what we seek. They represented a completely different *"culture,"* if I may use this term to mean that beneath the infinitely varied content of civilizations and groups lies a more fundamental way of structuring human-social experience. Unless we accept this meaning, history with all its periods of inertia and lethargy cannot be understood as growth. Over its longest *duree*, the main method for instituting societies excluded direct confrontation with the natural environment, excluded any immediate transforming grasp, a grasp only crystallized and expressed in the last century through the notion of labor. As I have already said, this was because this viewpoint integrated the relation to nature with the intra-social bond, since contact with objects was always mediated by the bond between beings.

Hence the division, so often noted by observers of traditional civilizations, between a humanized nature integrated into the system of signs and fabric of life and a separate, unoccupied nature, external despite its natural proximity.[9] Only in recent times has this duality broken down and nature been reunited, by being drained of any human presence or meaningful life-force while simultaneously drawing nearer to us as a unified object to be confronted. There is no participation in, ignorance of, familiarity with, or absence of nature: it lies before us, radically external and fully appropriable. The development of western art, particularly that of modern landscape painting, offers a parallel to this dual process of purification and elevation. Aesthetic emotion abandons the spectacle of a humanity steeped in nature, or a nature slotted into human space, in order to restore raw flesh to things and truth to sensations, before labeling or acting on them. By resisting any integration into appearances, we stop being so deeply moved by them. And what distances us from them simultaneously reveals their primordial strangeness, and returns us to that primal estrangement from the world, thus making it the object of our endeavors. There is a widely held belief that this pictorial quest is a reaction to science; an attempt to rescue a living contact with nature threatened by technical objectivization. But we are more likely dealing with two parallel approaches on separate levels, that of perception and understanding, two structurally homogeneous branches of the same encounter with the world. The painter's eye secretly prepares us for cold scientific objectivity; and conversely, technical domination initiates us into the emotional power of the purely sensory.

THE POLITICAL MACHINE

If we look at how the relation to nature is subjected to the social relation, we are surprised to see that the first major initiatives to reorganize and systematically exploit the environment beyond merely harnessing its resources, resulted from political domination. This human "megamachine" of despotism, the first real mechanical power, is both a prototype and an antithetical model of future transformational systems.[10] There is a regular influence on nature but this takes place from within and as a result of action on humans. Objects are approached and inspected by controlling humans. Slavery is the logical conclusion of this tendency: objects are transformed by first transforming humans into objects. In contrast, we can measure the extraordinary upheaval that the modern system of production represents, along with the structural link it establishes between artificially appropriating the world and the political emancipation of individuals. Humans are initially free because they are alone before an empty and totally accessible nature, and the power of labor is henceforth in principle unlimited because it expresses and guarantees human autonomy. We cannot pass from one universe to another simply by accelerating a linear accumulative process; the transition involves a complete reversal in the conditions and dispositions of human activity. With the State's appearance there is an unprecedented mobilization of resources, whereby the history-as-growth which still impels us begins. This does not mean that a practical and symbolic relation to nature prefigures the force that inspires us. This driving force was not the control of things but of people. There was at least initially no need or intention to enlarge the circle of available resources, but rather an internal dynamics of power exercized on fellow humans, a necessity for power to increase, to become firmly entrenched and exalted.

Extensive though it was, the change in the relation to the environment was not self-contained, but arose from the transformation of the interhuman relationship, without directly affecting the previous relation to the natural world. The manner in which the neolithic "revolution" in the means of subsistence, and its momentous expansion through the State's magnifying effect, was absorbed into the previous prevalent mode of apprehending the universe, may seem enigmatic, but is not. It is a sign, if one was needed, that this mode of apprehending the universe did more than just transpose the hunter-gatherers' material conditions of existence into the superstructure. There is always a temptation to interpret the appearance of agriculture and animal husbandry in terms of a transition from a "natural" hunting economy to one of proper production based on human intervention in the environment—the qualitative change in the means of acquiring resources counting for much more than any quantitative change which may have occurred. But however we interpret the sudden appearance of these techniques and practices, the fact is that the "superstructure"—the effectuating vision a society has of its position in the world—has proved stronger than developments in the "infrastructure". Furthermore, the primordial regulating schema of nature-as-partner, based on an unvaried balanced exchange, remained basically unaltered, despite the fact that very real control had been gained over the means for supplying nourishment. What we find in different forms at the heart of archaic peasant cosmologies, so characteristic of the unvarying fertility cycle, is that its regular recurrence both nourished humans and brought them the comforting reassurance of an unchanging mother earth. At a superficial level, humans tapped into nature, but maintained a respectful silence toward the inner order of things. Pastoral borrowing from nature adapted to the old equilibrium without the slightest disturbance, however subversive its underlying principle may have appeared. Moreover, the domestication of plants and animals did not bring with it any "revolutionary" social changes. Witness the fact that the majority of primitive societies we are familiar with are non-neolithic societies which have assimilated their altered mode of subsistence without having substantially modified the general pattern of their operations.

Changing the material base did have major effects, but only indirectly, by supplying indispensable conditions for the State's formation, though it should be remembered that this foundation did not contain the dynamic principle behind the State's sudden appearance. The State required this foundation, but did not necessarily have to develop from it. Nevertheless, only after the State was constituted, and its coercive mechanisms deployed, did the real potential of the resources contained in neolithic technology begin to be exploited. The *political* reorientation of economic logic to accumulate and distribute a surplus crystallized the latent energy of techniques which might just as well have been used differently in a primitive "subsistence" economy.[11] No doubt power alone would not have achieved anything without technique, but the latter could not have produced anything without the compulsion to work which constructed a new being, a new type of social actor: the peasant, who for thousands of years was the archetypal oppressed producer. This was a total reshaping of the human character and landscape (by force) from which emerged the open-ended process known as *history*. The arrival of the State revolutionized the way humans were grouped together, and also brought about an inevitable revolution in their numbers. But this change nevertheless took place by carefully fitting in to the previously established relationship with the natural surroundings, without displacing anything essential. Not that action did not have some reciprocal effect on representation. Practical mastery over physical processes must have somehow altered the scope of human possibilities. But it was not able to shake instituted powerlessness or to challenge the limits set on apprehending things. Though its effects undoubtedly undermined the established organization's credibility, the new authority did not in any way contain the basis for an alternative. The persistence of this relation of associating with nature also explains the basic limits to growth of old agrarian economies, which lacked any real foundation for progress. the endeavor to produce was stimulated either from above, or from below by sheer numbers; it did not originate from confronting things and systematically attempting to increase and deepen our hold on them. To move into the age of efficiency, the relation to nature had to free itself completely from its original incorporation and subordination to the social relation. Only then was there a possibility of circumventing the time-honored religious inclusion in a unified cosmos, namely by going beyond accommodation and collaboration with natural forces, by optimizing intervention into the inner structure of things—the complex of action and representation we call *production*.

THE VITALITY OF CHANGE

The major transformation of being-in-the-world was part of the reversal of the religious structure corresponding to the earlier unfolding of transcendence. The rearticulation of the visible and the invisible quietly set in motion what the lofty powers of the political machine could not bring about. As soon as divine oneness appeared, the conditions for a new relation to reality were set up. Distancing the creator from his creation dissociated intelligent creatures from the rest of created reality, breaking the comprehensive arrangement binding humans in a relationship of cohabitation with nature as a whole. Totality suffered a fracture separating the apprehension of the world from the relation with its foundation. Beyond immediately perceptible things and beings lay the cardinal principle of a wholly other order which created and governed them. The principle receives an unqualified respect not shown to the things and beings governed. The restrictive dispositions linked with participation in the Natural and Supernatural are thus theoretically removed.

I say "theoretically," because practice is different. I have already discussed monotheism's early ambiguities and the enormous gulf between the dawning idea of the transcendent god and his complete structural development. Similarly, as soon as the world was attributed to a separate subject, it became possible to separate humans from the cosmos. This possibility remained dormant as long as the ultimate unity of existing things was maintained along with God's close involvement in the world. But the opposition between the human sphere and the natural domain only became effective in the context of deploying the difference between the two orders of reality.

This movement at first sight appears to be a simple variant of the one I described as leading to the formation of an objective understanding of things. We have seen how the division between the visible and invisible simultaneously imparted a new status to reality and bestowed a new standpoint on the bearer of knowledge. This is actually only an implementation of the principle behind this transformation. One part of it, the complete freedom attained by the producer in relation to the world's materials, corresponds to the external position of the scientific subject. The other part, the indifferent availability of things, their openness to an action affecting their innermost workings, matches the silent autonomous physical nature of a thoroughly accessible reality

However true, this still does not explain the fundamental reorientation of human action. We are dealing here with a much deeper and more specific phenomenon, which developed from ontological duality. It does not mean just adapting to a hitherto unthinkable confrontational position. What really matters is what has given these new dispositions their irresistible efficacy, namely, a general redirecting of energy back toward appropriating this world, by transforming the concern with the other world. The increasing distancing of the beyond indicates a radical investment in the here-below. By this I do not mean that humans simply confer greater value on activity in the here-below or seek to penetrate it or be completely absorbed into it. The decisive feature of the change is its productiveness, its extraordinary liberalization and mobilization of forces. Our previous association with nature is now inverted into a possessive one; consent to the established is converted into a transforming offensive. The modern world intensifies activity and sets everything in motion, two traits which constitute an unconscious yet effective organizing imagination. This is perhaps the best concealed, yet most certain source of the energy of the ideal informing living practice. This schema of growth ultimately guarantees the unity of our civilization, a civilization permitting the co-existence of fragmented norms, from the private

quest for pleasure to the organization of political life, from technical systems to the course of individual lives. For this schema to take hold, the
following factors had to be harmoniously integrated on several levels: an
internal mobilization of beings, an increase in the exchanges between
them, a broadening of their social involvement, an accumulation of the
power to displace and change, and the development of all possible resources. But most decisive of all was the remarkable achievement of having turned religious indebtedness toward a created world into a duty to
create. The guarantee of a hold on the world was previously devoutly inscribed into an order determined from elsewhere; from now on, the
power to change what has been bequeathed to you, the power to alter the
mechanism and increase its quantity, output, or value will provide this
guarantee. What was once the source of the most enduring and powerful human emotion, immobility, now exhorts us to strive incessantly.

The Other World and Appropriating This World

I have focused on this area to highlight the distinctiveness of Western
Christianity, the structural factors determining its originality and scope.
I have said that the monotheistic idea alone could not do this. It could
quite easily exist as a belief without having any repercussions, for, in certain conditions it is fully compatible with the previous conserving integration inside a received world. The real question concerns God's position viz-a-viz the world, and whether there is a structural link between
the human world and the divine. The example of Islam shows how the
most austere and elaborate faith in divine oneness was reconciled with
an adherence to the law of an all-embracing universe conforming to its
creator's will. We could consider this a case of the radical exteriority of
this non-representable principle in relation to its creation, but that would
be misleading. For one thing, the connection between God and the world
was preserved, despite his theoretical exteriority, just as the practical
union between terrestrial existence and its governing principle was maintained. Both of these were assured by the intelligibility of the message
entrusted to the prophet and the law he decreed. In other words, a view
that does not go beyond doctrinal content overlooks the strict maintenance of ontological unity and the equally categorical preservation of an
existential structure, where being-in-this-world in accordance with religious norms was still valued in itself (whatever recompense it may bring
to the elect in the beyond), and where the relation to reality remained
actively sympathetic toward an inviolable universe.

It is only when there was an investment in the other world as *opposed*
to this one that the monotheistic creed became a destabilizing force, that

is, doctrinally speaking, in regard to salvation requirements. This assumes we understand salvation in the strict sense of the word, and do not restrict it to an outlook where the soul is somehow rewarded after death, but regard it rather as a feeling of strangeness toward, and rejection of, this lowly world, a total orientation of existence toward the other life. Believers were torn away from perceptible reality, as opposed to their previous integration into the cosmos, and humans in general earned a privileged position over the rest of creation, in so far as they were the only creatures in a position to hear the call of the beyond. Having been thus delivered from the common lot, they attained a freedom toward everything around them, which foreshadowed their theoretical right to be "lord and master of nature". Does this also mean that the detachment achieved by the need for salvation was enough, and that when this turmoil was unleashed we can say that all conditions required to establish an active transforming relation to reality were present? Something further was obviously needed, since if this lowly world is not our true homeland, we could simply lose interest in it, renounce it, or endeavor to escape it. At one end of the spectrum, we find simple believers, divided between what is due to God and what to Caesar, between their inner orientation toward the beyond and the works required in the world. At the other extreme we see several varieties of ascetic expression: the hermit's flight into the desert, gnostic escapism or deliverance through renunciation. It is quite easy to see how this summons issued by the invisible from beyond the sensory world (and no longer presented along with it) dissolved the principle of co-belonging and posed an insurmountable obstacle to any systematic attempt at transformation. But it is difficult to see how we could have gone from initially devaluing our earthly abode to upgrading and systematically exploiting it. Yet this is precisely what happened and to understand it we must return once again to the problem of ontological structure. The origin of this extreme escapism and pure indifference was an attempt to re-establish the One against the apparent duality of being, an attempt to recapture the ultimate oneness of the all-embracing truth. This occurred by abstractly denying the perceptible world's substantiality, interpreting it as superficial appearance, or absorbing it into an inferior degraded form of true being. Either way, it was regarded as a secondary emanation of a higher primordial reality. Buddhism is undoubtedly the purest example of this compromise between being other to the world and rescuing the One. There is both a total lack of involvement in our terrestrial prison and, by emphasizing the impermanence of the phenomenal universe, a diminution of its substantiality, so that once we passed through these appearances, all separation was abolished, along with the illusion of personality. This philosophy of deliverance presents a symmetrical counterpart to Islam where submission through belief was the keynote. On one side is monotheism without the salvation imperative; on the other a sustained effort toward salvation without monotheism, without any concern for the divine for that matter. But in both cases, there is an attempt to recapture the difference: either by making a (conceptual) disjunction between the creator and his creation; or finding a (perceptual) discrepancy, between the pain caused by appearances and the tranquillity of the real. On the one hand, there was a comprehensive adjustment to the world's law and God's will; on the other, any perceptible grief and error was dissolved into the intelligible nothing. In one instance the practical organization of the connection with the divine neutralized the distance attributed to it, while in the other, the radical depersonification of the supreme principle filled the hiatus between the kingdom of illusion and the domain of truth.

Heaven and Earth: Christianity's Specificity

Christianity's composite nature rendered the two stabilizing solutions just described impossible. For one thing, the idea of a personal creator god was scarcely compatible with reducing his creation to insubstantial phenomena. For another, the call of the true life beyond this life entailed not only uncompromising personal behavior, separate from any collective bond, but also further duality in the registers of meaning, thus making any clear straightforward reading of divine wisdom impossible and rendering it inappropriate for establishing the community of believers in an ideal union with the Almighty's unchallengeable law. There was no possibility for either a radically escapist doctrine or a moral code of complete submission or pure renunciation; nor was there any possibility of being completely at ease with divine order in the terrestrial city. Christianity's innate capacity to handle internal pressure and fluctuation depended on an interplay between the obligation to recognize this world's substantiality and life's value in their own terms, and the righteous refusal to adapt to either

Natural beauty created by God, the futility of life, the glorification of obedience—contradiction is intrinsic to Christianity and reconciliation a never ending task. From this relentless tension a new world, both religious and profane, is born. A structural link between the here-below and the beyond would not have been impossible. I have already suggested how a similar rearrangement of the two kingdoms within early Christianity was achieved by creating a complementary relation between inside and outside, both on the individual and collective levels. At the private level, it placed the unworldly deep within the self, while requiring external respect for the way of the world; publicly, it separated the righteous who renounce the world from the sinners who surrender to it. Despite the potential for deep antagonism between the personal and social selves, Christianity achieved a practical reconstruction of the one as well as encouraging devotion to and obligation toward the invisible. Moreover such integration implies that the cosmos continued to link the Natural and the Supernatural, despite doctrinal acosmism.

The Christian dogma of the Incarnation was the catalyst which unleashed the dynamic interplay of these contradictions. It was living testimony, at the heart of faith, of the irretrievable split between the two self-substantiating orders of reality. When God adopted a human form, he emerged as wholly other, so different and remote that without the assistance of revelation he would have remained unknown to humans. But at the same time the terrestrial sphere acquired autonomous substantiality and became ontologically complete, gaining enough dignity for the Word to become flesh. Through their mystical union in Christ, the human and the divine were differentiated, as the hierarchical intermixture of the earthly abode and the kingdom of heaven broke down into its basic constituents. However powerful the past, and whatever attempt was made to maintain the cosmic entanglement of the visible and the invisible, henceforth there would be an inexhaustible sustaining mystery at the heart of the belief system, namely, the mystery of separation and otherness condensed into the figure of the Saviour. Through the enigma of his presence and the unnatural union that occurred in him, the son of man rekindled the dialectic between monotheistic personification and rejection of the world. Christ evoked a difference that made any notions of radical escapism and deliverance from the here and now meaningless: in this life there was no escape from a world worthy of Christ's humanity. Nor was it still possible to find peace by strictly observing God's order. In the first place, since his order was based on an unthinkable notion, it was difficult to interpret his will and be assured of his truth; secondly, and more importantly, it was impossible not to feel completely overwhelmed by the very abyss separating us from him. The paradox of divine otherness, as reformulated within the framework of the Incarnation, is that while it intensified the call from without and reinforced mobilization toward salvation, it highlighted the impossibility of fleeing. This allowed an inversion of the religious process: we could devote ourselves completely to attaining salvation, not by turning away from this world, not by installing ourselves outside it, but, on the contrary, by investing in it and opening up to the plenitude of its own realization. In other words, we were no longer to seek a coincidence between the here-below and the beyond, either by dissolving immanent phenomena into transcendence or making the beyond present in the here-below by submission. We were now supposed to tolerate the difference and furthermore, strive to deepen it, since the internal realization of the terrestrial sphere's autonomy and integrity was the only means of attaining the separated absolute. So preoccupation with the other, which initially caused a turn away from the sensory, reached the point of demanding that it be completely appropriated and transformed. This did not result in any satisfaction, toleration of, or reconciliation with the other, but rather in attempts to grasp and change it, in a spirit of determined opposition. There was always a *rejection* operating, the same basic rejection of the immediately given, which did not encourage detachment from the world but action on it, and instead of giving rise to distanced contemplation, led to active negation.

I am of course only outlining one abstract possibility which tells us nothing about the complex and extremely varied conditions under which salvation values have historically been propagated. It is nevertheless extremely important to grasp the initial grounding of this reorientation within the world in the specifically Christian structural link between hope in the beyond and adherence to the here-below. This reorientation was a potentiality inscribed in the radically new bond, established and signified in Christ, between terrestrial closure and celestial otherness; and it was a potentiality deployed as part of the major reversal emerging from this central primordial transition from a system demanding the merger of the visible and the invisible, to one ensuring their mutual separation. This re-assessment both enhanced and relativized the significance of the doctrinal breakthrough that occurred as part of the Reformation.[12] There is no doubt that this sanctification of secular efficacy reveals a crucial dimension of Christian development, or more precisely a dimension of Christianity as development. This dimension is much more general and diffuse than the area in which it appeared. It existed for a very long time before becoming a code of behavior. Socially and historically, Max Weber's "ascetic Protestantism" is only the visible tip of an enormous underground movement which, having been continually concealed and denied, gradually replaced the former restrictive submission to the inviolable with the active optimization of the terrestrial sphere. I concede that maintaining the consistency ensured by the Protestant ethic between consciously espousing values and implementing them has had a practical reinforcing effect, but we should not exaggerate its significance by making it an explanatory paradigm. We are dealing here with a restricted superficial phenomenon, as against an overall restructuring of being-in-the-world from below, which the "spirit of capitalism" itself only partially expresses. As it progressed, this reshaping of the field of experience merged with the revolutionary change in the religious structure in modern Europe. Like the change itself, this reshaping continued until it in turn overthrew its earlier form; it took place everywhere to the same extent, even where rigid attitudes and dogma erected apparently insurmountable barriers against it. This reshaping ultimately overcame all barriers, whether by circumvention, infiltration or displacement. It was part of Christianity's continuity, which was distinguished by an original way of taking into account the physicality of human beings and the world. The greatly increased value placed on activity in modern times arose from a system of civilization which was itself already profoundly original from the standpoint of the occupation of space and time. And this distribution of humans, this social organization of their work, their installation in history, all of which so strongly distinguished the medieval West, is incomprehensible outside the framework of Christian harmony with the visible, a harmony informing their very basis.

ORTHODOXY AND HERESY

I do not intend to recreate the actual historical formation of this fateful community. Such a history would range from early dogmatic constructs up to the infiltration of key Christian values through the feudal transformation, and would include the establishment of the ecclesiastical system and the formation of monastic discipline.

Take for example the case of the Church, where the task would be to establish how the Christian structural link between the here-below and the beyond took shape through this absolutely original institutional creation. And by shape I do not mean merely translating a purposeful thought into action, but concretely establishing a meaning far removed from the actors' awareness and even against their will. The Church existed due to faith, that is, due to a necessity to break with received tradition and simple observance, a need for an inner proof, so as to find a god who can only be known through his revealed concern. There had to be functionaries whose role went beyond high-priests' ritualistic one, and who were qualified to interpret God's otherwise unfathomable messages. We needed dogma's assistance because inherited belief could not satisfy the basic uncertainty this unknown relation foisted on us. We did not have to be frozen in an externally guaranteed certainty, but had to participate in the truth through a mediating authority. So membership in this special society of the faithful, which was entirely oriented toward redemptive adherence to divine law, symbolized both a necessary internal distancing from worldly life and God's impenetrable transcendence in relation to this world. This theological line was adopted *de facto* by constituting the hierarchy so as to integrate ministers and believers within a perfect salvation society which created the explosive contradiction between faith's interiority and dogma's authority which previously justified each another. The necessity to rigidly regulate a body of doctrine against open-ended interpretation also legitimated an uncompromisingly personal understanding of the divine will. The difference from Islam is glaringly obvious. The Koran's revelation is itself the literal and indisputable presence of the transcendent in immanence and thus dispensed with interpreters, lest it succumb to the uncertainties of internal judgment or to an outbreak of subjective values. No clergy, no Reformation.[13] Christianity, by contrast, linked orthodoxy's austerity to an opening for heresy. We could even call it the religion of heresy, in so far as it was the only religion with a systematic project for recruiting and training souls by bureaucratizing interpretation. The more rigidly orthodoxy asserted itself and tightened its recruitment procedures, the more its truth appeared to come from beyond human reason, from beyond official language, since it was accessible primarily through inner experience. Dogma's prerogatives and the rights of conscience tended to jointly consolidate each other.

Western historical conditions allowed the Church to assert itself independently of temporal powers and, beginning with the Gregorian reform in the eleventh century, to develop a relatively centralized and integrated internal organization. It could be said that this was the first western bureaucracy, the first model of an organization formed separately and governed in its operations solely by the means required to achieve its end, even if it meant being at odds with the general social norms (in this case, delegated authority versus blood ties and feudal dependencies). By thus specifying its norms and requirements, or by indicating the necessary autonomy of the means for salvation, the Church established conditions for both a profession independent of the here-below and a personal religion. Indeed, the more our apprehension of the beyond was controlled by a specialized hierarchy, the more open this god and his problematic intentions was to being grasped in his innermost core. And the more the terrestrial sphere was freed from its restricted preoccupation with the Supernatural, the more self-sufficient it appeared. This created a huge gap which temporal power rushed to fill, in order to claim independence and power in its own realm. But it also represents a withdrawal opening up a new field of activity in this world, one that sustains the mobilization of spiritual reforming forces and the subjective reworking of modernity's faith. The papal monarchy achieved spectacular success by using theocratic language, that is, of the incarnate union of heaven and earth. But by highlighting the separation between heaven and earth, and isolating the responsibility for souls from the management of people, this actually served to widen the gap.

The Church's entire history thus revolves around this major ambiguity: its prevailing language is one of mediation, its central perspective one of mystical union between living beings and the spiritual realm, yet its very existence signifies the opposite. The impossibility of mediation, the irreversible fracture between the human city and the kingdom of the absolute invariably led it to focus on raising itself to the level of its ends. For Christians, mediation has *occurred* definitively in the person of the Word incarnate. This is an *event* that will never have a truly substantial *structure*. The best one could hope is to reach the level of an *image* of Christ without ever being able to occupy this intersection of the human and divine. The Son of Man occupied this space historically and it must remain unoccupied among humans until the end of history. We can invoke the presence of this supreme example every day, but though it is a mystical reenactment of the Saviour's actual arrival, the eucharistic sacrament is equally a commemoration of an absence, a ritualistic repetition of an unrepeatable event. As the reformers would point out, this says much about our distance from God the Father in opposition to the illusory participation of the invisible in the visible, as postulated by the dogma of the real presence. Nevertheless, the silent extraordinary tension associated with reliving daily an Incarnation whose very celebration attests its past fulfillment would have inevitably come into play, with or without such radical opposition.

INCARNATION AND INTERPRETATION

The dogma of the Incarnation was meticulously elaborated during the major fourth and fifth century christological disputes between two rival trends, one stressing the redeemer's divine nature and the other his humanity. Indeed, revelation's status, humans' relation to its meaning, and its reception, were all determined by the way in which Christ's nature is understood. If Christ was only a man (Adoptianism), the meaning expressed by his arrival in history tended to be eclipsed by the literal message God entrusted him to pass on. We are back with the model of a direct intervention among humans by a god present in the world, admittedly through the intermediary of a chosen individual, but one who is far surpassed by the role that has fallen on him and who expresses and definitively enshrines God's word. We have encountered a similar figure in our discussion of the Koran, a figure not entirely unrelated, via Nestorianism, to the doctrinal debates I have just mentioned, though here the Word incarnate, true God and true man, was naturally justified in expressing the Father's truth and freely accepted responsibility for adapting it to our needs. Furthermore, if he provided an accessible version in human language, his arrival as god was there to remind us of the chasm separating the thus accessible divine wisdom from its ultimate profundity. Through the god-man we can grasp something of the limitless nature of what lies beyond creation, but this only highlights our creaturely limitations. This may be due to the mediator's distance from the message: we do not hear

God's voice but his son's, and the attempt to return from there to the idea of the Father is essentially unending. Or it may be so because of the qualitative difference between what is transmitted and the absolute's inherent non-transmissibility: what we receive is God's thought put in human language and we know that this thought surpasses human language. In either case, *the religion of the Incarnation is basically a religion of interpretation*, involving the determination and imposition of a dogma, as well as freedom of conscience. And whenever the radical intervention of Christ's mediation was erased, either by being lowered to the human level or raised to the divine, this interpretive articulation disappeared. However, if Christ was only God assuming the outward appearance of man, we would end up with a doctrinal opposition like the previous one, where the immediate participation of the invisible in the visible, God's direct intervention in the world, requires total submission.

These are, of course, extreme positions. And deliberately so, since behind the discussion of dogma was a structural problem concerning the way in which relations between the divine source and the human world were organized. Extreme positions show us the truth of compromise, by showing how *only* the exact middle position, the total union of someone both completely human and fully divine, supplies the conditions for this hermeneutic opening where the divine other becomes forever answerable through his delegate—a delegate both absolutely authorized in his divine capacity and absolutely different in his human one. This is very useful for determining what is specific to Christianity. We can understand this deep, pronounced difficulty in tolerating the perfect union of the Word and the flesh in the same person. The problem is that, within such a conceptual framework, a *major* deity could not have legitimately embraced a station so far beneath him, since the slightest gap between the incarnator's two natures would have constantly put a strain on one of them by preserving the father's essential superiority. But the Christian God was more than a major deity and his might so far surpassed us that we could neither speak his name nor make his image. He was above all a god *who is other*—not a god crushing us from atop a hierarchy whose summit we cannot see, but a god whose absolute nature blossomed as he separated from our world. Not a god whose power was affirmed as our freedom decreased, but one whose own plenitude was deployed as our autonomy increased. What I am dealing with here, albeit in a cursory manner, are the metaphysical grounds for the possible dissolution of the hierarchical principle as it has been played out in our world. The revolution for equality began in, and with, the advent of the separated god.

The god who is other could only be the god of mediation, whose very being was revealed to us in the person of the son, and whose enigmatic withdrawal we would never stop questioning, from the moment of his annunciation. The mediation was both personal and institutional. Meaning was first given to the historical intervention of the god-man which took place at a specific historical date, and the church then incorporated this meaning as something to be repeated, by locating it in the living present while maintaining its permanence through the ages. The Church, in its never ending preoccupation with the content of belief, from exegesis to pastoral care, testified by its works to the problem at the heart of our understanding of God. In so doing, it sustained the necessity for a completely personal reception of, and quest for, divine wisdom, beyond what it claims to pass on. The basic ambiguity of the Church's status and role explains its capacity to survive any challenge because its mediating intervention expressed what was most specific to the Christian relation with God. At the same time this explains why the Church had to inevitably be challenged, since it could only maintain its position by creating conditions for surpassing it, in the form of faith developing independently of it. When that happened, personal mediation turned against institutional mediation. What occurred through a mediating event, by definition no longer had to be a substantial part of an organization whose permanent function was to reproduce the structure of revelation. The inner mediation of the Word's Incarnation sufficed and there was no need for the screen of an intermediary destined to perpetuate the principle among humans themselves. The awareness of time's irreversibility prevailed over the incorporated memory of ceremony and its eternal present. After the Church gained a monopoly over spiritual mediation the second wave of the western religious revolution occurred, namely, the challenge to the Church's mediating legitimacy. But the challenge was made in the name of divine truth's transcendence and the interpretative opening justifying the Church's existence. This may shed some light on its paradoxical capacity to resist and adapt when faced with the irresistible rise of the spirit of freedom. In its own way the Church bore within itself the seeds of opposition to it; in a sense it was built completely on what was opposed to it. We must keep in mind the ecclesiastical function's ambiguity if we really do want to appreciate the decisive re-orientation within Christianity toward the moral code of subjection inherent in the belief in a personal god. One might think the Church increased subjection and that, by constructing an authoritarian apparatus, pushed orthodoxy to the limits and established an exceptionally tight control over peoples innermost thoughts and feelings. This would be to misunderstand the origins of believers' incomparable personal freedom in their relation to God, a freedom presupposing the deployment of this administration of righteous belief. If subjection to dogma went further than anywhere else, it did so as a function of the autonomy of conscience.

There was a change in the moral code of subjection, but there was also a change in the moral code of renunciation, originating in the same logic of mediation. If the strict Christian conception of the Word's arrival introduced the fundamental indeterminacy of inwardness into our relation with the other world, it equally involved a necessary relativity in the rejection of this world, at least initially. Given the legitimation of the terrestrial sphere following from Christ's humanity, a condition embraced by God could not be totally bad or unsubstantial. But the Saviour's arrival on earth was also a sign of the earth's closure. Consequently, it was senseless attempting to flee our mortal condition, as if we were able to escape to the other side and attain true life. We could live with a mind to salvation in the beyond but not with one to overcoming the limits of the here-below. The Incarnation not only changed the conditions for receiving God's word, as compared with monotheism's absolute submission; it also involved a reshaping of attitudes toward salvation, in relation to the escapist seductiveness of the other. To observe the concrete realization of this great potential, we must trace the formation of western monastic discipline from the sixth to the tenth century.

The stakes are clear: both how we understand withdrawal from, and total rejection of, the world, and how we define the afterlife, involve a decision about the structure of being. Extreme figures such as the hermit, the ascete or the monk are ontological emblems: their behavior is an actual account of relations between visible and invisible, appearance and truth. Are we passing through insubstantial appearances to unite with the imminent presence, or are we confronting terrestrial closure, even when meditating exclusively on the true separate reality? Perhaps nowhere else was Christian hesitation and resoluteness between unity and duality more apparent.

The example of eastern hermits testifies to the great attraction of radical renunciation and, through it, the metaphysics of participation underlying ascetic liberation. After greatly devaluing the sensory and experiencing the required detachment, people logically began thinking about the One as the only true reality. Our visible abode was sufficiently insubstantial to allow our release, yet sufficiently imbued with invisible truth to allow us to attain this truth. A practical demonstration of this was given by spiritual virtuosi who placed themselves close to the divine by methodically tearing themselves away from human delusions, thus highlighting the futility of material things. By contrast, the monastic model was early testimony to a profoundly different orientation. Monasticism, which was set up as the dominant norm, limited extreme rejection. There could be no secession from the common condition and those striving for salvation had to pursue their ascent to God in conjunction with their peers. Even more important was the balance between contemplation and action, between commitment to the beyond and submission to the necessities of the here-below, a balance acknowledged in the code of St. Benedict. Behind the formulation of the ascetic ideal lay an implicit commitment to an ontological structure. The entire scope of religion was redefined, beginning with its boundary as represented by the monastic calling. Even the choice of dedicating oneself exclusively to serve God, separately from others, could not dispense with the tasks required to manage the terrestrial abode. In other words, there could be no internal setting aside of appearances, no abolishing the world's apparent stability, even for those supposedly dead to it; there was, rather, an obligation to accept the thickness of an unavoidable reality. For the man of God living only for salvation, work provided a minimum level of consent to this world and the discipline of the collective undertaking was proof he shares the human condition. The important thing here is less what was advocated—though we cannot ignore either the implications or effects of this legitimation of terrestrial works—than what was excluded, namely, any total rejection of the here-below with its accompanying cosmic-theological vision, which would have justified the attempt to overcome the separation from the beyond. The quest for the other life thus had to take place within the framework of this life. This exclusion was a decisive step, whereby the specific otherness of the Christian God took shape as an unavoidable obligation to the world, for the same reason as it did in the Church's hermeneutical apparatus and with the same historical ambiguities.

A god who is other is a god whose truth we can relate to by recognizing what separates us from him, and by taking into account the autonomous substantiality of our terrestrial sphere. The more we devote ourselves to caring for God's creation, the more we praise him. The internal dynamics of the articulation remains largely dormant as long as the hierarchical understanding of being prevailed, where the concern with heaven was linked to terrestrial preoccupations within an integrated hierarchy of obligations, in which all things, even the most humble, work harmoniously together.[14] Likewise, the potential conflict between direct personal understanding and dogmatic mediated understanding of God's word remained completely dormant: they were regarded as complementary stages of one and the same participation in the real. Nevertheless, the link had been made, and once we moved toward accepting the terrestrial closure, the stage was set for a development totally opposed to any known religious tradition, namely, the combination of God's deepening call with a simultaneous deepening interest in the world. Once God's distance had been accentuated and the hierarchical unity holding visible and invisible beings together collapsed, the joint process of gaining control of the world and individualizing faith would become more apparent. The more the commitment to the beyond was subjectivized within this framework, to the point of excluding any instituted mediation, and the more the here-below demanded autonomy, the more effective the mobilization on its behalf. This was diametrically opposite to all previous religious logic with its basic principle of subordination, which dictated that the greater the concern with the invisible, the less the interest in the visible. In Christianity, not only did both gain, but they did so *through* each other; any temptations of the invisible were countered by systematically recovering the visible. At the end of the process, there was no longer room for ascetics and salvation virtuosi, or specialists in sacramental or dogmatic mediation. Monastic withdrawal from the world, within the world it claimed to realize, no longer made sense. While completely submerged in and by dedicating themselves entirely to the world, believers acted in accordance with what would henceforth be a life for the sake of the other. The self-fulfillment of the absolute subject separately from the human sphere called for the latter's full realization through immense toil.[15] There was a genealogical solidarity uniting entrepreneurial asceticism to contemplative withdrawal, just as there was a link between the faithful subjugated to the Church and the inner human being, alone before God.

The Structure of Terrestrial Integrity

We must now turn to the encounter of social development with this latent logic of the religion of Incarnation, and disentangle its paths, a problematic task, since we are faced with two equally sustainable lines of interpretation: we can either admit the *influence* of the religious framework on the organizing significations at work within the social, or simply note the *convergence* between the system of civilization and the deep spirit of Christianity. However we interpret it, there is remarkable affinity between the most original developments in the society stemming from the feudal revolution and what is specifically new in the religion of the mediator, namely the principle of terrestrial autonomy. It may be that these two sets of phenomena were fundamentally independent and that the internal interaction of material causes and social forces explains the establishment of a system of civilization whose main traits just happened to be in agreement with basic Christian values. But we cannot completely exclude a possible infiltration by the systematic ontological presuppositions in the scriptural, sacramental and ecclesiastical understanding of the here-below/beyond relationship into the system actually governing the organization of beings and their habitation of the earth. In either case, part of the world still deeply affected by the old religious logic of dependence, appears to be the rudimentary materialization of a logic of self-sufficiency.

This is seen by the status of the principle of individuality in a hierarchically structured world, and especially by giving integrity to a world organized by subjection, fraught with scarcity, and marked by the inferiority of the visible. This process ranged from demographic expansion to the symbolic and practical installation of celestial eternity into a concurrent time frame, via the formation of a political body which discovers its reason for existence in itself. Again, even if these developments originated in strictly non-religious sources, they occurred in an arena informed by a vision of the divine and human, providing them with an overall coherence. Hence, social practice precludes religious consciousness from becoming explicit by actualizing some of its structural potential. This concrete reflection forced humans to decipher heaven's truth in the real world, which ultimately had to substantially contribute, however imperceptibly, to revealing faith's nature to itself.

The Crowded World

The basis of this transformation lies in the intensive appropriation of natural space which led, at the end of three centuries of crucial growth between the tenth and the thirteenth centuries, to what Pierre Chaunu has strikingly called the system of the *crowded world*.[16] This term refers first to the demographic growth and level of agricultural production making it possible. The combined effects of different population, socialization and production factors may provide a material explanation for this formative development that created the basis for all subsequent European history. But there was also an interaction between the crude development of this "unrelenting human presence" and the abstract Christian schema of a human world metaphysically self-enclosed, hence capable of being saturated and fully occupied. Though this mobilization of humans and their related activity was shaped by social changes, it also realized the investment in the here-below inherent in the Christian relation to the beyond. This phenomenon can be considered as a new logic of being-in-the-world whose effects can be seen in the ideal of global restriction and local expansion. Though it expanded occupied space, it did not initiate mass migrations, but on the contrary maximized the entrenchment and restriction of beings—which is precisely what occurred around 1300—generating the unbroken cellular network of fields and steeples, that incomparably tight fabric of control over the land, which is essential for understanding the endurance of subsequent major political constructions. And within this territorial, hierarchical and communitarian "incellulation"[17] there was slight, but crucial, room for maneuvering, seized on by the fragmented peasantry. By jointly altering both the work patterns and the relation to nature, the peasantry changed everything. Though they were completely subjugated, these peasants who managed to become domestic smallholders did not passively accept the pressure of numbers or the burden of domination, but used their fledgling freedom to respond to the situation by organizing their labor. Here we see the growing primacy of the relation to objects over the social bond, which constitutes the heart of economic individualism in modern society. Increased productivity, which doubled between the ninth and the thirteenth centuries, was surely related to the minuscule autonomization of the production unit.[18] Subsequent western economic growth would be forced to take this as a model and radicalize it. Nature would be increasingly exploited, not by increasing the weight of domination or strengthening constraints, but rather by making social agents autonomous. The increased concentration of beings, the escalation of their activity and the accumulation of possessions had a consequent liberating effect. This trend has a long history. The reversal linking the growth of resources to human emancipation began with populating the medieval world. From this emerged the novel compromise between dependence and independence, between village holism and possessive individualism, which would color the social nature of the countryside for centuries to come. No doubt the driving force behind the development of our system of production and ownership came from urban centers and from the other remarkable compromise between the individual and the collective, namely *guilds*. This would be even more so once we went beyond the high water mark of the end of the thirteenth century, when the leveling out of technical and demographic development would arrest the rural world in a "motionless history" for four centuries up to the beginning of the eighteenth century.[19] Yet we cannot consider this primary inscription of the principle of individuality in the agrarian base as unimportant, even though it was only partially successful. The immobilized presence of the principle of movement may not have physically caused any change but it participated much more than one might think in the effective significations precipitating the advent of universal mobility.

COLLECTIVE PERMANENCE

The formation of national monarchies may be considered complementary to the same transformation of being-in-the-world. The same logic controlling the occupation of natural space also controlled the occupation of human-social space. It must be said that the latter is easier to explain, since the breakdown of the old order was much clearer in regard to the State, where previous externalized authority was internalized. Territorial expansion became administrative demarcation. Power grew in order to incorporate increasingly large masses of people into a single world empire; its aim became one of gaining a deeper understanding of a supposedly clearer defined community which it controlled. Subjugating the human community as a whole to an ordering principle externally imposed through the emperor's mediation gave direction to the conquering enterprise. The internal coherence of a political body endowed with its own reason for existence now became the legitimizing principle of the sovereign's administrative actions.[20] This project's religious affiliation is easier to reconstruct since we can relate it to the temporal powers' attempt to secure independent and indisputable legitimacy. In the face of the papacy's imperial claim, national monarchies had to provide themselves with an equivalent religious rationale and were thus led to exploit the possibility of a politics of unmediated terrestrial autonomy whose origins were derived from the religion of mediation. The Church's ambition to mediate—to definitively unite heaven and earth by reuniting spiritual and temporal power in a single sovereign—revealed the incredible potential opened up by the arrival of a unique mediator, the Word Incarnate. It represented the human order's potential independence from the divine order, and hence the full Christian legitimacy of a power incarnating the plenitude proper to the human sphere. Monarchs strongly resisted this breach and blindly rushed to fill it. Thus another form of investment in the here-below, this time a political one, took shape under the theme of integrity. And on the horizon we can see two other elements crucial to modernity: state religion and the cult of the Nation.

A related, particularly original development, was our inclusion in the temporal dimension which justifies us speaking of a transformation of being-in-the-world, but of an unusual kind: being-in-time. This process began in the second half of the thirteenth century, just as the growth of the crowded world peaked. It was as if the conquest of the *duree* began once the appropriation of natural space reached its physical limit. It was as if a new frontier for the quest for terrestrial plenitude was opening up beyond the visible sphere and its material resources, one containing the invisible permanence of the human community and the instances of sovereign power and the national body shaping it.

The enterprise was part of the temporal powers self-reconstruction in order to rival, and imitate the Church. It systematized their long struggle to establish a sacrality for themselves equal to that administered by the spiritual hierarchy. Further sacralization would consist of raising the world's institutions to the level of heavenly entities by perpetuating them—by transforming terrestrial bodies into angelic beings. If humans are born and die, the associative bodies they shape remain, independently of their changing members. Actually, these collective bodies acquire the nature of transcendent beings similar to pure spirits from the other world. Though both are purely terrestrial realities, the "king who never dies", despite the succession of flesh and blood kings, and the kingdom that will last forever, become mystical entities with celestial status, despite their tangible material nature. So injecting an open-ended *duree* into human institutions tends to bring a part of divine eternity onto the earth. But it also gives rise to a new category of sacred beings, abstract individuals, collective apparitions, that we belong to and which crush us, immanent deities which, though never seen, continue to receive our devotion: the invisible State and the everlasting Nation. The personification and subjectivation of transcendent entities is the key to modern political development whose most original contribution, namely the system of impersonal institutions, is incomprehensible if we do not take into account the formation of these entities, as effective as they are fictitious. Because they personify immortality, the Nation or the State can only tolerate temporary *representatives*. If political power, like administrative authority, is only exercized through *delegation*, it is because both are credited with being true custodians, not to be confused either with the electoral body, which only momentarily lends its voice to the invisible Nation, or with the peoples' delegates, who cannot really help to perpetuate the State. Suffrage points to a more fundamental mechanism of representation, as does the bureaucratic principle of delegation. People who delegate are themselves always already delegated, and by something which cannot be embodied. It is as if the principle of collective order could only be returned to humans, to the visible, by setting up the invisible at the heart of the human order. It is as if we had to be dispossessed by collective-being's terrestrial transcendence if we were to be delivered from heaven's will. This is a remarkable example of realist fiction or effective symbolism. For these intangible abstractions, revised by us but inaccessible to our senses, these purely conceptual beings which, unlike God, will never be seen by anyone, have had just as great an influence on the organization of public and, to a certain extent, private action within our societies. This influence has extended from representative government and legal individuals to bureaucratic anonymity and the impersonal persistence of the public sphere.

Beneath this generalized representative logic lies an investment in the temporal under the sign of terrestrial self-sufficiency. The impermanence of everything human is the archetypal sign of the basic imperfection and inferiority of this world below compared with divine eternity. This hypothetical perpetuity was absorbed into the theologico-political movement of the last two centuries of the middle ages, until it finally crystallized in the abstract notion of the State, during which time the orders of reality were reshaped. A hierarchical logic, where the visible world's shortcomings and its temporal fragility was a necessary physical sign of its dependence on something more perfect than itself, was replaced by a logic of difference. The inequality of the two orders still existed, since the perpetuity of human creations in time was not the same as divine eternity outside time, but each was fully and freely itself, and the internal principle of integrity erected by the visible (in this instance in the form of invisible personification) confirmed its ontological independence. This was an extraordinary political-religious alchemy which succeeded in transforming becoming into a principle of indestructible self-identity. Ours is without doubt the only civilization to have ever had the idea of constructing the stable ground of collective identity out of this seamless network of beings and the universal mobility of things. We can immediately see how much our societies' highly distinctive ability to accommodate history owes to this special disposition. Far from threatening the self-presence of the encompassing collective, and our corresponding assurance of living in the same world, changing the basic constituents of our world contributes to its maintenance, another reason why we manage to adapt to them. In other words, if we no longer need to exorcize becoming by clutching to tradition or origin, it is because we are situated within a frame of reference assuring us that we will retain our identity. Permanence used to be affirmed by repetition; now it is experienced through change. It used to demand that time be frozen; now it presupposes being immersed in its flow and systematically turning it to our use. We used to have to bow before the law; now it has become our duty to make use of it. It is not our orientation in time which has been redefined but our ability to make use of it.

I am only briefly sketching this to highlight the historical depth of the new mode of being-in-the-world whose potential was part of Christianity's structure. The Reformation brought the beginnings of an appropriate awareness of divine otherness and its consequences, whereby whole sections of social practice were informed and wrought by the dynamics of terrestrial appropriation demanded by a separated god. In other words, the Protestant ethic was an epiphenomenon superimposed on an enormous transformation of both the experiential field and the orientations of human activity. This transformation had long been underway in the darkest recesses of collective behavior not just outside any awareness, but in opposition to the dominant values of the civilization in which they secretly took shape. The new ethics of salvation was opportune because it (partially) alleviated the contradiction between the emerging form of practices and the fixed content of beliefs. But it did not ultimately cause but rather furthered an already deeply entrenched silent revolution. What it promoted as an ethic for economic practices was only one aspect of a general trend expressing itself in other areas, such as political principles.

It could be said that the change revealed in the prospects for terrestrial action was only one instance of a *general inversion of the various logics of power*, the other main example being the dynamics of the modern State. Previously, power grew through territorial expansion, by the terrifying affirmation of the sovereign's distance from us and by the greatly increased grasp on, and control of, production and exchange. We can already glimpse signs of a radical reversal in the early attempts to build nations: the process begins by intensively adopting the administration of a territory taken into its orbit, and over time makes power conform to the will of its subjects, makes the citizens participate, emancipates interests and frees up civic action. The secret to the unprecedented strengthening of public authorities in the age of freedom lies in growth through setting limits. Contrary to appearances, democracy and the cacophony of the masses, the opening to the humble and weak, the fight for equal rights, all constitute the true foundations of power. Both the conservative mind with its fear of anarchy, and the progressive mind with its hope in collective morals, completely misunderstand these sources of social strength. The practical concrete equivalent of this inversion of political logic can be seen in the reorganized relation to the world which began in the Reformation. Before then, real power lay properly within the framework of political power and it presupposed the domination of humans. The great innovation was the turn toward the domination of nature. Previously, exploitation was only brought to bear on human beings; now it would devote itself to transforming things.

PEACE

We can use the *idea of peace* to establish a connection between effective historical innovation and the explicit values of the Christian tradition. I will restrict myself here to noting that the notion of peace summarizes and conveys in an exemplary fashion something of the basic distinction between the two orders: "My kingdom is not of this world." It allows a certain freeing up of the individual. The duty to be violent and to wage war constituted the very fabric of social obligation: the legitimate necessity of power from above and the unavoidable duty of reciprocity from below as seen in *conquest and vengeance*, the will to dominate, and the constraints of honor. But when the right and obligation to peace were set against this, the prospect of two separate behavioral patterns was introduced: there was the law of the world, and the call of blood; then came

the relation to the Wholly Other, which released you from these constraints by obliging you not to reciprocate, and to forgive offenses.

In other words, the value bestowed on peace was equivalent to the
metaphysical hypothesis regarding God's relation to this world: he was
not welded to the ladder of human hierarchies, nor was he consigned to
the chain of dependencies forming the immanent legality of the social,
along with the violence required for their administration. The god of
peace is a god from somewhere else, an individualistic god desiring harmony among individuals in an environment where communities disagree.
But also, on that account, a god who radiates out into the universal,
without needing a power or a people to extend his domination. *A god
with no empire*: this is what separates the Christian God from the terrifying God of Israel, pre-occupied with the victory of his followers, or
from the God of Mohammed and his true believers' duty to expand the
realm of the true faith through arms. The temptation for religious expansion was not absent from the Christian world, but it was ambiguous.
From the Crusades to the missionary campaigns undertaken after the
sixteenth century, there were wars of faith and outbreaks of conversion-
ary zeal, usually backed by arms. We should, however, carefully distinguish Christianity's approach from the dynamic ideal of Islam, for example. The Christian system of civilization dominated by martial values,
contained at its very center either a direct or indirect religious enhance-
ment of the value of activities turning people away from confrontation.
But this was not non-violence, understood as total disengagement from
inter-human bonds and as indifference to the world. Here again we encounter a feature of the religion of the god who is other, which has already been analyzed: he is not satisfied with totally renouncing and ab-
senting himself from the reality of the here-below; on the contrary, he
demands that we be present. Hence Christian peace could not be a gen-
tle or desperate withdrawal from either beings or things, but a conver-
gent irreversible merging between conciliatory independence from others
and the possession of the world. On the one hand, inter-human struggle
was prohibited in the name of human autonomy and the blood ties inherent in collective obligation were spiritually rejected; on the other,
God's total withdrawal into the invisible produced a mobilization preserving the integrity of the visible.

Due to this twofold injunction, power in this world was redirected toward apprehending nature. The force, the splendor, and the wealth that
was provided by conquering an increasingly larger number of subjugated
people at will, was from now on expected to come from an ever broader
and deeper appropriation of the physical universe. In this case, pacifica-
tion actually meant displacing war. It was not disarmament, but rather

a transferal (and correlative transformation) of what previously divided human beings, onto the order of things. Previously, the scheme of domination and self-affirmation by conquering the other was carried out entirely within the social bond. From now on it would be applied within the relationship connecting humans to their natural surroundings.

Homo Oeconomicus

By changing its target, domination changed its supporting or operative basis. What was a collective function became an individual task. It used to pass through the medium of personal relations; it now presupposed the isolation of the actor confronted with nature. This is the birth of modern individualism as *economic* individualism—using economic in the sense of a general scheme of relating to things. Modern man's relation to nature, which is both possessive and transformative, is inseparable from individualism as the organizing vision of the human-social phenomenon. Similarly, political individualism presupposes peaceful indifference between peers engaged in a primordial struggle with things. Committing power to the project of controlling the physical world created the signatories to the social pact who reach agreement in a state of primitive independence they try to preserve. They were free from all ties and from any intention to enslave their partners as they were mainly concerned with controlling reality and augmenting its resources. We have seen how the religion of the One involves favoring the societal bond over the relation to nature. This bond could only be grasped from within the human-social space and by means of a hierarchical relation between beings. The underlying dynamics was produced by reducing those who deal with objects to the same level as objects. The more senior you were in the hierarchy, the more responsible you were for governing humans and the less you were concerned with things; the more you aspired to the greatness attained by possessing things, the more you had to transform those who obtain them into objects. Here we see one of the most far-reaching expressions of the change in being-in-the-world generated by the transition to religious duality, namely, the autonomization of Individuals acting in their own economic interests in relation to the community of their peers. It is worth pointing out that democratic capitalism is thus industrial, technical, and scientific before it is commercial (in this instance running counter to history from a logical viewpoint). Democratic capitalism is more a way of relating to the world's overall situation than one of accumulating and distributing wealth. Here the accumulation of physical goods is not only inseparable from the general and systematic optimization of natural resources, but is subordinate to it. There was initially a stronger hold and more power over the order of things in order to get a stronger hold over available resources. Growth became an end in itself, in the sense of being an optimizing approach to one's possessions, rather than possession in itself.

It is as if, by passing from the system of hierarchical values to liberal values, we exchanged one misunderstanding for another. We used to cover over nature with the social; now we cover over the social with nature. It is as if we had to choose between either denying man's humanity, which requires passing through the other to act on things, or denying the primordial sociableness which goes with his being constituted as a free and efficient producer.

. . .

As God withdrew, the world changed from something *presented* as unalterable to something to be *constituted*. God having become Other to the world, the world now became Other to humans, in two ways: by its objectivity at the level of representation, and by its ability to be transformed at the level of action. In the framework of the interpenetration of the visible sphere with its invisible source, nature was in theory codependent with man and in practice inviolable for him. It was conceived as "human" and experienced anthropomorphically in terms of physical proximity and spiritual involvement; at the same time it was accepted as superhuman with regard to any possible hold over it; it was revealed as unalterable and approached as though it was immutable. Disentangling the visible from the invisible made it "inhuman" in our minds, by reducing it to mere matter. At the same time, this made it appear capable of being wholly adapted to humans, malleable in every aspect and open to unlimited appropriation.

We must carefully maintain this dual perspective if we wish to avoid the cliche of the "predator" unleashed by the loss of solidarity with nature. The realization of divine transcendence placed nature in man's care and he became metaphysically responsible for it. And if he entered into a relation of otherness, it was within and according to a defined goal, namely to realize his ontological independence. Herein lies the central schema shaping the universe bequeathed by Christianity's religious revolution. The schema supplies the goal and explains the methods of human activity. It describes its hidden purpose, which is to demonstrate and constitute the intrinsic integrity of the world left to humans. The key paradox here can only be clarified by tracing the history of the religious organization of experience. That is, when the world appears to the intellect as a self-contained and self-sufficient objective reality, it becomes for *practical purposes* the object of a systematic negation of its givenness, in the very name of this self-sufficiency which it promises to realize and which it must continually make more concrete. This negation is put in the service of an ideal increase in magnitude and value. Such is the articulation of our relationship to reality, taken as a continuation of previous general structurings of being-in-the-world and understood as the final metamorphosis of religious otherness—the one through which we cease to be determined by religion in the strict sense.

Actually, we have always experienced the other, but now it is a driving rather than an inhibiting force. The cult of the other amounted to denying the power of humans over what was given to them. Our particular practice in relation to the other consists of refusing and negating the given as such. This is done along two basic lines: either by neutralizing otherness—by assimilating, understanding, and arranging for it to be mobilized at all levels—or by producing otherness—by transforming, reinventing, or optimizing it. Any simple acceptance and continuation of it has been ruled out. This puts us in line with the age-old tradition of religious rejection and its more recent expressions in the form of the unacceptability of the real. The difference is that rejection previously had a constricting effect whereas now it has an expansive one. The negation of what exists, the active feeling that things are inadequate, is directed to realizing a surplus of terrestrial being. Whether it is related to an attempt to overcome the world's otherness by appropriating it, or to make it yield more than it offers, the driving aim is the same: to reveal—materially, socially, symbolically—the autonomy of the visible sphere which gives us the basis to completely occupy it, and simultaneously to fully realize this partial autonomy. This is not the goal of realizing a worldly absolute. It is the more ambitious, yet more modest, one of bringing the world of humans and the natural world they inhabit to the stage of complete internal congruence that would internally signify their ultimate ontological self-sufficiency.

This is an open and infinite task, which is to be constantly resumed, always opening new frontiers. This may mean, for example, sustaining the democratic claim for an increasingly deeper participation of citizens to manage their own affairs, and an increasingly more self-confident correspondence between the actions of those governing and the will of those governed. It may mean taking hold of human bodies to inform them of the full potential of the powers and the pleasures they are capable of. This example is most telling with regard to the appropriating and optimizing trend that interests us, which is neither simple liberation, nor diabolical transgression, nor ordinary hedonism, but bears the seriousness of a duty and the constraint of an onerous task. It is the refusal to suffer one's bequeathed lot, the concern to control its mysteries and functions, and the attempt to maximize its capabilities and resources. To understand, to master, and to increase. Beauty, achievements, or enjoyments are all part of a mobilization to embrace our own flesh, which is the archetypal given. It represents a mobilization sustained by this obscure central source, which calls for an endless reworking of the entire terrestrial condition and which allows contemporary activism to communicate with the past's immobility. For what makes us increasingly turn our backs on our predecessors' world is also what makes us more deeply their heirs. The universal reverence for the given, which used to drive our predecessors, has become the uncontrollable necessity to innovate spurring us on. The latter continues to tie us to what inspired our predecessors for thousands of years, while increasingly distancing us from it.

PART TWO

The Apogee and Death of God

CHRISTIANITY AND

WESTERN DEVELOPMENT

CHAPTER 5

The Powers of the Divine Subject

A Religion for Departing from Religion

THE TERMS "end" of, or "departing from" religion make sense in terms of the actors' practices rather than of their consciousness. What matters is not what the members of a given society personally think and believe, but the pattern of their thought processes, their mode of coexistence, the form of their integration with being and the dynamics of their actions. We can imagine the extreme case of a society comprised entirely of believers, yet beyond the religious. Religion was initially a general shaping of humans' material, social, and mental life. All that remains of it today are individual experiences and belief systems, while actions affecting things, and the link between beings and the mind's organizing categories contradict the logic of dependence that initially governed them. This constitutes our departure from the age of religions. We cannot pronounce religion's meaninglessness, or predict its imminent demise from the decline in the Church's influence, or the number of its members and the strength of their belief. But we can do so on the grounds that the conserving logic integrating us into being, nature, and culture has been inverted; and further, on the grounds that the necessity of being attached to the hierarchy has disappeared, and that the constraints to conceive the world as united with its origins (mythical thought) and in accord with itself (symbolic thought) have disappeared.

Even after we have reached the conclusion of this process and are outside it, there may still exist groups formed freely on the basis of similar beliefs, in a society completely free from belief's structuring influence. And even if every type of official dogma were to vanish, every form of sociability based on shared faith and any cult with common observances were to disappear, individual religious experiences could exist indefinitely. Even though its collective function has been neutralized, there is probably an irreducible element of openness to the invisible, from the viewpoint of both internal thought processes and inner self-apprehension. I hark back to this last bastion of potential religiosity, which is both

a logical and psychological one, because it throws light on a side of the
phenomenon that I have deliberately avoided: its deep-seated anthropological roots. This side has caused the greatest misunderstanding on the
topic in modern times, a misunderstanding which is, however, based on
a fundamentally sound insight. I have avoided it because it seemed
preferable to tackle the real issue only after establishing some solid facts.
The sound insight is that there is a subjective source underlying socially
determined and organized belief, a source which is exposed as belief sub-
sides—the "religious sentiment" that Benjamin Constant distinguishes
from "religious institutions."[21] But this insight is accompanied by the
misleading inference, also made by Benjamin Constant, that through
"religious sentiment" we can attain the true "center" of the religious
phenomenon, its invariable core, and the inexhaustible seminal principle
whose dogmatic or cultural constructs are only derivative forms. The
source is supposedly permanent and the content variable, depending on
the context and the "level of civilization." This perspective creates the
false belief that the more religion declines, the more its permanence is assured by this inner quality which has been uncovered and highlighted by
its public demise. To say that we have departed from religion itself, but
are still under its sway, is to make a very serious error: there could be no
surer way to close ourselves off from understanding religion as history,
as well from understanding the precise import of this subjective inscription which can withstand the weakening of its collective meaning. Once
again, it is not the reality of this phenomenon which is in question, but
its nature and role. There is no doubting its necessity as an anthropological prop, as a transhistorical condition for the possibility of the reign
of the other. In order for religion to exist, it was necessary for individuals' spontaneous psychological and intellectual functioning to adapt itself
specifically to its investment in the invisible. And the otherwordly perspective, and the confrontation with otherness, most certainly constitute
a major organizing factor of the human imagination. Similarly, the encounter with the undifferentiated, unrepresentable infinite presents an
ineradicable horizon for structuring thought, just as the double-edged
and contradictory experience of self-abrogation and inextinguishable
self-presence echoes, at the deepest level, the problematic tension determining being-a-subject. But that tension does not make this substratum
a creative principle. It does not tell us what religions' essential function
was, and consequently tells us nothing about their internal logic and the
possible ramifications of successive changes to their content. *A fortiori*,
this tension does not allow us to understand the very possibility that they
may lose their substance and be reabsorbed. Furthermore, there is no evidence that the indisputable correspondence between the registers of sub-

jective organization and the modalities of religious experience signals a need that would require an explicit outlet, or instituted forms, in order to be satisfied. On the contrary, the evidence suggests that this inner sense of otherness is socially neutral, and that if organized religions need to rely on it, it can on the other hand survive quite well without established religion, whether it is directed elsewhere or somehow operates in a vacuum. In other words, any attempt to reunite the two poles, the personal and the institutional, that have gradually been separated by the divine's inexorable withdrawal, is futile. The subject's permanent needs do not reflect any timeless religious essence. We will gain a greater understanding of both by looking at them separately. On the one hand, we must decipher the subject's timeless truth in light of what was its ultimately transitory guarantor in the social order; and on the other, we must understand the religious in light of its final phase, this possible future when nothing which used to strike a chord in us will be recognizable in it anymore.

The end of religion must be mapped out in great detail, not just to understand its proper essence and its historical nature, but to grasp our world's originality. For out of the decline of systematic exteriority has emerged the totality of factors distinguishing our civilization's foundations from those of previous societies. Politics based on representation, systematic investment in the future, knowledge based on objective causes, controlling nature, increasing material productivity as an end in itself, are so many key elements of modernity. Their common origin and general cohesiveness only becomes intelligible after it has been reintegrated into the central process of reversing sacral otherness, a process whose formative background was supplied by Christianity. The wholesale reconstruction of human space under the influence of God's paradoxical absolutization/withdrawal is the hidden source behind the expanding fragmented components of our democratic, individualizing state-based, historical, technological, capitalist world, which seem contradictory but are essentially unified. And we can also see the seminal focal point illuminating the profound organization and development of each of these autonomous zones of activity. If we really want to understand how a society controlling itself operates, and the possible lines of force behind its development, we must start out from a subjugated society. As with the internal dynamics of the transforming relationship with nature, we must here start with the practical constraints of religious otherness. The same applies to the formal and material possibilities of a thought based on the opposition of subject and object in a system where the cognizable world and the cognitive subject participate equally. Leaving religion is not like waking from a dream. We originated in religion, we continue to explain ourselves through it, and always will. Only by examining the change that has drawn us away from religion do we have any chance of determining the imperatives that condition and regulate our actions. These imperatives have not become clearer by ceasing to be externally imposed. Though they now come from us alone, they are no less mysterious than when they derived from the supernatural—except now they may be partially elucidated in light of the internal reversal of their ties to the supernatural.

.   .   .

The crucial step in understanding this dual history lies in precisely gauging the singularity of Christianity's trajectory. It was neither the culmination of a "development of religious ideas" which retrospectively illuminates the phenomenon's less advanced stages, nor was it one religion among others. It was rather a highly individualized branching off from the shared destiny of the other "major religions" (including its own eastern branch) with whom it initially had much in common. And it was above all the beginning of a movement which took the questioning of religion's very principle to its conclusion. All this occurred through and in time with the complete deployment of a structural link between the human and the divine, which corresponded in every detail to the inversion of the primordial structure of indebtedness to the invisible.

I have already described the essentials of this process in terms of its internal logic, thus running the risk of suggesting necessary connections or a nonexistent overall progression. Reversing the hitherto adopted viewpoint, I will now highlight the fortuitousness and contingency of the conditions determining the major turning points. Although separating the structural order from the order of events is somewhat artificial, it reflects a partition inherent in the very nature of the object—a separation between the narrowly defined limits of the displacement and transformation of religious organization, and the radical indeterminacy of its actual accomplishment. The possible orientations and content of the historical change are determined by a rigid logic; on the other hand, the very fact that the change occurred depended on the event's contingency and on a sort of freedom at work in the midst of becoming. Its essence was determined, but its existence was a matter of choice. Or more precisely, it was essential to the deep organization of the religious that its actual realization displayed an ultimate indeterminacy.

There are basically two possible religious organizational patterns, and we have seen how the general course of Christianity can be described as the transition from a regime of the united social body and its extrinsic foundation, to a regime of duality. What occurred within the framework of this transfer followed an inexorable logic. Nevertheless, the fact that this transformation took place, that it went to the limits, appears at every stage to be the outcome of an historical decision whose content was in no way incomprehensible, but whose actual existence will always remain a mystery.

. . .

One of the best possible illustrations of this ambiguity is the change distinguishing Judaism from the other great spiritual upheavals of the period, namely, the birth of monotheism. Its originality was so great that there is a huge temptation to see in this new attribution of the deity the sign of an absolute break. It was rather a reorganization of the previously dominant structuring of the other—a reorganization that simply exploited in a more systematic manner the possibilities present throughout the entire political matrix of "great civilizations." From this viewpoint it was an operation whose necessary structural transformation involved a reorientation away from the past toward the present and correlatively concentrated a fragmented intraworldly divinity into a unique extraworldly subject. Still, when we look at the concrete conditions under which this crystallization took place, in a tiny marginalized tribe responding to its oppressive situation, we are again faced with the enigma of a radical improbability. Appearance is misleading, as we will see at every crucial stage in this process. The transition could not have occurred by chance, and we can reconstruct the determining factors; nothing compelled it to happen, but nothing can remove the indeterminacy involved in its having taken place.

Even though this change was indeterminate, we must still precisely define its limits. We cannot simply say that the appearance of the new god-as-one is in itself an inexplicable sudden appearance. We have seen how the intrinsic dynamics of the State's actions—an internal one of oppression and an external one of expansion—created the conditions for a religious thought free from the primitive structure of the One preserved in classical polytheism. And these conditions developed in three main ways: first, an increasing subjectivation of the sacral foundation as its embodiment among humans progressively took hold; second, a universalization of the terrestrial perspective as the world-empire expanded, along with its effective relativization of every type of local or group affiliation; and finally, a separation between the here-below and the beyond, by exalting the master in-this-world and assigning the visible to him, both of which combined to push the ultimate principle back into the realm of the separated.

Unlimited conquest constitutes only one extreme possibility open to the State, the other being its complete withdrawal into "magic" royalty, for which African history provides an almost unique example. Instead of following the logic of separation and expansion, such royalty concentrates the tasks of perpetuating and renewing the world's order into the biological frame of an individual. But the magical confinement imposed by this incarnation of the Natural and the Supernatural does not necessarily entail many of the other prerogatives of authority. Furthermore, this personification of the human order's inclusion among cosmic forces does not destabilize the primitive religious framework: it breaks decisively with the essential anonymity of the process instituting the social, but remains compatible with its underlying systematization. At the other extreme, the dynamics of empire virtually dismantled all previous established beliefs and provoked an eager quest for another spiritual solution. Between the two extremes lay a wide range of intermediary positions, whose limits were determined mainly by the cultural isolationism which halted the majority of major despotic formations. The empire is (or should be) world; but world is deemed to be what is effectively or potentially covered by the sovereign's dominion. The ideal of the highest power was limited by its congruence with a relatively homogeneous civilized area outside which it becomes barbarism. There was both a real and a symbolic lack of mobility that effectively limited any possible challenge to the union with the ancestral order and to the immersion in the impersonal cycle of cosmic forces whose living pivot was the sovereign. So it would be possible to develop a typology of imperial formations establishing a connection between the extent of the opening foreshadowed by its expansionary trend, and the scope of the spiritual possibilities raised in the complex dialectic between absorption by the center and a decentering process. Of course the transition from one level to another was never automatic, and their influence could work in either direction. In any case, at a certain point the goal of conquest could also arise from within religion. Moreover, the triumph of the universal religion of the personal god came at the end (and in the sphere) of a series of unprecedented imperial upheavals. Roman expansion provided the immediate formative context, but the general background was Alexander's conquests and the Persian unification of the Near and Middle East prior to them. The most thoroughgoing religious transformation, that represented by the Christian break, came at the end of a prodigious broadening of national horizons. It was carried out at the point where the intermingling of heterogeneous elements and the consequent decentering of human perspectives had gone furthest.

Israel: Inventing God-as-One

The remarkable thing is that this change started at the periphery before capturing the heart of the most powerful imperial system. Moses' reinvention of the divine always presupposed both subversion and revelation and was borne by the dynamics of empire. And in a sense, who could have been better placed to feel its effects than a tiny peripheral group, hemmed in between two major spheres of influence, sometimes submissive, sometimes captive, sometimes in exile, half-barbarian and half-assimilated, half-fascinated by those above it and half-jealous of its identity? But, it is also likely that in order for this radical formulation of a monotheistic faith to occur, there was a need to encounter imperialism and then formulate a desperate plan to be free of it.[22] From Moses to St. Paul, the complete deployment of a religion of duality took place through a repeated shift between appropriating and rejecting, between resuming and distancing oneself from the principle of empire. The entire process leading up to Christianity, including the Incarnation, should thus be understood in terms of the spiritual reversal of the system of universal power. To accomplish this, special types of beings were required, both sufficiently inside the system to have internalized its spirit and sufficiently outside it to seek freedom.

We can see this in the neighboring Mesopotamian or Egyptian religions from which the god of Israel emerged. They also contained movements which in certain respects—or at certain moments—clearly brought them close to Israelite Yahvism, as numerous studies have indicated. Scholars have pointed out the tendency to simplify their pantheons and concentrate the divine, so that the ethnic god, Marduk or Assur, became the preeminent deity of Babylonian and Assyrian religions.[23] There have thus been disputes as to the true content of the reform introduced by the enigmatic Pharaoh Akhenaton and its role in the beginnings of Israel's faith.[24] But when we compare these transformations with the specific characteristics of the religion of Moses, we are struck by their inherent limits. However strong the emphasis placed on the main god in the Mesopotamian pantheon, for example, the other divinities were not rejected and there was no need to do so. The new was incorporated or grafted onto the old without clashing with its organizing principles. Similarly, as thorough as the spiritualization of the solar principle in the reforming Pharaoh's speculations were, this did not involve any subversion of the long-standing religious logic. It simply supplied an extreme, but internal, variation of the system constituted by the imperial mediator between the Natural and Supernatural. The Pharaoh not only remained a

mediator, but became one to an even greater extent when his role required him to guarantee the living connection between the human order
and the world soul. His person confirmed the unshakable unity of the
two sides of being, whereas the change begun by Moses was character-
ized by its negative logic, its exclusivist dynamics.

Moses: Dominating Domination

We are dealing here with the *response* to the religious system guaranteeing an oppressive power, a response introduced *externally* as a result of
a situation of extreme inferiority and revolt. But paradoxically, this response borrowed from its adversary. It incorporated the conflict between
divine oneness and separation at work in despotic organization, and gave
them radical expression by turning them against the despot and his legitimacy. It thus invented a god whose like had never been known. This
was the god of the exodus from Egypt, a god far beyond the measure of
the Egyptian gods, far more powerful and thus potentially the one true
god.

Herein lies the distinctive origin of the monotheistic break. It arose
from the creative confrontation of the weak with the strong, in which
comparing, going one better, and then rejecting, are indissolubly mixed.
Monotheism lacked any syncretizing goodwill by the conqueror toward
the idols and beliefs of subjugated peoples, which he then annexed to his
own. Here, on the contrary, the gaze was directed up from below; it was
that of the wretched gazing at the munificent, and was inspired more by
the desperate determination to escape the conqueror's hold than by the
idea of revolt. How could they imagine a power capable of freeing them
from the highest power in this world? The radical originality of the Israelite's response derived from the highly unusual standpoint of the
questioner and the penetrating nature of the question. It was because of
this extremely special need to dominate what dominated them, and to
guarantee their identity in the face of assimilation, that the use of spiritual possibilities latent in despotism's matrix went beyond normal limits.

This was a miracle of history: the consequential turning point that redefined the balance between the weight of tradition and the forces of
revolution, carried out in the most improbable manner from the most
contingent situation. The conserving principle of the One, of the inner
conjunction of the human and the divine, was by no means absent in this
situation. It was even entirely protected by the Covenant formed between
the new god and his people. The difference is that the alliance with this
vengeful god was not based on ancestral order, but on blind confidence
in his saving intervention. He was not to be grasped from within the
community of his believers, at the top of a ladder of visible and invisible

beings connecting you to him. He was beyond any terrestrial power, hence beyond any imaginable hierarchy or perceptible embodiment. He was not the highest, but the sole one; he could not be thought of comparatively only exclusively; he did not present himself in the context of continuity but in that of separation; he did not complement the human world but stood opposed to it. The dynamics of challenge led to this inversion of the divine's previous structure by reversing the earlier structural link between the same and the other, the near and the far. The founding past's archetypal absence, changed into presence, in the form of the supreme organizer's constitutive capacity to intervene at any moment in human affairs. And the archetypal presence of the ordering principle welding beings to their originating law, became absence, in the separated nonrepresentable person. Thus one possible system for uniting the human world with its ultimate truth was translated by separation from the divine into its symmetrical opposite. We moved from the *actuality of the original source* to the *presence of the transcendent*. This decisive bifurcation resulting in ontological duality can only be explained on the basis of appropriation coupled with fascination, a situation whereby Egypt's deep turmoil precipitated the formation of Israel's distinctive god. Although attempts to concentrate the divine were at work, wherever a similar crystallization occurred—Iran, India, China—the religious reformulation ultimately slid back into the traditional mold of the One. In these cases, no separate person appeared but there was a reabsorption of all separation into impersonal ultimate being; the world was divided by a merciless war between gods, which nevertheless kept it united with itself. The cosmic struggle of the two principles took place within one and the same world; the hint of a split in being was turned into an internal conflict.[25] It was, as it were, impossible to overcome the heritage of the old conceptual framework from within.

The Covenant and Trial by Adversity

The decisive factor, which for convenience I will attribute to Moses, was not the new faith's specific content, but the background to its emergence. Early monotheism's rigor or clarity are far less relevant than the political mechanism allowing its formulation. For, once in place, this mechanism clarified monotheism in two ways.

It did so first by reinvigorating Yahveh's people through their trials and tribulations. Even after they triumphantly entered the promised land and become a kingdom, the threat of being submerged and enslaved remained a factor permanently affecting their outlook, existing as they did at the crossroads of three dynamic empires. We know the catastrophes that rained down on the defenseless chosen people, from the destruction of Samaria to the Babylonian captivity. Now the formative logic of Yahvism—where God is great because he is greater than the world's most fearsome sovereign—was constructed in such a way that the worst trials experienced by his followers could only reinforce in their minds the divine's complete omnipotence. Only Yahveh's will could lie at the origin of the evil striking his people through the conqueror, and only this will could deliver them from the conqueror, by commanding his armies to retreat just as it commands the seas to flow or the stars to move. The more Israel was crushed by terrestrial forces surpassing its own, the more its god appeared as the supreme sovereign of the universe, absolutely beyond the visible sphere and its actors.

Along with this was an additional factor, namely the obligation to turn back into oneself. What have we done to invoke this punishment? the faithful ask. In the eyes of a god who must be the source of all adversity, humans became blameworthy. In other words, ethics became problematical. Whereas previously ethics was basically positive, it now mainly tended to raise questions. It used to operate by adhering to the order of a world which, due to the gods' support, was the best imaginable. It now began to turn to conscience to justify the action of actors uncertain about God's ways.

By proceeding along these lines monotheism, as inscribed in the Covenant's internal dynamics, culminated in the figure of the righteous individual overwhelmed by inexplicable trials and tribulations, who nevertheless submits to supreme wisdom. Between Moses' triumphant god, who supports the weak over the mighty, and the incomprehensible transcendence of Job's god, who overturns any semblance of meaning, the human understanding yielded all it could. In one respect at least, God now belonged to the other world.

THE PROPHETS

A second factor deepening faith in the one true god was prophecy. The lesson to be drawn from Israel's misfortunes and the call for sinners to turn back into themselves was formulated partly by the prophets. Both developments—trials and prophecies—have their own specific natures, and each can be imagined in isolation. There could have been prophets without Israel's sufferings and, conversely, the latter could have been interpreted without the prophets' assistance.

A god superior to the most exalted being is a god to whom *any human being* can appeal *against* the collective behavior of one's equals—in particular, against their failure to recognize his law or their idolatrous failure to observe true religious practices. This critical exteriority constituted the distinctive nature of the prophet's intervention, an exteriority dependent on the extraneous nature of the principle presumed to be expressed through it, and which bestowed on it a significance different to that of the simple "seer" familiar to Middle Eastern civilizations. Seers operated from within the forest of being; their clear-sightedness put them in a position to read its signs and to perceive hidden correspondences. Their powers allowed them to be in touch with the spirits who inspired them, and thereby discern the future and pass on the reprimands and desires of the forces of the invisible, unveiling the source of misfortunes and advising which course to take. But the messages they passed on in this way remained essentially contemporary and specific. The prophet made sweeping comments on human conduct in absolute and general terms, even if he put the blame on one particular individual's misconduct. That is because the prophet spoke wholly from outside his community, released from it, as it were. And this notional distance existed because he spoke in the name of a supreme law-making power, which itself was separated from the human sphere, and therefore possibly unrecognized or flouted by humans, although it was directly concerned with their loyalty or base deeds. There were therefore two gaps reinforcing each other: one between God and humans, another between a single individual and the rest. Here we see the circular logic of the prophetic model.[26] The more the prophet made his own voice heard, the more God was located outside the cosmos, separate from everything created; and the more God was thus separated from it, the more his spokesman had a right to claim a personal tie with him. God's difference legitimated the prophet's rancor and, in return, the prophet's secession affirmed the deity's unity by emphasizing its withdrawal—the third intermediary term in the equation was his creatures' sinful freedom. Hence the exemplary figure of the ignored prophet: the inconceivable folly of those refusing to hear him highlighted the human capacity for error and the opposition between the true path and common opinion. Consequently, it carried transcendence to the interpretive limits of its dual development of inner certainty and ultimate intelligibility.

Still, prophecy in the strict sense of a discourse breaking with the present state of affairs by appealing against it in the name of a wholly other, could have existed without a personal separated god. Helene Clastres' fine comparison of Israel's prophets with the preaching of the Tupi-Guarani *Karai* is most illuminating on this very point. At the formal level, in both their separation from the community and the radical nature of their denunciation, the structural similarity is striking. The Guarani *Karai* conspicuously and systematically avoids common social ties: he sets himself up alone away from the villages, he claims extraterritorial status (in a war-orientated society, he does not acknowledge the distinction between friends and enemies); in a society articulated by blood ties, he puts himself outside kinship (since he has no father).[27] And his condemnation of our miserable world is irrevocable. But he clearly differs from the Israelite prophets in his proposal to abandon everything, to leave this irretrievably wicked abode without any intention of returning, and go in search of its counterpart, which has neither constraints nor limits nor death—the "Land-Without-Evil." In other words, if he makes an absolutely negative judgment about present reality, he does not, properly speaking, criticize it. He does not turn against it; on the contrary he suggests that we turn and flee it. We can assess the basically different orientation concealed by the external similarity of their methods of operation. If in both cases the essence of the phenomenon is opposition to the existing state of affairs, in the Guarani case the opposition is directed outwards, while in Israel's case, it is directed inwards (in a positive or negative manner, in a spirit of denunciation or exhortation toward spiritual reform). This is a divergence that naturally relates to the enormous gap between the underlying theologies. The inspiration of the Guarani prophet is controlled by the model of a community at one with its law, without a gap between what is and what ought-to-be. The community would remain at one with its law, even if, through some extraordinary change, the prospect of reversing the unconditional pro to the radical contra began to effect the assessment of the world and its order. But even if it thus made sense to break with the world and its order as a whole, it would not make sense to oppose their deviation in the name of the pristine purity of the foundation. This world is all that can exist; our hope can only lie in transferring it elsewhere into a world of abundance, freedom, and immortality. The prophet of Israel, on the other hand, exploited this internal gap between practice and norm, between the feats and gestures of individuals and the law that is supposed to govern them. He became the spokesman for a living extraworldly will, which provided a defined goal for intraworldly creatures. The remoteness of this will allows us to understand humans' forgetful casual attitude toward its decrees, just as this will's omnipresent vigilance requires that they be bluntly reminded of their duty. In such a framework it does not make any sense to claim to go beyond the range of obligations laid down by the deity; there is rather the endlessly renewed attempt to gain his favor through strict observance of his law. The prophet's dissent is proportionate to the gap between human actions and the code governing them, a gap showing the extent of the opposition between the human and the divine. It so happens that the innovative ferment comes less from the prophets themselves than from the way their connection with monotheism led them to direct themselves to their society. The inspired person's dissociation changed the religious system's nature and content less than the community's consequent turn against itself. Contrary to the ancient ideal of uniting foundation and deed, there is a tension between humans' spontaneous conduct and the law that should structure this conduct. In a world where the archetypal normative order is to be accepted and repeated, the prophets' intransigence *questions* the underlying principle motivating and justifying action.

The danger of analyzing such a phenomenon in systematic logical terms is that it might lead us to overestimate its effective contextual impact. It is one thing for the inner dynamics of the prophet's call to mobilize interiority as part of a personal relation with the living god, it is another to say that Israel's prophets were preoccupied with this. Their task was not to deepen the inner side of Yahvism in relation to its routinization, but to firmly establish Yahvism in the face of the henotheism posed by the Canaanite pantheon. The god they invoked was not the universal god who speaks directly to humans but the jealous god of the Covenant infuriated by his people's inconstancy. The target of the prophet's wrath was less the need for purity of heart in harmony with God's living will than the need to observe the pact with Yahveh to the letter. Nothing could better demonstrate the boundaries of the prophesying trend than its disappearance, once the Covenant was renewed and Judaism was stabilized by its definitive codification into a text of divine Law. The goal that justified prophecy was attained when the conditions had thus been established for Israel's conduct to come completely into line with the goals of the one true God. Once the promise contained in the Mosaic creation was realized there was no further reason to protest. The fact is that within these limits, the prophets in their turn revealed the promise of something completely different. Beyond the limited use they made of the promise, they brought to light the structural resourcefulness of the solitary revolt of faith, the personal claim of the beyond against the here-below, which developed when God was separated from any terrestrial materialization.

Yahveh's spokesman was thus ultimately deeply distinguished from his savage counterpart by his exemplary status. The Guarani *Karai* responds to his society's evolution or drifting; so does the Israelite prophet but he thereby reveals an ongoing possibility of relating to the supernatural foundation. The eulogist of the Land-Without-Evil entreats us to follow him, as does Yahveh's watchdog—however the latter, through his preaching, also maps out a position that theoretically any of his listeners could occupy. Not only do the prophet's listeners not rely on his discourse, they are in a way called on to identify with his direct relation to God. The *Karai* remains to the end a separated being who is blindly followed. Yahveh's prophet was a chosen, inspired, exceptional person, but he was at the same time a model. His distance made the general potentialities of a spiritual order legible. For two thousand years, this figure played a symbolic and exemplary role in the people's memory, which had little in common with the scope of his actual historical intervention. The Elijahs, Isaiahs, and Jeremiahs, quite independently of the truth of their entreaties, embody the inexhaustible reference point for attempts to deepen the inner religion against the religion of tradition, thus legitimating the individual against common propensities.

The internal trajectory of the movement lifting prophets out of, and lowering them back into, the ranks, is a marvelous illustration of monotheism's inherent political ambiguity. In one respect it increased human dependency since it encouraged embracing and internalizing the decrees of a living will. The prophets worked to obtain such adherence; they rose up to obtain obedience. But in another respect, the all-powerful God became the one whose essence and aims will forever remain unfathomable. This in turn justified, if not demanded, our questioning the gap separating human achievements from his true will. This god opened up the infinite possibility of personal questioning, of inner dissent and spiritual challenge. The model for this was for a very long time prophetic mobilization. From the very start, divine oneness contained two tendencies: first, tightening external obligations and enlarging internal room for maneuver; second, a decreased duty to submit and the sudden emergence of the right to revolt. The enhanced delineation of human obligation goes hand in hand with opening up an unprecedented indeterminacy. Monotheism's political path could have led just as easily to an immobile reinforced servitude.

Everything depends on each religion's practical understanding of how the one true god's will is to be communicated with, laid down, and administered. There might be a direct transmission producing a clearly and definitively determined Text or Code, as in the Judaic law, "the law of Moses laid down by Yahveh for Israel," or, as in the Koran, there might be a compilation of God's word itself, eliminating any margin for indeterminacy. The Book is true in every detail and therefore puts you in the presence of the Transcendent; its possible commentaries, however contentious, could not imply dissenting interpretations. Commentary itself appears as blasphemous license toward the literal reception appropriate to the decrees of supreme wisdom. Christianity's liberating originality lay in its indirect transmission. God delegated his son, in the shape of a man, to address humans. As a result, the message of salvation appeared as a partition between ultimate truth and what we know of it. This partition created a mystery requiring exegesis and the assistance of interpreters specially appointed to guide the flock. These interpreters could not content themselves with preserving or increasing our understanding of revelation, but became indispensable intermediaries between the faithful and the mystery's true meaning. Yet it was a mystery which also justified inner illumination, the lonely conviction of having recognized its true import or having gone deeper into it than the clerics and the scholars, and justified the regular questioning of previously accepted interpretations. Well-defined historical conditions were required to actualize the interpretive and conflictual possibilities contained in the Christian idea of revelation, and to reawaken the prophetic spirit, this time in heresy, schism, reformation, or dissent.

Jesus: The God-Man

Just as Judaism had settled down and stabilized itself, Jesus arrived and surpassed it while fulfilling it—for in my opinion we can only understand the Messiah's appearance as a further development of the process initiated by Moses. His preaching deepened a certain idea of God that had two main dimensions: a background of trials that were repeated and meditated on, and the exemplary nature of the prophets' separation from the community. Jesus' teaching was actually, if not doctrinally, the resolution of Yahvism's basic contradiction, exacerbated within Judaism, between God's universality and covenantal exclusiveness. I have already stressed that the stakes invested in this contradiction were high: it was the price to be paid for resolutely maintaining a religion of oneness that harbored the prospect of a religion of duality. By having chosen his people, the unique and separated god remained intimately tied to this world. His loss of immanence to the world does not matter since his indissoluble union with Israel kept him intimately connected to the human sphere—above all to his *locus* among humans, to his Temple, his Village, his Land, all equally imbued with his sanctity. What was at stake in the belief in this pact is the final organizational stratagem of the religious, the last-ditch attempt to preserve what had always been the basic structure of religious experience, to preserve the last nonidolatrous means for holding on to it, once transcendence had been largely inverted. This explains its extraordinarily deep-seated entrenchment.

Messianism

However immensely powerful the motives to retain it may have been, from a certain point onwards this defensive compromise between two religious eras appeared logically highly problematic. This question did not clearly present itself while Yahvism was establishing itself against raising idols or local customs. During this phase, the problem for the religious-minded was not one of the status of God's will in itself; it was the much more prosaic one of having it recognized and making it prevail. On the other hand, once the Covenant had been solemnly renewed, once the idea of the divine had been considerably refined by the prophets, and an appropriate balance achieved between Moses' law and his people's conduct, the difficulty inevitably arose of how to reconcile this god's universal mission with his exclusive choice of Israel out of all the nations. Only in the formative experience of oppression and persecution can we glimpse any sort of solution. There at least the role and place of other nations was clear: they were God's instruments to punish Israel for its sins. But in every other case the unavoidable and disconcerting question arose: what was the relationship of Israel's god to other peoples or other humans?

The proof that this question was perceived as a deeply pressing concern is that it generated the religious response of *messianism*—which is nothing less than *mystical imperialism*. Israel's ultimate destiny, justifying its unique status, was to subdue all other nations, so as to spread Yahveh's law throughout the entire world, "from coast to coast, from the Euphrates to the ends of the earth." A great King, sent especially by God, would come to unite the world, whether this meant Israel would become the spiritual center of a pacified humanity or, would triumph by the sword, or even remain alone on soil completely purged of idolaters and enemies. So whereas monotheism was formed in opposition to the logic of empire, the latter reappeared in the former as its obligatory horizon once it had been properly established: a universal God demands universal domination. The original context of a defense against oppression, of being wrenched from the threat of assimilation, changed to its opposite, that of an unrestricted expansion of covenantal law—which was the only possible logical outcome of the deeply felt contradiction between God's vastness and his limited attestation by humans. It was unthinkable that almost all creation might remain forever unaware of its true creator and master, and live without any knowledge of his will. This scandal had to be resolved. There were several versions—some pleasant, some cruel, some apocalyptic some sentimental—of this reconciliation between the divine essence and its earthly manifestation. They all boil down to some kind of extension or generalization of the Covenant, placing Israel at the head of nations, and extending Yahveh's reign to the entire human race. And we cannot dismiss out of hand the possibility that a Judaic expansion similar to the Islamic conquest could have taken place under certain conditions, both external (weak neighboring powers) and internal (a suitable Messiah). In a favorable context, the trend toward an exclusive isolationist withdrawal could have been reversed into a universalizing process. Its outlook would have been the imperial dream in its most classical form: the complete union of all beings and things with their true ordering principle and their proper code of behavior. With such a dream the ferment of unrest introduced and maintained by Israel's religion would have been buried under the reign of the One. This ferment was brought about by God's distance from the things of the world, which was clearly foreshadowed by his people's isolation from other nations. As long as the Elect were suppressed, history remained unfulfilled and divided between presence and the burden of the future. Israel's solitude was a sign of this axial distance between the prefigured possibility and reality; for this reason it virtually attested God's withdrawal from a world even more remote than it would be if it completely and universally recognized his will. The Covenant's exclusive nature kept the transcendent difference minimally open, since although it inwardly denied difference, expectation reintroduced what custom concealed. Conversely, imperial messianism would have abolished or reabsorbed the difference by reuniting the all-encompassing terrestrial order with the celestial One.

The Second Moses

It is important to explain this background with its unfulfilled possibilities because everything in it demanded Jesus' intervention. His person was entirely a response to this distinctive situation—a response to the internal tensions operating in it, to the expectations it opened up, to the prospects that the basic thrust of the politico-religious brought to life. It was the most radical response imaginable in this context, with a powerful implicit legitimacy, since it actually repeated Moses' founding act. Indeed, like his, it both resumed and broke with the imperial schema's universalizing process. Except this time it was no longer just a matter of *enduring* imperialism, but also of *implementing* it through internally developing Israel's faith in a messianic form. However, the response was not just a tearing oneself away from the oppressor's physical embrace, but a secession of minds. The break no longer took place (either really or mythically) in the visible external world, but in the invisible inner world of souls. Moses had to free his people from Pharaoh's hands. Jesus extracted his followers from Caesar's grasp, not by leading them toward a terrestrial promised land, but by removing them from the world, while remaining in it. There were two pressing requirements, one traditional and one new, which combined to inspire him from the very beginning, and his remarkable genius was to accept both together and regulate each through the other. The traditional requirement was to counter a fatal domination, and the proven formula here was to appeal to the power beyond all power, in the tradition of the Mosaic invention. At the same time, there was the more recent, but equally powerful, spiritual requirement to resolve the contradiction immanent to the covenantal god who, though universal, only recognized a particular people. The edge to Jesus' preaching comes from the interacting solutions to these two questions in that the god he appealed to, a rediscovered Mosaic god, was an unparalleled liberator freed from the restricting aporias of a chosen people.

Unlike the prophets, Jesus could not content himself with urging sinners to repent and the righteous to hope. He was a guide, a leader, and one had to follow him to obtain the salvation he promised—he was a second Moses. But he was no longer an ordinary Messiah who could have called, in Israel's name, for an uprising against the occupying power, and a final war to establish the reign of the Law. The resistance and flight he proposed were of a wholly different nature. For his god was so far removed from this world's ties that it would not have made any sense to confront terrestrial thrones and principalities in his name. His battle was in the soul's inner recess, far removed from Caesar demands, in the quiet conviction that the true kingdom lay elsewhere. God's universal omnipotence would not emerge in the coming world empire, but was attested here and now; he did not recognize any nation but only inner beings, who were made more receptive to his message by their withdrawal from worldly things into themselves. Where the prophet attested the distance of the one and only god by repudiating his community, Christ's believers bore witness to the unlimited nature of transcendence by completely cutting off their inner selves from the entire sensory world. Faith was no longer only what legitimated opposition to others, it now became the justification to feel oneself profoundly other to the world as a whole. The circle was thus complete and the identification of the universal god was achieved in this repetition of the inaugurating act giving rise to his figure, and was at the same time a reversal of the Covenant's exclusiveness. This identification occurred at the speculative level by intensifying divine exteriority in relation to creation, by making the believer "other" in relation to this lowly world. This change freed God from even partial involvement in human affairs, and turned the relationship with him into a purely individual one, open to all. That is to say, it took place through what was identified above as the specifically Christian merger between submitting to the world's ruler and rejecting the world, between the spirit of obedience and salvation values.

An Inverted Messiah

If we wish to accurately measure the impact of Christ's preaching, we must focus as much on actions as on words. There is what Jesus said, and there is what his discourse *conveyed*, what it symbolically implied, which goes far beyond its immediate content due to the *position* he occupied. The *space* he occupied—which was not only the one he claimed, but the one in which he was actually installed—is more revealing than all his words put together. Or more precisely, it was this space that silently gave his words their real significance and explained how they were to be received and understood.

Jesus thus claimed to be the Messiah.[28] This meant choosing, in a situation whose details were well-defined, an equally well-defined status and role. But Jesus was not just any sort of Messiah: he actually operated like *an inverted Messiah*. Of course he did not say as much, but the way he presented himself meant he had to be seen as such. What actually is a Messiah? The king of the end of time, the great sovereign sent by Yahveh to bring about His people's victory, the universal emperor who will mystically reconcile the entire earth with heaven's law—hence a being with two natures, both human and superhuman, in whose body both realms are destined to be united. The difference is that Jesus simultaneously occupied an inverse position. While the monarch of the world was *at the top* of the human pyramid, Jesus was *at the bottom*, just like any other ordinary human. His sublime self-conception did not prevent him from assuming a humble birth, and the enormous mission he invoked did not cause him to claim prestige or dominion. He was the perfect *counterpart* to the imperial mediator, only *at the opposite pole*. But this shift within human space gave the encounter between two levels of reality in one and the same person a radically different meaning. The incarnation of the invisible used to be the archetypal means for showing the continuity between the earthly hierarchy and the celestial order; here it became the very signifier of their mutual exteriority. We have already had the opportunity to see, in regard to Akhenaton's reform and its limits, how the monotheistic endeavor was inspired by the Pharaoh's office and was bound to become entangled in the coparticipation of the human and the divine in the sovereign: the interweaving of the Natural and the Supernatural, as represented by Pharaoh, conclusively established an invincible barrier to the idea of a unique and separated god. Jesus, the exact opposite of this systematic obstruction, showed how it could be overcome: having definitively opened up transcendence, he would sustain this opening for centuries to come.

When the human and the divine actually joined together in an ordinary man, far removed from power, this junction began to signify the opposite of what it traditionally had. Instead of attesting to the other's substantial proximity, it began to refer to its infinite distance; instead of identifying the collective body with its external foundation, it highlighted the enormous gap separating them. For God's truth to reach us, he had to adopt a shape analogous to ours, a spectacular way of announcing his unimaginably foreign nature. His proximity through Christ is an inexhaustible sign of his unrepresentable remoteness. The central pivotal point in the system remained the same: the notion of the man-god was nothing new. On the other hand, what has been less noticed is the reversal of its symbolic function, achieved by displacing him from the top to the bottom of the social ladder. We switched from a logic of *superiority*, where the general and permanent contact of beings with the sacred source occurs through the network of dependencies whose keystone was the sovereign, to a logic of *otherness*. Here the special communication divine wisdom granted us through its messenger could only be repeated by contemplating its incarnator's unique example within each individual, since only a retreat into the inner self opens up the meaning of God's unknowable withdrawal. The extraordinary radiance of Christ's figure, the exemplary nature it has so persistently assumed, its symbolic power, can ultimately only be explained by this logical operation. It was an operation whose significance, both as a well-defined historical form of the human community, and as its political articulation, was incomparable. There is a long polemical tradition that has continually stressed the fundamental anomaly of the idea of a man-god and scoffed at its incoherence. Putting aside all belief in the mystery itself, this polemical tradition misunderstands the quite clearly defined stakes in this context and the compelling necessity orchestrating it. The hidden source of its effectiveness is that it embodied the inversion of this key figure in the human world who, for an entire phase of its history, had been its highest-ranking member, bordering on the nonhuman. Collective-being was previously exemplified in him alone and the unifying perspective of the secular order was to be found in his personage.

Not only did he now place himself directly opposite the position allocated to the messianic monarch, he also inverted what should have been the latter's message. Where the Prince of the apocalypse would have called for war, Jesus preached love. In other words, the law to which he bore witness had nothing to do with the cardinal imperatives of power in this world. True faith's victory would not be the gathering together of all humans in a single kingdom uniting heaven and earth; it would be the complete reversal of what used to be the universal code for all humans. Living according to the truth of the other world meant freeing ourselves from the archetypal worldly obligation, namely, violent reciprocity, the call for blood, the necessity for revenge as a communal duty. The very constraint of the social bond was the primary cause of war, from the lowest level of group solidarity and the tribute due to it, to the highest political ideal, namely the realization of peace through war by uniting the world. From the everyday law of retaliation to the unlimited goal of conquest, war's necessity was neither more nor less than a reaffirmation of the collective's primacy; but love was the interior distance of individuals from the social bond, their inner release from the original communal obligation. This did not mean rejecting or openly contesting them but rather silently and privately abandoning them. Jesus did not want to dissolve the previous principle of adherence and the system of duties accompanying it. He instaurated a wholly different understanding of obligation, based on the autonomy of the heart. He did not establish an order of individuals. He created individuals who, judged from the code they followed and the ends they pursued, were internally removed from the law of inclusion ruling the world.

So this *doctrinal* inversion ended up *inverting* destiny. Jesus was not heading for victory but defeat. He was not heading toward the glorious attestation of his truth; he was headed for abandonment and the uncertainty of an ignominious death. He did not mobilize his people in a worldly mission; he sacrificed himself, alone and unrecognized, to save everyone else. Just as he was mysteriously forsaken in his agony, so would the true path, salvation in another life, remain clearly opposed to the greatest worldly victory imaginable. Reversing the reversal through the resurrection, triumphing over death after death's victory, took place so as to confirm the exemplary necessity of passing through extreme abandonment and humiliation. The encounter with the otherworldly god was not just the conclusion of one among several terrestrial paths, but rather the realization of the highest goal the human mind could ever conceive, which no conqueror had even remotely approached. It was quite unlike, and contrary to, all other paths.

At the same time Jesus' preaching was wholly and constantly in keeping with the eschatological messianism whose perspective it reversed. Since the horizon it foretold was of the approaching end of time, it revitalized itself on this very point. In other words, it did not completely abandon the space for compromise available in Judaism; it displaced it without ruining it. If his preaching made us conceive divine transcendence beyond and against the possibility of terrestrial alliance, this was in order to restore the perspective of an ultimate union between heaven and earth by announcing the imminent arrival of universal upheaval. Despite everything, the radical separation it outlined was counterbalanced by the apocalyptic reunion it simultaneously postulated. The latter, of course, expressed itself outside the framework of the election of Yahveh's people. It broadly reversed the order prevailing among humans rather than extended by the Covenant; it was a surge of otherness rather than an establishment of sameness. This changed its content to mean the exact opposite without in any way changing its function. The two separate kingdoms would one day see their differences reduced—and whether this day was imminent or far-off scarcely affected the basic teaching promising the end of time. If there was a duality of the human and the divine, it was destined to return to unity. Future history would resolve the present split. In Judaism, what was both carried by present observances and guaranteed by the Messiah's future arrival was transferred by Jesus into a future far removed from the present. But with him also, the radically new reached a compromise with the old—quite simply, it compromised by adopting an original form through the intermediary of the temporal element. There is no need to dwell again on the part this factor had to play in making the message acceptable. And we scarcely need stress the decisive role this balance between present and future continued to play throughout Christian history. The unfolding of transcendence was accompanied by the completion of history: the second coming has never ceased to counterbalance the Incarnation, and the infinite distance opened up by God's son becoming man was supposed to be ultimately canceled out by Christ's second coming, this time as a glorious king. Here we have the unshakable buttress, the ultimate bulwark of resistance by which the Christian vision continued to be related to the philosophy of the One. Once everything originating in analogical or miraculous consubstantiality of the visible and the invisible had been removed, there was still the prospect of a final reabsorption of this world into the other. While this contact may have been remote, diffuse, and imperceptible, it was nevertheless necessary. The major difference regarding the normal modes connecting the Natural and the Supernatural was the possibility of conceiving their strict separation in light of their primary encounter in Christ. What had been separated by the deeply disturbing union of the human and the divine in a Messiah, would one day merge together. Until then, we could never cease examining both the enormous discrepancy between God's absolute nature and human understanding, and his remoteness to the world as indicated by the law of love, preordained humiliation, and his messenger's unfathomable proximity.

Initially a resolution of Judaism's internal contradiction, the Incarnation ended up becoming the pivotal point of a whole new religious sensibility. It combined, in a unique manner, the personal god's universality with the believer's extraneous relation to the world. This god created the world whose creatures felt basically other to the universe established for them. The Christian synthesis united two different lines of development of religious otherness, and this union, though essential to western development, was nonetheless a challenge to reason. So for it to occur, something more and other than a detached movement of ideas or a rationally organized development was necessary. What was needed was *an event*, without which we could not have grasped how this unnatural union between rejecting the world and submitting to the creator's will could have taken place. Only by reversing all possible mediation between heaven and earth, as Jesus did, could such a system of dual otherness crystallize, a system where God's distance from the world corresponded symmetrically to humans' distance from it, where extricating believers from the cosmos was a counterpart to separating the all-powerful one who so willed it. The system is structurally quite intelligible, but appears rather odd when translated materially into the idea of a creator who encouraged his creatures to flee the abode designed for them. There thus emerged a structural link between a God separate from the world and a believer outside-the-world, through which the reign of the other (God) against man became the reign of man against the other (things). For the structural link, as improbable as it was effective, to occur, a series of contingent circumstances and conditions was necessary. A prophet's devotion to truth and Job's sufferings themselves were not enough to bring it about: what was needed was for him to sacrifice his own flesh in a specific location. He had to do more than put himself completely in God's service: he had to give himself completely. And for there to be such a man, there had to be a special combination of a past and a present, of a memory and a problem. The problem, once again, was how a god meant for all humans was worshipped by only one people. Jesus' genius was to resolve the problem by using the memory of the chosen people, of Moses and his founding actions, as the source for a new god, by breaking free from terrestrial domination. Jesus urged an even more radical repudiation since his was no longer a removal from the world's empire, but from the world itself. His god thus became the truly universal god, directly accessible to all. This is what has made us Christians. The significance of the gradual deployment of transcendence from these humble beginnings should not make us forget its origin's extremely peculiar and fragile nature.

I must stress that this interpretation does not require the protagonist's clear awareness. There is no need to attribute to Jesus a well-considered plan to resolve Judaism's basic contradiction by inverting the messianic figure. His cultural context is one where the imperial outlook was a living factor structuring being-in-the-world, just as the image of the mediator uniting heaven and earth in his body was the basic symbolic articulation of human space, immediately perceptible to anyone—and Jesus was part of a tradition defining itself through opposition to imperial milestones. The status of Israel's god was not a question of pure speculation, but once again, of a problem binding the very organization of ordinary existence to the balance between legality and inwardness, to the balance between collective submission and personal latitude. These factors were experienced before they were understood and we should try to position ourselves effectively in relation to them, rather than understand them abstractly. The creative operation that interests me did not develop on the reflective but the active level, a symbolic sort of action in contact with the deep logic of the social totality, expressing itself through examples rather than ideas. This does not in the least mean we must consider Jesus' discourse to be negligible, devoid of any originality. But it does mean we must measure the influence of his discourse in terms of the implicit action it represents rather than that of its explicit content. Its purpose only gained meaning in relation to the axial reference points of the collective operation. He was a thinker insofar as he silently subverted schemas which had up to then structured the human world, as well as subverting dependence on the other world's foundation. This means that he said far more than he expressed literally, and certainly far more than he himself believed he was formulating. We do not have to determine the extent of his clear-sightedness retrospectively, but must rather establish that there was no necessity for him to know in order to act. There was no need for him to intellectually control a situation to respond intuitively to it, as he did.

What is true of Jesus' inspiration applies equally to the reception of his message. Otherwise, we could not understand how the extraordinarily captivating force condensed into this peripheral figure was sufficient to push his teaching from a remote outpost into the heart of the greatest civilized power of its time, not to mention the central position his example would occupy for twenty centuries of spiritual life. Renan, who was well aware of Jesus' magnetism, attributed it to the influence of an admirable individual who mobilized the total dedication of a group of disciples to seize the attention of more extensive groups. This explanation, though not necessarily false, does not go far enough. I think we can only really clarify its extraordinarily attractive power by taking into account the symbolic background of Jesus' preaching, which constituted its unconscious motivation along with its inexhaustible reserves of meaning. The captivating power of this model remains unintelligible unless we look at the effect on the world order caused by his person and his word, and look at the renewed relation between the here-below and the beyond highlighted by his simple style of living among humans. By the structure of his role, by the gesture constituting the heart of his teaching, by the mysterious trajectory of his destiny, he implied something unutterably *new*—about life, truths, values. This did not have to be explicitly thought in order to be inwardly accepted.

SAINT PAUL: THE UNIVERSAL GOD

This perspective allows us, if not to avoid, at least to relativize some classical problems related to early Christianity—problems concerning the constitution and clarification of its doctrine. The most significant was the second and decisive foundation brought about by Saint Paul. Indeed, subsequent history undoubtedly rested on how he conceived the universal god, went beyond the limits of the synagogue, separated the new faith from the Jewish religion to open it up to gentiles, and deduced its missionary implications. Paul's god is truly universal because he is wholly internal and, being ethnically disaffiliated, possibly not the one Jesus proclaimed. On the other hand, this god was certainly delineated in the wake of Jesus' terrestrial activity. Paul's work must be understood as explicating what Christ conveyed by his actions. This is why it was so enthusiastically received: it did not graft an invented message onto a silent base, but unfolded the meaning of an extremely revealing symbolic figure. Paul's message merged the Christ-model with its theological implications, thereby enhancing the splendor of both.

Here we must pay attention to the structural necessity of events and individuals as well as their contingency. Jesus might not have appeared, even under favorable conditions. But once he appeared, the general direction of his actions was established. Not that he was condemned to do everything the situation demanded of him. But his intervention inevitably had to remain within a range of clearly defined possibilities, which he used in an original way. He exploited, in a contingent manner, possibilities that were themselves necessarily linked. Similarly, Paul might not have found his way to Damascus. But from the moment he followed in Christ's path, integrating the fact and the meaning of Christ's coming into this world, he was thrown into a restrictive domain whose transformation controlled his movements. He embraced both the faith and the inner necessity determining its possible developments. It certainly required an exceptional person to bring them about, but even the most exceptional person would have had to follow in a certain predetermined direction to be understood. Both Paul and Jesus provided an appropriate individual solution to an obscurely, but widely perceived problem. Jesus appeared where there was a space for concluding Moses' redefinition of the divine; his absolute legitimacy was to have logically realized the spiritual possibilities that were created within the imperial dynamics but could only crystallize in its margin. And Paul completed this process by revealing the universal impact of the Messiah's declaration. He released the otherworldly one true god from his original ties; he moved this god from the periphery to the center of the melting pot kindled by the world empire, so to speak. In both cases, the greater the encounter between open understanding and latent possibility, the more surprising its success.

CHRISTOLOGY

Another example is the Christological debate of the fourth and fifth centuries. I have already identified the main ontological stakes involved: when dealing with the union of the human and the divine in Christ, we are really dealing with the structural link between the here-below and the beyond. However, we cannot just judge it by its consequences. We must further consider its cultural reference point and the structural support giving it meaning. The inanity of the subject matter, the arbitrary nature of its argumentations, the incomprehensible discrepancy between the small stakes involved and the vicious emotions invested in these murderous disputes, have become the very image of madness, and the mobilization of entire populations in these theological disputes gave them both a tragic and ludicrous character. If ever there was an emblem of human propensity to mindless and pointless self-destruction, this is it. Such a judgment arises from the absence of those reference points behind this confrontation, which when taken into account shows that these discussions about the true nature of God's messenger were directly linked to the structural process at the heart of Christ's intervention, namely the inversion of the classical figure of the man-god. The central issue in the debate was between a traditional understanding of any possible contact between the two orders of reality, and a radically new understanding of it inspired by Jesus. On one side were those for whom the encounter between the human and the divine remained essentially hierarchical, and the question of whether Christ's divine or human nature predominated was posed within the same conceptual framework. And on the other side, there were those trying to interpret Christ's exceptionalism, and the de-hierarchization implied in the advent of a Messiah from the lowest order. For this faction, the Incarnation was no longer to be understood in terms of the old political logic of higher and lower, but in terms of a purely metaphysical logic of otherness; and in this framework the absolute difference of the human and the divine allowed us to think their complete union. As the famous formula of the Council of Chalcedon put it, "without confusion, without change, without division, without separation; the distinction of natures being in no way abolished because of the union, but rather the characteristic property of each nature being preserved, and concurring into one Person and one subsistence."[29] Here, the complete union of both natures in Christ—"the same perfect in Godhead, and the same perfect in manhood, truly God and truly man"—draws our attention to the complete disjunction of the human and the divine. I cannot overemphasize the decisive importance of this debate, whose outcome for determining the possibilities inscribed in the figure of Christ can be legitimately considered the first decisive step toward the western deconstruction of the hierarchical principle. Once the orthodox interpretation of the hypostatic union was determined, an irreversible step had been made away from a central plank of the unitarian, nonegalitarian understanding of being.

But to completely understand a confrontation of this type it is vital to be aware of the symbolic framework underlying it. We must go behind the opposing positions to grasp the structural schemas maintaining and controlling the thought. The debate's abstraction only seems extravagant. The theses were determined by a reasoning whose principles, as far as the actors are concerned, were as nameless as their effects were tangible, so to speak. An idea as peculiar and gratuitous as the hypostatic union becomes obvious and necessary when seen in its formative context.

It corresponds to a mathematically precise locus and a clearly defined role obtained by reversing to the last detail the more customary, but also totally determined, figure of the mediating sovereign. Let us imagine, as the ordinary humanity of Jesus entreats us to do, a being who follows the example of the King of Kings and unites heaven and earth within himself, but occupies the position directly opposed to this king's. If this is done we cannot think of him other than as the complete conjunction of the human and the divine in a fully maintained disjunction, rather than a classic mediator. We are not dealing with a challenge to reason but, on the contrary, with the relentless logic of a cultural system whose major reference points must be pieced together to understand its logical pattern. By virtue of his unprecedented position in the human sphere, Christ can only be understood as realizing the perfect union ("without division or separation") of two natures which, just as profoundly, remain completely distinct ("without confusion or change"). Only contradiction can supply the logic required to understand this position, as it was the only satisfactory way of simultaneously thinking about the encounter of the here-below and the beyond in one body and in a neutral position in human space, opposite to that of power. It was a faithful, and on its own grounds incontrovertible, expression of an unavoidable structural outcome. The dogma of the Incarnation was not believed because it was absurd; it was accepted because it was reasonable. There was nothing arbitrary in this unusual proposition; it contained only what had been determined by clearly identifiable operations on the basic articulations of the human establishment—which explains why so many minds were able to be mobilized around such esoteric questions. However high these speculations aimed, they remained embedded in common soil and affected our modes of collective-being. There was a vibrant flesh to thoughts about the other world, one whose unreality was so attractive that humans would devote themselves to it, and would be as savagely punished for their image of heaven, as it were, as for their worldly interests. There was wisdom behind the folly, and careful calculation behind the detachment, because what was really at stake, disguised as extremely tenuous speculations about heaven, were the deepest and most enduring forms of the terrestrial bond.

CONQUERING THE CONQUERORS

My analysis can be broadened and systematized by going beyond the two examples I have just discussed. Indeed, I believe that theoretically it could be applied to the phenomenon of the establishment of Christianity as a whole. This will not of course exhaust its mysterious depths but it may throw some light on it.

The historical life of religious ideas can only be understood through their collective roots, where the conditions for their formulation and reception were articulated, where the possibilities for thinking and receiving the new jointly emerged and clarified each other. Once again, there was no guarantee: latent ideas might not have been formulated even though they were capable of expression, and properly expressed ideas could be totally rejected. To go from an idea's conditions of possibility to its effective implementation is an enormous step, to be elucidated by the historian staying as close as possible to the actual course of events. By confining myself to the logical blueprint of the process, I have at best indicated the considerable gap separating the general conditions for the appearance of a monotheistic faith from the paths through which they were actually realized. So we cannot simply assert that Christianity's triumphant expansion inevitably followed the dismantling of previous representational frameworks, the unsettling of minds, and the disclosure of unknown spiritual horizons brought about, in Rome as elsewhere, by the dynamics of empire. Just as the complex roundabout path of Mosaic founding and its Christ-centered inversion were necessary for the successful separation of the divine, there was also the need for highly specific conditions. No one up to now has succeeded in throwing light on their interplay in an even remotely satisfactory way. The fact remains that even beginning to understand an event such as the diffusion of Christianity presupposes taking into account the massive contradiction working deep within the empire, between the inherited religious order and the religious world vision implied by the actual logic of the system of domination.

In this context, the new faith immediately appears less unusual. Christianity came from a totally different place, but this was true of many other cults admitted to Rome. This new faith had a unique history making it difficult to present to those in a world where it was yet to prevail. And it would ultimately collide head-on with paganism as a whole—not just paganism's content but the very basis of its intellectual organization. And yet this foreign body, which appeared so completely non-appropriable, and whose very incongruity seemed calculated to trigger universal rejection, was much less unintelligible than it might seem at first glance. It appears that even the extraordinary image of the world and of human destiny put forward by Christians secretly colluded with the potential space for feelings and thoughts foreshadowed by the move toward the universal expansion of the political realm and the hidden but fatal inner discredit it brought to the previous harmonious integration with beings.

We must return to the central phenomenon which almost everywhere caused the downfall of the human race's religious outlook: the unifying expansion of power and the destabilizing effects brought about by the ongoing project to gather every being together under a single power.

There was a radical incompatibility between residual primeval religion, which for a while, continued to organize the empire's nuclear community, and the vast horizons opened up by the unlimited nature of the expansionary goal. There was no imperial undertaking which did not delegitimize or devitalize every articulation of being-in-the-world made in terms of the religion of the past, of allegiance to the received order. Its correlates were self-centered exclusivism and a plural structure of the deity. The spirit of conquest led to the death of the pagan gods. Installing the legitimizing principle of the ancestral past inside the universal power tended to restore it to the living present. This installation tended, as it were, to unify the heart of the world. It also led to a redefinition of each country's codes, whereby the requirement for personal and rational conformity to a universal law was substituted for the spirit of custom and the strict observance of community practices.[30] It created, either on the margins of or within the ruling culture, the space for another cosmology, for another moral code, for another legal code—for another understanding of what was right and necessary. In the Greco-Roman framework, the development of Stoicism from Alexander to Marcus Aurelius remarkably illustrates this. Polytheism was buried by the conquering city, whose rise was paid for by the slow demise of its guardian deities and its forefather's beliefs. There was an invisible upheaval whose shock wave left everything externally as before, but internally without any real substance. In the midst of this intangible disintegration appeared the most successful ever transmutation of minds, brought about by the crushing and intermixing of peoples. This does not explain why Roman concerns yielded to Christian convictions, but it does make their convergence less improbable. Despite appearances, the certainties arising from the outcast peoples' tribulations and the agony undermining minds in the highest civilization were in agreement. Though nothing in their destiny forced them to converge, the fascination of the strong for the faith of the weak seems less improbable, and the conversion of the imperial metropolis no longer looks like an internal surrender to barbarians.

At this point structural analysis reaches its limits. It does allow us to state the problem differently by identifying the common roots through which such distinctly separate mental systems were able to converge, but to go further and explain how the above mentioned convergence actually did occur is the historian's task. We must move from reconstructing logical connections to measuring distinctive features. It is no longer a question of relating Rome's fate to a general history of political forms, but of distinguishing Rome from other empires and explaining its particular receptiveness to the Jewish Messiah's teaching and example. We can guess the major axes of such a powerfully determining force. First there was an empire based on the city, a major realignment of the balance between collective and individual principles, along with all the possibilities for in-

dividualism conveyed by the internal and extra-worldly Christian god.
Next, there was an imperial republic whose domestically driven expansion transformed the image of terrestrial power and the representation of
the world community. In short, it was an empire imposed on the emperor
rather than arising from him. This is probably the main distinctive feature to consider when assessing the way in which a figure like Christ
could be perceived in the context of the "Roman revolution" and its successors. All this concerns the basic elements, but says nothing about the
integrating process's actual sequence and operation, or about the conjunction between internal crisis and external threat; or how social difference was able to integrate the status of the outsider (the foreigner, the
slave) with the doctrine of supernatural extraneousness. To describe all
this would exceed both my concerns and competence. I am raising the
point to counter the impression the approach here adopted may create,
by emphasizing that paying attention to the constraints of symbolic organization does not exclude paying attention to the facts and events, but
should ideally combine all three. Taking into account the structural factor behind the history of religious phenomena, with its radical reduction-
ism, should not lead us to neglect the abundance of facts, but rather to
enlarge the breadth and number of those we should consider significant.

The Christian Revolution: Faith, Church, King

What exactly is a believer in Christ? In other words, how does the representation of the other world introduced by God's becoming-man affect
the definition of being-in-the-world? In purely structural terms, we can
reduce the matter to three core dispositions whose combination and interaction contain the logical possibilities for all subsequent developments
of transcendent religion. There is one central disposition controlling the
relationship to visible reality in general, and two others resulting from its
direct application. One relates to the conditions of terrestrial legitimacy
(existing in this world) and the other to the conditions of religious life
(existing for the other world).

1. The only way to attain God's invisible extraneous level was to separate oneself from visible reality and withdraw through contemplation
into one's own invisible inwardness. Unlike the former gods concretely
present through the normative texture of their "works and days," the
separated god demands *an act of faith*, a *conversion*. This god's truth
could only be grasped by breaking with sensory self-evidence, hence is a
god whose separation from nature is reflected in an obligation to cut ourselves off from the realm of appearances. So whoever scrupulously followed the message delivered by the Incarnation became "an individual-

outside-the-world," to borrow the phrase recently suggested by Louis Dumont's extension of Troeltsch's "the individual-in-relation-to-god."[31] By this I mean beings inwardly freed from any worldly affiliation by their secret dealings with the extra-worldly god. This phrase, however, does not fully take account of the dynamic tension inherent in the individualizing structural link between the here-below and the beyond, a tension crucial to the development of history. There is a dual tension, one in faith's relation to itself, and the other in its relation to external reality. These individuals inwardly isolated from the world were still outwardly subjugated to it, both as corporeal and social beings. They had to win their spiritual autonomy by first turning against that part of themselves dependent on physical reality and controlled by it. Their individual liberty was won at the price of a personal split. In other words, the religious division was played out within them, it traversed and dwelt in them. But at the same time, God had willed and organized the sensory world from which we must separate ourselves in order to reach the heavens. How could the sensory be totally rejected when it was judged worthy for the Word-Made-Flesh? So if we are to radically distance ourselves from the sensory, we must also to some extent consent to it. We cannot completely reject the world, however impossible it may be to accommodate ourselves to it. We must reach a compromise between acceptance and rejection, a compromise that cannot be definitively defined. We find ourselves in a vicious circle of obligations: we must hold ourselves outside the world while admitting we live in it.[32] The true originality of the relation to the world established by Christianity lay in this axiomized ambiguity, which was a direct refraction of the union of two natures in Christ. It made the Christian into a being torn between a duty of belonging and one of distancing, between forming an alliance with the world and being estranged from it. But also a being in whom this shuttling between worlds is to come to an end—a being who will one day reconcile choice for the beyond and systematic commitment to the here-below.

We see the same tension at the heart of the individual actor's relation not only to objective reality but to collective power. Inwardly, they only have to justify themselves to God. But that does not release them from their obligations to Caesar. If their private consciences are their sole ultimate judges, they still must be integrated into the community of their peers, and they continue to owe allegiance to established rules and authorities willed by God. Indeed, how could they exist without at least the tacit consent of the All-Powerful? The individual-outside-the-world by necessity compromises with secular law. Though internally free, Christians were still subjugated as social beings. As Luther's reform showed, Christians could extol the rights of conscience which advanced the secularization of the established powers and the destabilizing dynamics in-

evitably accompanying it. However strong the desire to strictly separate
the two domains, in reality they must interact. The external obligation to
submit and the right of inner appeal were doomed to clash. It was impossible to make an avowed sacred authority coexist with subjects having a direct relationship with its source, without somehow transforming
the idea of legitimate authority. The more so because increasing God's
extraneousness, the foundation for autonomous conscience, renders terrestrial legitimacy more indirect while simultaneously aligning the external individual with the internal one. Here again, the static formula of the
individual outside-the-world does not give us a complete view of the situation. It omits the tension in this individual outside-the-world's relation
to the world, and how this relation is replicated in a simultaneous submission to, and withdrawal from, the world.

But to fully appreciate this new stance thrust on believers by their
faith, we must incorporate two factors relating to the social repercussions
of Christianity's primordial essence. Though the new being-in-the-world
instaurated by God's becoming-man was a new mode of being-a-self, it
prepared new forms of collective-being. We first see the appearance of a
special society of believers within the broader society, then we see an ultimately decisive reorganization of political power's relation to religious
authority.

2. Early Christianity's Christ-inspired stratagem was to organize the
faithful into one Church. This was simply a transposition into the collective, of each individual's internal distance from the world. This movement, which required focusing on the other world, simultaneously demanded that beings who made the same choice gather themselves into a
separate community. They had to jointly form a salvation society whose
intrinsic difference from ordinary society accorded with God's exteriority. The difference is that changing the scale of the problem changed its
nature. By becoming collective, the religious secession became open and
at the same time institutionally problematic. The question of Christians'
relation to the world turned into the permanent practical question of the
relation between their particular society and the broader society they still
belonged to.

Needless to say, everything here depends on context. Christians' situation as a persecuted minority or secret society differed from when they
constituted society as a whole, when the Church's structure got mixed up
with that of the worldly community. What concerns me here is the underlying structural feature: the refraction of ontological duality into an
irreducible duality of social adherence and legitimacy in Christianity.
Their overlapping administrative structures suggests the recreation of a
classic hierarchical structural link between ecclesiastical and temporal

powers. There was functional specialization and circular complementarity: the priest was subordinated to the sovereign in the temporal sphere and the sovereign was subordinated to the priest in the spiritual sphere, both contributing to the operation of a unique order.[33] In actual fact, such a joining of the two powers was *de jure* impossible. There would basically always be room for two independent orders of authority and two principles of sociability, each complete in its own terms, and impossible to weld together in a stable hierarchy. This is because for a Christian there cannot ultimately be only one unique order, since Jesus' god was not the totally superior being, but the absolute other. There are accordingly two spheres and two legitimacies which in principle must remain distinct. There is life according to this world's rules and life directed toward the other world: two coexisting systems of requirements, but also two systems for organizing existence which, because of God's difference, have autonomous necessity. If the spiritual gathering together of the faithful did not encroach on the privileges of temporal power, it no longer had to *depend* on it, and vice versa. From the outset, the division between spiritual and temporal allegiance attested by the Church and the hierarchical separation of the two powers, placed the Church far beyond the traditional relation of priestly and sovereign function. The Church did not arise from the harmonious cooperation of two spheres; its existence signified the breakdown of any possible organic connection between administering the world and concern with heaven. We must understand this when we relate the differentiation of the two societies to its source, namely, the gap between the two orders of reality.

Historically, and somewhat paradoxically, this central de-hierarchization began to manifest itself in the clash between two rival hegemonic claims: each of the powers considered itself expressly capable of coping with everything and absorbing the other. The first approach was to reabsorb the Church into the imperial administration, placing it under the sovereign's terrestrial responsibility. The second pointed toward a papal theocracy, needed to orient this life toward salvation. Though both deny any dual affiliation, their very antagonism attests it, demonstrating the existence of two world views, independent enough to encroach on each other. This aspiration to absorb the other cannot be attributed to traditional hierarchical thought, but rather shows how the tradition had collapsed due to its inability to cope with a binding difference. It shows how extremely difficult it is to imagine, within a Christian framework, a harmonious union between duties here-below and obligations to the beyond. Instead of reciprocal adjustment, we see here an illustration of their propensity for mutual exclusion. The western "miracle" was due precisely to this tension between two orders of necessity, each so firmly entrenched that it could resist the other—this tension completely satisfied the needs of the here-below while fully devoting itself to the imperatives of the beyond. There was no successful primitive copenetration of the spiritual and the temporal, hence no lessening of tension. Though this seems to have nearly occurred, as in the case of Byzantine Caesaro-Papism, it never had any real foundation. Beneath the apparent reunion of heaven and earth, of faith's champions with the law's champions, Christianity always kept the two spheres separate. The Christian god, who is other, did not guarantee the common structure of hierarchical authority. Hence the fracturing and discord, at the heart of Christian society, between the means for salvation and the mechanism of domination.

Up to now I have looked at the general conditions for the existence of a Church embedded in the Christ-inspired apparatus. I now want to demonstrate the unshakable legitimacy of demarcating a second, theoretically autonomous, society within the broader one. I am not concerned with its internal organization, only its ability to form an autonomous self-regulating society which could ultimately encompass and absorb society as a whole. It nevertheless remained unable to ever completely eliminate the legitimacy of a secular society organized on Christian foundations, yet independent and completely terrestrial in its aims. This was because the West's dynamics arose from confrontation between two equally comprehensive and equally Christian legitimating systems, which could not be made hierarchical. After all, this religious society could have run counter to the broader society it was immersed in by becoming a republic of souls, a federation of communities of spiritual equals. Common sense may object that, ensnared as it was in worldly life, religious society quite naturally followed the model of imperial government and its bureaucracy. Though not false, this view does not do justice to this religious society's systematic nature and its religious inspiration. Though it may have borrowed the oppressive machinery of Roman centralism, it arose from a profoundly original aspiration grafted directly onto Christianity's founding nucleus, an aspiration whose deployment would make the ecclesial system a new model for succeeding centuries.

At the origins of the Church's existence was a special type of mediating claim, one grafted directly onto the Christ-centered mediation it tried to make permanent. Christ revealed the abyss between the human and the divine by showing that God's will could only reach us through the Word becoming flesh. By this fact, by the immeasurable gap between the human words through which we have received this will and the infinite wisdom behind them, this abyss became something we had to continually contemplate and interpret. In other words, the purpose of the Incarnation was to open up a yawning gap hermeneutically impossible to close. And it was the Church's nature to be at the heart of the irrepara-

ble gap between the message and its source, in order to both embody its
conspicuous obviousness and fill it. The Church's position, ambition and
role made it a wholly original institution: the first bureaucracy to give
history meaning, the first administration of ultimate meaning. It had to
administer a definitively determined doctrine and body of regulations.
On the one hand, it had to constantly redefine them, dispel the shadows,
remove uncertainties, and determine their dogmatic content; on the
other, it had to examine all their possible ramifications, so as to maintain
a living communication between the spirit and the letter. The Church's
claim to authority arises from a central openness onto the abyss of truth,
to which it continually calls attention, while striving to mitigate the vertigo that abyss induced. Hence the inherent equivocation of its undertaking to train the faithful and control belief. The clerics desire to enter
hearts and minds accords with the underlying uncertainty as to the foundation of the beyond. If there was a need for a centralized system to simultaneously determine the doctrine, organize its propagation, and mon-
itor inner adherence, this is because there was a gap in the code and
meaning this system was supposed to administer. When belief and law
were clearly received through their time-honored source or when God's
voice itself was given directly to us, as in the Koran, there was no need
for a monarch to control dogma and for a mechanism to integrate souls.
The agreement of minds on the basic issues was presumed to be self-ev-
ident and spreading centers of worship became the norm. Conversely, it
was necessary to enforce the detailed contents of practices and belief,
and even more, to exert a guiding control over each individual act of
faith because determining God's living will was seen to be a deeply questionable undertaking. The explosive paradox of spiritual subjugation is
that it legitimates a direct appeal by believers, over the system's head
and over its administrators, to the ultimate source of all justice and reason. The bureaucracy of belief could not work without tacitly recognizing the autonomy of conscience.

The split between the here-below and the beyond, implied by their
union in Christ, was necessary to develop these previously unseen things:
the organization of dogma and the policing of souls. The Church was
born of Jesus' revolutionary mediation between heaven and earth—a mediation which, rather than welding the two orders into an unshakable
spiritual and physical amalgamation through the enigma of his body, did
the opposite, namely, revealed the infinite distance separating human reality from the divine foundation, and at one stroke installed the question
of the limits of the Church's knowledge and understanding of the ultimate cause into the center of human understanding. The ecclesial edifice
arose from this necessity for interpretation but it is just as much a structural necessity (though not, I repeat, a historical one). The Church, in its
role as a salvation society, was the direct obligatory and inevitable mate-

rialization of the differing aims of the beyond. However in its other role, as a hermeneutical authority, it did not have to exist or could have done so completely differently. The Church indisputably substantialized a potential present in the new structural link between the physical and the supernatural, a potential which did not have to be realized. Christ's intervention made it possible to design an institutional hermeneutics, or to put it more broadly, raised the problem of an understanding lying between the divine message and its reception by the faithful. It did not demand the construction of an institution claiming a monopoly on the mediation between God and humans, insofar as it continuously re-emphasized the son's mediation. To understand this particular development, we must introduce the formative component of transcendent religion which desperately attempts to preserve the dimension of ontological unity—the possibility of a living interpenetration, a bond between every moment of the visible and the invisible, even though the logic of the Incarnation deems it impossible. This had to be done through the mediating event itself, whose effects had to be neutralized by constantly reenacting it in a ritual, the Eucharist, and perpetuating it in an institution, the Church.

The signifier of separation thus became the symbol of the relation. Through the daily repetition of the sacrifice, Christ continued to be present among humans. The faithful continued to participate in the actual reunion of heaven and earth through the great ecclesial body, headed by Christ and continuing his work. In both cases, the alliance and balance between *repetition* and *commemoration* are extremely precarious. The union of rite and memory here is in fact inherently contradictory. The repetition of the event which was the Word becoming flesh—I mean the action designed to restore the event to our presence and keep it there—symbolically contradicts the event's historical significance, as grasped by memory. Herein lies the entire difference of Christian ritual. It is, like any pagan ritual, the actualization of an origin. But with Christianity, the origin was an event which actually occurred at a given historical moment and was seen as such—not as a timeless beginning, but as a turning point in the world's history, inscribed long ago in human memory, an originating event whose main thrust is to proclaim the impossibility of any future actualization of the founding principle.

The same difference appears when we turn from the ritual repetition of Jesus' sacrifice to the institutionalization of his role as intermediary between God and humans. It is as Christ, as the everlasting mystical prolongation of the Word's arrival, that the Church is justified in assuming exclusive control of commerce with the other world and making relations between the Creator and the faithful pass through its authority. But in actual fact it is only justified in carrying out this function in memory of Christ. The Church is actually the mediator of God's word as it reached humans through the teaching of the god-man. It is not the interpreter of God's direct will from the beginning to the end of time, but of what has come to our knowledge through his messenger. This messenger was living proof, both in the mystery of his being and the charity of his action, without which the truth of our destiny would remain hidden, that there could be no other conceivable conjunction between the Natural and the Supernatural than what occurred through him. If it makes any sense for the Church to set itself up between God and humans, this is due to what the Son revealed about the mystery of the Father—a disclosure which, while demanding exegesis, denounces the futility of any claim to organically bind heaven and earth. It was a problematical grafting of the metaphysical demand for the One onto the hermeneutical imperative, the actualization of the non-actualizable, the perpetuation of the non-repeatable. In other words, what legitimated the Church's existence— the human understanding's uncertainty about revealed truth—simultaneously justifies challenging its authority. For if God is truly the other, inexhaustibly different, in his supreme wisdom, from what we manage to understand of him, then we can only accommodate the enigmatic, disturbing surplus of meaning deep in our hearts. Any claim by the Church to interpose itself between ultimate otherness and extreme inwardness becomes an absurd hoax, any communitarian bridge thrown across the abyss toward heaven seems an idolatrous misunderstanding of transcendence. To institutionalize communication with the invisible, enabling the faithful to bask continually in the proper interpretation of the Law, guided by inspired pastors, is to clearly ignore our distance from the divine. Ecclesial mediation was thus built on something that cast doubt on the very possibility of mediation. This imitation and continuation of Christ was an open-ended invitation to call on his unique example for the purpose of questioning its assigned role. Its fate can be summed up in this peculiar equation: if room existed for mediation (between divine reason and human intelligence), this was also because there could no longer be any possible mediation, or any further living conjunction between God and humans. The interpreter's role as an intermediary was challenged by the very development that called for it. This was the cause of both its deep-seatedness and the merciless opposition it would arouse.

I have previously spoken about the tension, inherent to Christian being-in-the world, between the principle of authority and that of freedom, between the obligation to submit to established powers and the intractable right to inner autonomy. We can see how this constituting tension was intensified and culminated in the Church. For the Church's authority not only touched on matters dependent on the world's exteriority; it concerned the very substance of the relation to the other world. Not only did it not leave the realm of conscience alone, it increasingly legitimized its own opposition to independent minds by tightening its control. By affirming its power over souls, the Church deepened the difference with the beyond which justified the autonomy of consciences. Also behind each major re-organization of ecclesial machinery, of reinforcing the training of the faithful, of strengthening the pastorate—for example, the Gregorian and Protestant reforms—we can see a claim for a more personal religion, freed from clerical interference and dogmatic appropriation. The god of the heart versus the god of dogma. It is even possible that the Church's perfection was more dangerous to it than its corruption. Naturally, its declining interest in its spiritual mission and its collapse as a secular power provoked short-term indignation. But in the long run, returning to the original spirit of its role and regaining its concern for souls had a far greater effect: these two trends imperceptibly removed believers from its grasp, taught them to have a direct relation with the creator, and introduced them to faith without clergy. Herein lies the entire paradox of this unprecedented authoritarian enterprise. The Church's dogmatic rigidity and its incredible goal of directing the faithful contributed more than anything else to entrench the spirit of freedom it continually opposed. Its unique attempt to make the community of inner beings participate in God's living mystery, largely brought about the demise of independent investigation's staunchest enemy: the spirit of custom and the received order. The Church's desire to go beyond adherence to the letter and obtain wholehearted acquiescence, made it the major instigator of the demand to understand over and above the age-old obligation to believe. These socially substantial but historically improbable beings, who determined themselves by their own knowledge, whether in relation to the beyond or to their equals here-below, appeared in and through the Church, even when they opposed it. The Church, though unfaithful to Christ's mediation because of its excessive claims to mediate, would nevertheless be decisive in realizing the possibility inscribed in the advent of the god-man: the power of inwardness. Its effects will range from disaffiliating the act of faith to making the rational being independent; from withdrawal from the world, brought about by converting to the otherworldly god, to inner autonomy bestowed by the search for the truth of divine reason.

The Church, whether regarded as the salvation society in its relation to secular society, or as a hermeneutical authority in its relation to believers' freedom, was the locus where all the tensions born of Christ's partition emerged. How could we reconcile the legitimate concern of the here-below with the only worthwhile preoccupation, the beyond? What does it mean to truthfully receive God's message, which requires both submitting to a revelation far beyond the puny forces of human understanding, and attempting to understand its transcendent meaning? From this viewpoint the Church was, historically speaking, a second Christ. Due to its existence, the questions opened up by the Jewish Messiah continued to affect humans. Both in its legitimate separation and in its highly ambitious pursuit of meaning, it offered them the refuge of a permanent body and the chance to have a second life.

3. The revolution in the mediation between visible and invisible brought about by Christ's instauration obviously affected not only religious but political mediation. It changed the nature of the political realm as much as it changed the essence of the priesthood, though not in the same way. From the outset, the Incarnation made the relationship to the beyond problematic by giving it an intrinsically open meaning. The Church replied to this by making the priest much more than the traditional specialist in religious dealings with the supernatural, and he became an intermediary of what could be thought, between the mystery of foundation and the faithfuls' unease and bewilderment. No such essential function was demanded from the order of socially established powers. The believer outside-the-world had to yield to these powers outside his domain, but it was never appropriate for him to be involved with them. This implicit withdrawal caused the terrestrial powers to emerge radically changed by their confrontation with the Word-made-flesh. Whether he liked it or not, a Christian prince could no longer ever be what a pre-Christian prince ideally had to be. This is because the place of the perfect mediator had been occupied, and no one after Christ could claim to occupy the pivotal point where the Natural and Supernatural had come together in one body. This is, I believe, the meaning of the famous Gelasian doctrine on the separation of the two offices, namely that, after Christ, no one could simultaneously be both priest and king.[34] This means that, before Christ, sovereigns were able to claim (either falsely, from the Christian viewpoint, or on the grounds of foreshadowing, like Melchisidech) that they were living embodiments of the sacred foundation and divine law. In this way, they were able to claim to reunite in their person the management of terrestrial affairs and the administration of celestial matters. Once the divine had been genuinely incarnated in the human—that is, once the real priest-king, who united the right of domination here-below and the power of communicating with the beyond, had arrived—the very possibility of wanting to legitimately recombine what Christ had clearly shown to be irretrievably separate, was eliminated. Roles were organized in two orders just as there were two orders of reality, separated by being consubstantial in Christ. One order was dependent on the governing of this lowly world and one was concerned with obligations to the other world. One had authority over the body, and the other managed souls. The terrestrial power's sacrality could no longer originate in a personification of the invisible source of

every rule and every life. Yet its sacral nature was not denied. It was even expressly confirmed since, if sovereign authority existed, the All-Powerful had clearly sanctioned it. But terrestrial power was no longer justified in calling itself the physical manifestation of heaven's law. Political power now found its symbolic foundation had been revolutionized because the traditional support for its sacral identity and its mediating legitimacy had been withdrawn. When the effects of this phenomenon became obvious long after, they were enormous. The beginnings of the radically original form of public power that developed in the mainstream of European history, reversing the previous articulation between the top and the bottom of society, must be sought in the Christian break with the logic of an organic interlocking of the Natural and the Supernatural.

In practice, this break remained concealed for a long time. The basic ambiguity regarding the sacral nature of power lent itself quite naturally to a confusing renewal of previous forms. There was also the weighty tradition of the One, fuelling the attempt to keep Christ's union of heaven and earth alive and continually present. Because of this favorable background, the appearances of the old sacral royalty were preserved and reconstructed within a Christian framework, particularly the intimate alliance between priesthood and sovereignty which had been theoretically excluded since the Saviour's coming. If it was unthinkable for someone to fully occupy Christ's position, at least it was possible to perpetuate its spirit by reproducing its image. The commemorative actualization of the mediation would compensate for the impossibility of repeating this mediation and make us forget it. Unable to be what Christ was, the king would be like Christ. If he could never be both priest and monarch as fully as his supreme model, he could nevertheless be so to the extent that he made Christ's absence present and symbolized his truth. And the fact that power was conferred by God would be sacramentally sanctioned and confirmed. However they varied, these three traits—divine devolution guaranteed by anointing, the priestly character of the king's function, and his symbolic participation in the father's power—all tended to reinstate the Christian king in the long line of royalty which incarnated the sacred foundation and was capable of absorbing it. I concede to Marc Bloc that there is no major difference, but rather a strong similarity, between the role and appearance of this sovereign in the flesh, and the magical force implied by the personified copenetration of the visible and the invisible, and the African monarchs shown to us by ethnology. However, beneath this superficial kinship, the very legitimation of the Christian prince contained a destabilizing fermenting factor, a potential constraint to displace, a transforming possibility whose equivalent we will seek in vain in African monarchies, where the symbolic foundation is far more secure. What sustained and guaranteed the

Christian monarch was also likely to dislodge him. He maintained his sacral legitimacy by being compared, either directly or indirectly, to a mediator whose incomparably greater legitimacy quietly deflated any of his pretensions to be like Christ.

Despite the internal contradiction in representing the non-representable, it was still quite possible for the system to remain stable, as we see in the example of the Byzantine *Basileus* and *Christomimetes*. This representation required both a theological and an institutional aspect to maintain itself. In the first place, it required the continuation of a conceptual framework based on the unity of being. Only within a vision of the cosmos structured in terms of hierarchical copenetration of the visible and the invisible could the sovereign conjunction of the two orders retain its meaning and necessity—like the Church's sacramental union between the terrestrial abode and the realm of true ends. Next, the credibility of christomorphic royalty had to be safeguarded by the institutional figure of an intellectual organization centered on the representation of a unique order, a combination of priesthood and kingdom sufficiently cohesive for them to appear as two cogs in the same apparatus. The problem was not about the monolithic behavior of practical authority; it was rather that of a global system of representation and action, where it was understood that, behind *factual* conflicts and dissensions arising from human weakness, temporal power and spiritual authority constituted two *legal* functions working toward the same goal. The result was that the sovereign mystically shared in the understanding of the divine mystery, just as the pontiff actively participated in the domination linking terrestrial figures with the celestial hierarchy.

The equilibrium was twice as vulnerable within the Christian framework. On the one hand the Church was justified in closing in on itself, by alleging that its salvation mission was specific to it and that its responsibilities were related exclusively to the other world. By highlighting the completely irreducible nature of the gap between living for the beyond and living for the here-below, this autonomization had the crucial effect of shaking the ideal of a physical alliance between the two spheres embodied in the mediating king's sacred person. As we know, this specification of the Church's function would be pursued further, in the West, by the papal ambition to subordinate lay governments and become a universal monarchy, whereby the necessity of anointing the sacred king was used as an argument in favor of the pope's imperial supremacy. Having thus been put on the defensive and finding his privileges threatened, the temporal sovereign responded by mobilizing nature's resources in order to guarantee an independent legitimacy, something already inscribed in transcendent religion. On the other hand, if the Church was justified in affirming its originality as an instrument of salvation, then the political power was no less justified in claiming a sacrality *sui generis*, directly dependent on God alone and free from any obligation to the spiritual power. The difference between the necessities of the here-below and the urgent requirements of the beyond, which justified the clergy's exclusivism, and simultaneously justified the complete autonomy of a terrestrial authority established by the sovereign master of all and not responsible to anyone else. In this case the royal consecration ratified a divine decree in an order of reality beyond the Church's responsibility, to which it had to piously submit. The sacred serving heaven had to kneel before the figure of terrestrial sacrality. But the moment royalty claimed its divine independence, its essence tacitly changed. It ceased to be dependent on a truly christomorphic mediating sacrality. By endorsing this new political sacrality, it actually ceased to be a sacred royalty in the traditional "ethnographic" sense of the word. While retaining the same forms and words, it became completely different from the former composite being who, like the Word incarnate, made the divine present in the human.

This invisible revolution contained the beginnings of modern politics. It was the major turning point of the thirteenth to fourteenth centuries, one which would constitute the national monarchies in the westernmost lands—especially the English and French—from which would ultimately arise an astonishing innovation: representative power. As strange as it may appear, representative power was distantly but directly related to the initial metamorphosis sacralizing the king, made possible by Christian duality, and actively undertaken when the princes were forced to reply to the Church's imperial claims. A complete reversal of the essence of political legitimacy was brought about only through a tortuous narrow path and an extraordinary symbolic alchemy, which permanently modified the old categories. This was no brutal rupture, but an imperceptible evolution, where the continuity of appearances conceals the most crucial shifts. So when the sovereign ceased to be a truly sacred king, that is, a spiritual incarnator, his appearance as mediator remained intact by establishing mediation in a register removed from the spiritual power's control, the register of justice. The appearances remained intact up to the next stage, when the development of symbols of political incorporation established the monarch as the archetypal mediating figure in the collective sphere, as opposed to individual mediation between souls and God, guaranteed by the sacraments' absolving power. Secular power's attempt to further entrench itself and independently deify its role in opposition to Christ's monopoly under the deceptive cover of continuity, made the royal function the exact opposite of what it once was. At stake in this process of autonomizing a terrestrial sacral order (which at a certain point became the divine right of kings) was a radical turnaround of the relation between power and society. The monarch gradually evolved from incarnating sacral dissimilarity into realizing the collective body's internal self-congruence. He slowly changed from being a symbol of dependence on the organizing other into a legal representative and coercive force for bringing the political community (of the nation) into line with its autonomous reason for existence and its own principle. The development of the political in the modern age was the practical deployment of this symbolic turnaround, along two major lines. One was the deployment of a type of State oriented toward taking complete control of collective organization; the other was a form of legitimacy based on the convergence of power and society, as well as the coincidence of action applied to the society and the expression of the society. The bureaucratic State and representative legitimacy, the power of administration and the power of delegation: two completely successful expressions of political power originally set up outside sacral mediation. Political power was obliged to accept full responsibility for the whole of collective life refracted in it; and it only had the right to exist by establishing a connection between the parts of the social whole, from top to bottom. There were thus two prominent incarnations of the beyond's difference and the correlative autonomy of the here-below, as originally revealed and instituted by Jesus.

.   .   .

So the three main components of the Christian revolution would seem to be as follows: first, it changed the basis of political power by displacing the sovereign incarnator; second, it transformed religious sociability both by specifying a salvation community and by increasing priestly authority through a hermeneutics of divine mystery; and finally, it brought about a more general reform of being-in-the-world by dividing imperatives and making impossible a stable hierarchy of consent and refusal, independence and submission. These are the three main lines of development whose combinations and interactions would supply the intrinsic dynamic potential for Christian civilization. Put differently, Christians were beings divided by their perception of the world and their relations to worldly powers. But there was also a further division between the desire to balance belonging to reality with transcending reality, and the ultimate inability to do so. Christians were beings integrated into a spiritual community *de jure* separated from secular society, an integration which on the other hand made them subject to an authority responsible for ultimate meaning. They were subjects of a Prince who, instead of embodying the indispensable link with the celestial hierarchy, had to repre-

sent the internal necessity of administering the terrestrial bond. All these
characteristics have made we moderns into Christians of a sort, direct in-
heritors of the many-sided mutation whose rudiments were contained in
these primary dispositions.

The Greeks: The Religion of Reason

To repeat, all this might not have taken place. The timeless order of the
One might have overcome the Christian breakthrough and contained its
effects through compromise. This compromise would have been progressive, but would certainly not have favored the intellectual explosion, the
economic growth, and the political transformation which eventually
arose from the miraculously liberated dynamics of transcendence. Christian civilization, even with the theological base which brought about this
capitalist-rational-democratic world, might have returned to the tardi-
ness and inertia of the East. Only one key ingredient was needed for
everything to be reunited: the re-hierarchization of the de-hierarchizing
principle inscribed in Christ's division of the divine and the human. If we
can imagine a system where priestly authority and temporal power were
reintegrated into a hierarchy, where a stable balance was reached between the high and the low, between the concern with salvation and terrestrial needs, a system which organized the division of labor between
the faithful in the world and the spiritual individuals outside the world,
then we can imagine a system accommodating Christianity's major elements without their inherent tensions. We can get some idea of this from
the fate of the second Rome and from the general spirit of orthodox
theology.

Among the factors favoring such stabilization, we must count first and
foremost the encounter with, and absorption of, Greek reason by Christian speculation. By integrating within a hierarchically ordered representation of the cosmic whole the antinomies tied to the duality of the
realms, philosophy gave exegesis an incomparably powerful instrument
for mitigating these antinomies.[35] This is not to say that Greek thought
was itself exempt from internal tensions. Far from it. However these tensions operated within a continually renewed framework of the One. For
example, when the intelligible's radical "transcendence" in relation to
the sensory was affirmed, the sphere of the pure intelligible continued to
be understood from within the same all-encompassing framework as the
sensory sphere. In any case, the latter was no more substantial than its
diminished reflection, so that we might go from one to the other as from
the lower to the higher. This "transcendence," along with the consequent
expulsion of the world soul outside the world, had nothing in common

with the transcendence potentially contained in the idea of the Christian god—even if for several centuries Greek thought lent Christianity its vocabulary while curbing the latter's possibilities for division. Let me say in passing that I believe this difference can give us the key to the limits of Greek naturalism with regard to modern science, whose formative background was supplied by the Christian vision. The Christian god's transcendence was necessary for the conception of a purely physical and completely isomorphic world. This world was removed from any spiritual animating force and from all meaningful correspondences between the parts and the whole, between the parts and the cardinal principle coordinating and justifying the world's basic elements.

The emergence of rational thought and the development of monotheistic faith are to be understood as two expressions, or two moments of the same process that transformed the magic-mythical world. The same fundamental logical facts were mobilized in both cases and both operations were part of the same metamorphosis of the previous conceptual order. They provide two somewhat differing versions, in keeping with the discrepancies between their contexts and the constraints that drove them. But beneath their diverging modes of existence, lay a similar dual movement, which on the one hand brought the instituting principle back into our presence, and hence, on the other, differentiated the explanatory principle from the reality it justifies. This applies to God in relation to the world, truth in relation to appearance, the intelligible in relation to the sensory, form in relation to matter. So the idea of creation broke just as much with origin-based thought as did Ionian physics' demand for immanent explanation. Even though one of these breaks occurred in the register of belief and the other in the register of concepts, they both had to happen through a logical restructuring of the previously dominant representation. Similarly, these breaks reversed the dual articulation of the instituting omnipotence of the past (mythical) and the contemporaneous multiplicity of influences and invisible forces (magical)—along with its implications for the classification of beings and the things of the world, what we can say about our origins, and how we say it. Both likewise inverted the temporal axis: now the present justified the past. And both likewise unified the prime mover of being and broadly substituted a reductive unity for an unlimited classificatory plurality (the latter being the mythical mode of apprehending reality with its dynamics of "rushing blindly ahead," as opposed to rational thought's structuring imperative to return to itself). Everything that exists can and should be related to the One—however this One may be conceived. From the moment this organizing postulate was put to work, a new form of thought had to be developed. Now we had to seek the truth of the One behind the appearances of the many, we had to perceive self-identity behind the varied shiftings, we had to go beyond the simple sensory given to intelligible coherence. All these processes presuppose a horizon of endless examination and a continual application of thought to itself and against itself, all aimed at achieving a more radical explication-reduction—an application to be tested against the thought of others, in this common struggle toward the ultimate sameness which will reconcile minds. Thus thought was called on to organize itself at every level around an internal difference, from its basic instruments (concrete/abstract), through its regulatory ideal (a goal transcending any possible outcomes) up to its social use (the opening up of criticism with a common aim). The formative background for a rational reflection thus emerged from the destabilized mythical framework.

The Christian instauration, however, did not take place here, despite the fact that by mobilizing these premises it participated in the material and formal metamorphosis of our apprehension of the real which had been given positive expression in Greece. In the environment in which it was propagated, Christianity was immediately forced to come to terms with the already existing understanding of being. But we still must consider what allows Christianity to come to terms with this understanding and predisposes it to adopt it. This faith had a certain need for reason.[36] We can even conjecture retrospectively that sooner or later faith would have called for both speculation on the divine mystery and the rational ordering of the cosmos—in the original sense of structuring our thought processes from the One's viewpoint. Faith would at least have contained this possibility, due to its primordial theological principles and the logic of its potential deployment.

But we could with equal justification say that Greek reason was destined to encounter the religious problem at some point in its development. At a given time, the ontology of the One had to necessarily lead into a theology. In fact, the invisible principle's unification was accompanied its differentiation. Within the framework of magic pluralism, invisible forces could not be separated from their visible manifestations. They were the very flesh of the world's animated plurality where there was neither physics nor theology. On the other hand, when the world came to be apprehended as unity, it could in one respect be explained in general terms and by internal necessity, and hence become the object of "physics." But it also raised the fateful problem of this ultimate invisible principle to which it could be related; it required a metaphysics, which tended to be a theology, insofar as there was an inevitable subjectivizing of the supreme principle. In other words, rational thought about the world's unity at a certain point had to face the question of the duality of the visible and the invisible justifying it. What are we to make of this absolute One over the many? The trend toward specifying the One, both internally and externally, both by distancing it from the sensory and by purifying its intrinsic essence, led to assimilating it to absolute self-identity, thus giving it a subjective form. Hence, the drift toward an onto-theology.[37]

Here we discover the limits of Greek thought in relation to the historical potentialities of the Christian vision. This rational Greek ontology was in the impossible situation of bestowing a wholly personal status on its ultimate principle of self-intelligible presence—it could only conceive that presence as being in harmony with the diverse sensory world to which it was opposed, within an all-encompassing cosmos where it merely constituted the upper region. Meanwhile Christian speculation, by separating the personal god, sanctioned an external deployment of the absolute subject, allowing the world to be grasped as an object, and then allowing human actors to set themselves up as cognitive subjects radically detached from the world-as-object. All this was totally foreign to Greek reason, which was organized by the primacy of the all-inclusive One. From this ensued a series of restrictive schemas affecting the self-enclosing cosmos, its deeply hierarchical internal organization, and the vitalist principle animating it. But it also resulted in a definition of knowledge which could only be seen as an outstanding manifestation of the cohabitation of being and intellect, or more broadly, of the integration of humans into the world—and therefore it was a direct and passive knowledge, acquired through reception, participation, or intuition, ranging from common perception to elevated contemplation. These organizing constraints were directly related to the social mold where this new power of thought was invented. The *polis'* constitutive ambiguity was extended and refracted into the equivocation of the *logos.* The limits of Greek thought compared to modern thought correspond precisely with the limits of Greek democracy compared to modern political individualism.

In fact, the extraordinary thing about the birth of the city was its union of innovation and conservation. This occurred by amalgamating otherwise contradictory terms: the pre-eminence of the collective whole and the equal right of the parts. There was a revolution in the hierarchical order, a dissolution (within sovereignty-as-citizenship) of the bond subjugating the lower to the higher, a dissolution affirming the social foundation's exteriority. By establishing equality before the law, a sort of individualism is instaurated, since all the members of the political body find themselves in possession of an independent and equal share of public authority. Thus the common intellectual reason for existence is put back into the midst of humans, and a field of confrontation, of argumentation, of persuasion, opened up where the power of the word determines the outcome and the agreement of minds decides the issue.[38] But all this takes place within, and as part of, the rigorous preservation of the deepest tendencies of the hierarchical principle: the priority of the global order over its local components and the primacy of the whole over its parts. This hierarchical principle's appearance is completely reshaped without changing its essence. The distribution of social power among members of the political community does not prevent their actual, physical grouping together to hold power, so that individual prerogative acquires scope and meaning solely through its obligatory participation in collective sovereignty and its contribution to assisting its expression. Here Benjamin Constant's astute diagnosis in *The freedom of the ancients compared to that of the moderns* remains unsurpassed. The equal redistribution of political functions was carried out on the basis of an undiminished integrating compulsion within a logic of belonging whose underlying principles were unaffected by the transformation. Within this framework, individuals simply have a direct relation to the whole through participative engagement, rather than through dependency on those above them, as was traditionally the case. But this has nothing to do with the primal independence and priority of individuals in relation to the political bond, not to mention the private exteriority they maintain toward it, which according to the moderns is the formative basis for sovereign authority. Hence this city of equal's capacity for hierarchical exclusion: outside political functions, the city could only see itself as part of a global order involving subordinate functions, whether of reproduction (women) or production as such (slaves). Equality only made sense within a sphere whose pre-eminence demanded subjugation in another way. Not only did this sphere allow certain people to be reduced to instruments or objects, it presupposed it. This has nothing in common with the general human identity postulated by the moderns, and the trend toward similarity this identity initiated.

It is quite obvious that by now basic conceptual divergences had appeared within this general mechanism which itself had liberated, sustained, and encouraged interpretative conflict. It did not impose any monolithic framework for reflection, quite the contrary. The ambiguity of its constituting principle, which could be called hierarchical individualism, involved an almost inevitable polarization of minds around two major contradictory tendencies. There was, on the one hand, a "hierarchical" tendency which, as in the civil situation, steadfastly oriented thought toward collective membership and ultimately made exchange and agreement between humans the "measure of all things." It was a tendency toward conventionalism which, pushed to its limits, brought about a challenge to the primordial given it presupposed and exemplified, the founding bond of the City. On the other hand, there was a reactive "individualist" tendency, more ethical than civic, emphasizing both the inner distance from obligations to the City and the demand for self-possession. In this situation, reason aimed to gain power over the self rather than outwardly take action against others. Reason was therefore an affirmation of personal difference and independence, along with all the individual differences, or the withdrawal into the sect or school, that the ideal of the autonomous sage involved. But now the same results were achieved by somehow going deep into oneself, by turning toward one's very own capacity which, by going beyond fragile human conventions and assimilating the solid ground of the one truth into the quest for freedom, provides inner freedom. For what legitimated and required the sage's distance, was the gap between appearance and reality, the difference between the intelligible One and the unstable illusions common humanity wallows in. Only the contemplation of the absolutely inviolable was capable of providing a solid foundation for mastering one's own destiny. Starting out by assuming an opposition between the (individual) path of truth and the (common) path of error, the philosophical path toward personal power led back to a strong reaffirmation of the One as the code of life, back to self-knowledge as recognition of the individual's place within the Whole, in the light of the supreme organizing principle constituting human duty. This trend would be translated politically into the reforming vision of an ideal city—*The Republic*—organically subject to the pre-eminence of the only real values. We turn away from subordination to the City's actual viewpoint in order to recover it at a deeper level.

Thus a new struggle takes shape between proponents of social affiliation who internally undermine the primacy of the inter-human space they base themselves on, and proponents of philosophical withdrawal who reaffirm the necessity of subjugation to a higher order from which they initially intended distancing themselves. How could one fail to combat the corrosive discord of minds with the intelligible order in which everything has its proper place? But this discord expresses the unavoidable obligation of citizens to the order predating them, it expresses the primacy of organized speech over particular speakers who are heard in it, and it allowed the condemnation of someone who, like Socrates, defied opinion by appealing to the oneness of truth. I am not confining Greek thought to a rigid framework. Greek thought thrived on conflictual limiting situations, so that what might seem restrictive to us was productive for it, which is why it continues to profoundly engage us. Greek thought operated in a context where the counter-model had the same hierarchical inspiration as the model, where, both in intellectual activity and city governance, the horizon of affiliation to and participative dependence on the totality to which it belongs remained unsurpassable.

Greek thought continues to fascinate us because it exemplified, during the major upheaval of the "axial age," a successful conjunction of opposites. It departed from the magical-mythical-hierarchical world while simultaneously rescuing its ultimate religious articulation, i.e., ontological unity. The transformation took place much earlier in Greece than anywhere else, but as elsewhere, the new was forced to compromise with the old, in a "miraculous" balance between innovation and conservation. A startling confirmation, if any was needed, of this organizing schema's extraordinary attraction for human thought, which encouraged it to reunite the visible and the invisible within a single being. The onus fell on Christian thought to overcome this schema after having embraced it for several centuries in its Greek form, and having expressed itself almost entirely through Greek philosophical language. The break only occurred because de-hierarchizing ideas, such as the dogma of Incarnation, were preserved in the midst of the inherited vision of an hierarchical cosmos.[39]

Could it have been otherwise? Was the projection of Christianity's salvation doctrine into the categories of Greek logos and its subsequent reinterpretation, unnecessary, as a certain critical tradition likes to claim? Against the thesis that Jewish revelation and Hellenic wisdom were antipathetic, I would mention two major affinities which made their cross-fertilization probable. First, there was faith's "rational" possibilities, even necessities. These called for restoring order to a world which broke away from the earlier mythical-magical vision of the Natural and the Supernatural. Faith encountered a highly developed and demanding reflection that, through its own spiritual preoccupations, and through its individualizing, ascetic and contemplative inclinations, lent itself remarkably to theological appropriation. How could fascination with this neighboring other have possibly remained dormant? But apart from this foundational aspect, there was also a conjunctural one linked to the way in which a triumphant Christianity established itself in the secular world in a manner which resolved its internal doubts by steering it toward the One-as-God-as-World, a conjunction attested by the Church's and the sovereign's dual mediation. Greek thought appeared as the ideal tool to conceptually translate this reinstatement into being into theology. The philosophical notion of "the intelligible" became the language and substance of what was theologically reasonable in terms of the strong tendency to neutralize founding dichotomies and stabilize instituting partitions. This notion was an incomparable tool consolidating for ten centuries the Christian synthesis between the two worlds, the two powers in this world and the two requirements struggling within the individual, until the incompatible element of the difference signified by Christ was rekindled. Furthermore, once the ancient legacy reached its peak in St. Thomas's *Summa*, the ultimate monument to conciliation and the Christian hierarchizing of being, any future attempt to unite what had been irretrievably separated became superfluous. There could be no further integration of opposites. Original tensions were unleashed through the insuperable division of swords and realms, and this rending would generate a way of reasoning wholly different to that born of the Greek city.

The Turn toward Equality

The tensions contained in the Christian instauration were not spontaneously self-initiated. They developed under the influence of external circumstances, with the help of a historically given configuration and according to parameters completely foreign to the inner logic of religious schemas. The breakdown of political authority and its enduring emptiness was decisive, despite repeated attempts in the West to reconstitute it after the fall of the Empire. Had the Empire continued as it was, evidence suggests that Christian civilization would have allowed the creative forces at its center to remain dormant. Christian civilization would probably have been frozen in a harmonizing compromise neutralizing the interplay of the dualities established in Christ. However, there was a major break, a decisive collapse that imperceptibly committed God's followers, and others in succession, to release the original mechanism's dynamic possibilities. The event did not substantially modify the conserving ideal, which was subverted in the name of the One. The de-hierarchizing process began when hierarchical affirmation and order were coming to an end. There was no sudden realization of a previously repressed theological truth, but rather a stubbornly maintained repression of the logic of the other in favor of the logic of identity, by hierarchically integrating dissimilarities. Medieval Christianity's explicit ideal, mental framework and visible operation remained completely dominated by this systematic union of opposites harmoniously linking priesthood and realm, soul and body, the tasks of salvation and terrestrial needs, in a world itself seen as coparticipating in the visible and the invisible.[40] But if this systematic union continued to organize people's minds, it no longer controlled their everyday actions; if it still organized the social symbols, it no longer constituted the keystone of the civilizing apparatus. A fundamentally adverse movement was at work beneath this apparently comprehensive integration of the divine essence, the order of things, human nature, and the social bond—a trend that would eventually blow this integrating mechanism to pieces.

This movement began in the vacuum created by the collapse of imperial power, a vacuum that committed ecclesial power to fill the symbolic gap thus created. I am of course speaking metaphorically about a fairly complicated history whose meanderings should be followed through Papal history, from the turning point in 754 to the Gregorian reform, from the moment the papacy was driven to play the card of western royalty— Stephen II's investiture of Pepin the Short—to the pontiff's claim to the imperial *plenitudo potestatis*.[41] What concerns me here is the Church's increasing tendency to aspire to universal government, to absorb the two powers into it, to subordinate temporal dominions to the spiritual. This development could scarcely have occurred without the long-term weakening of the archetypal figure of the emperor, the supreme representation of the One in this world. The Carolingian or Ottonian instances of restoration or renovation of the *imperium*, paradoxically only served to crystallize the ideal of a Church-Empire. To survive, a pontifical government would have had to coexist permanently with a corresponding political body secure in its foundations, functions, and legitimacy, like the Byzantine *Basileus*. These two bodies would naturally have retained the formula of a balanced partition and reciprocal submission. But due to the symbolic vacuum created by the imperial See's instability, and the consequent absence of a crucial pole in the human world, the Church was instead unexpectedly called on to extend its apex into the visible, while orienting its axis toward the invisible. The common will to power does not sufficiently explain these increasing theocratic ambitions, even if we include the illusory remembrance of Roman glory. What was at stake was primarily an actual gap to be filled, then the living attraction of a community model, and finally an ideal of power—the very things which, throughout civilization's (i.e. the State's) existence, defined the horizon of terrestrial action. Real power is what recognizes and fleshes out the unity of the human race, the only collective form which bestows the fullness of its meaning on existence. These three factors came to life again in the Church, due to the secular power's failure to even begin to make them concrete. And they came to life in the Church because they found there a primal opening up of one of Christianity's constitutive ambiguities—namely, its inability to provide a steady path between the demands of the beyond and the obligations of the here-below, between the legitimacy and illegitimacy of life in this world compared to life directed toward the other world.

These circumstances will produce a total collapse of salvation values. For Christians, what really matters was what would become of their souls in the other life; consequently everything in this life had to be subjugated to this supreme goal. This naturally applied to personal life, but it also applied to collective life, in the framework of a Christian society whose operators bore responsibility for their flock's spiritual destiny. So it was natural for the paths of imperial vision and pastoral concern to cross. The true Christian community, which was the highest worldly goal that could ever be imagined, would unite all the faithful within a City-World, where the executive mechanisms and the wheels of authority would be subordinate to eternal aims, under the leadership of a single shepherd, who was himself closest to God. The political unification of the human race was thus the materialization of the unity of ultimate values regarding the one and only god. Though the rigid subordination of the lower (the temporal power) to the higher (the spiritual authority) would suggest that we are still within the hierarchical domain, we have in fact moved into the domain of de-hierarchization. For the real axiom of the hierarchical order was of course unity, but unity through difference, through the recognition of the other. This unity results from the subjugation of the parts to the greater goal of the whole, but presupposes the rigorous specification of the parts, which was achieved by separating the different registers, demarcating the spheres, and mutually externalizing functions. The differentiation of the elements, their reciprocal otherness, is precisely what gives meaning to their inner orientation toward the common goal. Deep down nothing was more foreign to the authentic spirit of hierarchy than this absorption of the temporal into the spiritual by fusing them in what is commonly called "political Augustinism."[42] Here encroachment replaced interlocking, intrusive domination replaced the subordination of differences, the reduction to sameness replaced the complementary articulation of opposites. On the other hand, this absorption had to conform with one of the basic possibilities of the mechanism modelled on Christ: from the moment this world was disjoined from the other, there was no rule for a balanced coexistence between clearly defined spheres. Nothing technically prevented us from wanting to subject existence as a whole to the goals of the beyond. Again, this does not at all mean that this orientation came to be accepted merely through realizing a theoretical possibility. It was rather a typical instance of the encounter between structural necessity and historical contingence. The actors involved continued for a long time to see each other in traditional terms until the truth of their conduct was imposed on them by the collusion between reality's demands and their faith's presuppositions. By thus liberating the contradictory potential of Christ's revelation, which lay behind the West's dynamics, an unforeseeable historical movement achieved what individuals could not have willingly achieved.

As soon as one of the two possible hegemonic claims—in this case, the primacy of the spiritual—was openly asserted, it literally provoked the expression of an opposed claim, the autonomy of the temporal. The structural outcome was that the desire to subjugate everything to the beyond disclosed the irreducible independence of the here-below; this very desire legitimated its opposite. If serving God not only demands participation in this world, but also its organization as a whole, this was because God himself is not simply the pinnacle of the world, but its wholly other. There was, therefore, room for an authority lending substance and form to the autonomous legitimacy and intrinsic validity of the terrestrial order. This is why the affirmation of royal prerogative inevitably arose in protest against pontifical imperialism. And it would switch to the offensive, since its logical conclusion was that the Church must be subordinated, because the personal relation to God it guarantees must take place within a collective organization whose basis lies outside its jurisdiction and to whose rules each and every person must submit. The will to establish the City of God, and to place the secular arm in the service of the world community of believers and its spiritual head, was destined to stumble over the competing claims of a human City and to allege the respectable sacredness of its own natural order, which brings with it the absorption of the Church as a social entity.

We are of course dealing with conventional power rivalry; but at a deeper level, we are dealing with their conflicting legitimacies from the Christian viewpoint, whose fundamental complicity in setting them at odds should be assessed. Both claims were anchored in the basic articulation of the new faith, the one announced by the Redeemer's humanity, whose contradictory and interdependent potentialities it expresses. This allows us to understand the kind of unconscious pact and complicity existing in the midst of the confrontation through which the two opposing sides increase their influence. These two parties between them deploy the full extent of the Christian possibility. Even if the temporal power's aim to be all-inclusive in a basically spiritual society, and the religious authority's similar aim are mutually exclusive, they ultimately complement each other from the viewpoint of Christ's dual nature. So the two projects of reinforcing and specifying the pastoral bond and of sacralizing temporal sovereignty are jointly pursued. The opposed protagonists clasp each other without questioning allegiances to pontiff and prince—the rift between the believer's duties and the subject's obligations remain. And, furthermore, all this takes place without openly shaking the conceptual framework of the One: the exclusive nature of the spirit of salvation, and the exclusive nature of the spirit of terrestrial plenitude were developed, while the reconciliation of the "two suns," of the priesthood and the realm, remained a dream. This illusion continued until it was destroyed by "primitive accumulation" concerning terrestrial economic, political, symbolic, and intellectual self-sufficiency. Its destruction took place by gradually making the organizing schema of coparticipation between the visible and the invisible untenable. This gradually made it possible to think unprecedented things about the gods, things which were to be the sources of modern thought and its practical extensions: a world without the organizing and nourishing meaningfulness of the invisible; a bond

between humans without constraining carnal dependency on its instituting other. This movement was initiated by the mediating Church whose
power to mediate between heaven and earth, now imagined separately,
would soon be challenged.

The modern turning point occurred precisely when—as in the Radical
Reformation—we adjusted to the separation of the terms and took it as
given. As a result, instead of separating heavenly concerns and worldly
achievements in order to rearrange them, we forced them to coexist. The
human sphere was thus self-contained. We could not satisfy the imperatives of the true life by idolatrously dedicating ourselves to this world's
symbols; but by working to perfect the world, created beings could devise an appropriate relation to the separated other. This relation involved
passing from hierarchical alternatives (one rather than the other, at the
expense of the other) to egalitarian coextension (one simultaneously with
the other, and through the other), turning a static-logic of dependency
into an acquisitive dynamics of worldly self-sufficiency. This was the
founding of the modern spirit of growth. It would not have been thinkable without the primordial accumulation carried out through long creative confrontation between these two totalizing aims, one attempting to
absorb the secular into the sacred, and the other to absorb the sacred
into the secular.

To describe this process in terms of the internal logic of symbolic
structures, which could only effectively exist in a certain context, is not
simplistic idealism. The pontiff's portentous imperial option only became
a decisive catalyst in the fertile context of a social-historical mutation
that allowed terrestrial autonomy to become a substantial option. The
turn imposed on Church authorities from 1073 to 1085 by Gregory VII
would have been ineffectual or different, had it not been part of the feudal revolution and accompanied by the decisive growth that led to the
"crowded world" at the end of the thirteenth century. It so happened
that the theocratic option was endorsed and highlighted at the very moment that economic and demographic trends, the reconstruction of the
social bond, and new political alliances provided tangible support for
this undertaking.[43] Establishing the world's independence ceased to be a
purely abstract possibility when it discovered its equivalent in the material dynamics of spatial appropriation, for example. It does not matter
that the latter depended on factual causes unrelated to the society it operates in: it set about creating meaning within the network of possible interpretations. The same phenomenon of the "crowded world" would per-
form completely different functions in a world stigmatized throughout as
sacrally impaired, and in one where, however vaguely, the human
sphere's internal integrity acquired meaning. The entire system of civi-

lization must be reread in terms of supporting, substantiating, and symbolizing the new legitimation of human activity, liberated from within
the depths of the religious bond.

It is particularly important to stress the elements of practical individualization operating within medieval "holism" if we are to grasp, at its
most basic level, how the energy for continually reorienting people toward
secular involvement was able to develop alongside the individualization
of souls at work in the domain of faith. Hence the feudal reformulation
of the hierarchical principle, the consequential individualization of the
bond of political dependence, and the tendency to shift from group solidarity to the interpersonal relation. Hence the individualization of labor
which, along with serfdom, made its way between commands from above
and communitarian constraints. Hence, finally, the personalized mar-
riage bond, which introduced an interaction between the cultural code
and religious control. We must also consider the special place the urban
world carved out for itself in feudalism, and the forms of the collective
bond invented in it—the municipalities born from the voluntary association of their "conspirators," or corporations endowed with the identity
and perpetuity of ethical individuals.

But the crystallization of being-in-the-world came about through the
sudden appearance of a new ideal of political community and the establishment of an unknown type of State. It did so in accordance with the
split between the human and the divine, in contrast to humans' willing
subjugation to the divine incarnated in the Church. It was through the
confrontation of authorities that the consciously promoted divergence
between the parties of heaven and earth acquired reality and meaning.
Contingency was always present: we could not imagine the Empire,
united in the face of papal opposition, playing the same role as territorial States slowly reassembled from feudal fragments. Nor was there a
force with universal ambitions capable of sacralizing the secular order,
law and politics, which national monarchies by their very limitations
were in a better position to do—even if this process was initiated under
the banner of Frederick II's universal Empire.[44] The imperial schema's
inexorable constraints meant sacralization was caught up in a mediating
mystique, like that of the priests' claim to give substance to the sacramental union of heaven and earth (the charter laid down at Malfi in 1231
by Frederick gives us a clear idea of this). This was far removed from
the principle of difference between the here-below and the beyond,
which gradually took shape through the universal particularism of the
national sovereign State. Here again we encounter history's radical unpredictability: the irreversible polycentrism of European space arising
from the major disintegration of the ninth and tenth centuries, and the
consequent appearance, in Europe's western extremity, of stable limited

monarchical centers, which would be the crucible for the theological-political amalgamation of ingredients from the religious substratum. The overall process may be described as interactive: the Gregorian reform came about in reply to threats of absorption into secular life and disintegration due to feudalism; while political dispersion provoked a revival of the ideal of imperial unification, which worked against the multiplicity of territorial monarchies. Thus the features of a centralized government began to emerge, one that proceeded by enacting rules of law and delegating functions to individuals, in a universe of lineal and patrimonial appropriation of public power. We could say this was the first rudimentary form of "rational bureaucracy" in Western history, above all, the first organization to go beyond the simple administration of beings and things and to be defined according to a global project of meaning. Temporal powers would reply to this with imitation (particularly in the area of law) and different claims to legitimacy, especially territorial claims against papal universalism

It is impossible to disentangle what arose from accommodation to factual limits and what from the intervention of an organizing schema valuing limited rather than unlimited power. A decisive reversal of political logic took place very early in the formative mold of the modern State and the phenomenon of the nation. Action was redirected inwards; there was a move from extensive to intensive power, from the imperative of conquest to the need for administration. Defining territorial limits was obviously nothing new in itself. The novelty lay in making it the basis for the ideal political form by transferring the universal perspective associated with world expansion into national boundaries. The imperial project was not simply abandoned, but was completely transformed by being harnessed within the frontiers of a State that, like the emperor, had nothing over it, but where the growth of power, as distinct from the emperor's, proceeded by deepening its inner control, rather than broadening its external hold. Of course this does not prevent centuries of war to "round off the domain" and take the kingdom to its supposed ideal "natural" boundaries. From here on, universal power would be limited by its particular national characteristics and its universality would arise from the political body's internal self-congruence. The latter was produced by the action of an administrative power taken to its logical conclusion, by developing the principle of the community's self-correspondence, which the administrative power initiated and which would be transformed into representative power. The religious process of autonomizing a sector of profane sacrality received its ultimate expression within the framework of this emerging political form, whereby the inner realization of the political community acting within the gestating State incarnated the principle of terrestrial integrity. Faced with the will, incarnated in the

Church, to make the world part of heaven, this new type of sovereign, representing the nation, lent flesh to the human order's independent legitimacy. This legitimacy was derived unmediated from God, attesting his separation and the legitimacy of his creatures' sphere. This was no "secularization" of power, but a transfusion of sacrality into politics, a unique sacrality, which arose by breaking away from its clerical form. On the one hand, there was the power of the priest's mediation connecting the here-below and the beyond; on the other, there is the equally legitimate Christian embodiment, through the king's "divine right," of the self-enclosed human City, with the full dignity of terrestrial action. On the one hand was a salvation community aiming to encompass everyone in its concern with the future life and striving to control the soul's inner participation in mysterious divine truths. On the other, there was the government of a political body presumed to hold its purposes within itself, striving to take complete responsibility for the law tying beings together, and aspiring to monopolize the allegiance of those under its jurisdiction. There were two broad social aspirations, at once exclusive, complementary, and equal—living testimony to the insoluble tensions in the Christian mode of being-in-the-world.

The gap between the logic of these projects and their effective realization was certainly quite large, whether it concerned the Church's compromises with worldly life, its precarious hold on the faithful, or the fledgling State's weak control over justice—not to mention contingent events such as the great Schism or the Hundred Years' War. Indeed, this gap is nothing other than history's source and substance. The fact remains that the gap was most effective in the symbolic order and that evoking or mobilizing such aims produced influential significations, however vague and confused, enormously disproportionate to the initial attempts at implementing them. We must define the true significance of these attempts relative to the instituting core underlying everyday faith. Their influence went far beyond the actor's representations, in that they liberated basic dispositions latent within the Christian institution, which would subsequently influence events in their own way. The lag in consciousness relative to action, the divergence between the actual that can be controlled and the potential to be harnessed, the conscious striving for implemented meaning, along with the doubts and resistance it involved, would eventually prove to be constituting dimensions of this history. Limited though these shared legitimacies remained in their expression and justification, it was through this sharing that the central fission between affirming and devaluing the world, embedded in the mystery of Christ's two natures, gradually acquired irreversible paradigmatic status and substantiality.

If the requirement now arose for the true faith's restoration against deviation, then the only possibility for a return to the original spirit was to rush blindly forward. In terms of the depth of reality attained by the world, it was impossible simply to revert to a determined commitment to the beyond through an unequivocal restoration of the hierarchy of values. Like it or not, we had to begin with the fact that, alongside the imperative to restore salvation's importance, there was also the terrestrial sovereign's divine legitimacy, the human community's intrinsic necessity, and the rightfulness of actively operating within the world. These could no longer be reunited by subordinating the incidental to the essential within a unique hierarchy. They had imperceptibly become two orders, each *de jure* valid in itself, and logically equivalent for this very reason. To keep them together, we had to simultaneously embrace both: we could no longer turn away from this inferior world toward eternal life, but had to devote ourselves to the fundamental hope of attaining salvation through dedicating ourselves fully to terrestrial autonomy. The act of founding the world of equality was an operation which, by reversing its ontological principle, destabilized the hierarchical world's very basis, and was the decisive option by which, starting out from within religion, we left the religious logic of dependency. This is what made the Reformation the effective inaugurating force of the modern era. It was the most explicit sign of the change that would influence the modern age's other developments: the effective dehierarchizing and equalizing of the here-below and the beyond, which is the cornerstone of the general transformation of future human activity.

This was not a secularizing process due to the exhaustion of sacral values presumably pushed aside to make room for secular ones, but rather a sacral legitimizing of the lay sector, independent of and alongside the properly religious one. It could even be considered a positive religious revaluation of lay activity that jointly transformed being-for-the-otherworld and being-in-this-world. Four centuries before Luther and the spark of 1517, the founding of Cîteaux in 1118 as a way of reforming the monastic ideal promoted the flight into the desert as against compromises with worldly life. Yet this reform was undertaken so that people could dedicate themselves to intense manual labor, an action taking place within a religious logic where the radical rejection of the world was structurally linked to an acceptance of its stability and an obligation to confront its reality, which differed from other traditions of spiritual refusal. The Protestant breakaway was an open admission of the major consequence of the actual split between the two spheres of religiosity, namely the impossibility of mediation. If the Prince had a sacral character bestowed on him directly by God, if every individual had a duty to accept the creation and exploit it for its own purposes, then the Church's claim to be the authorized intermediary between heaven and earth was based on deception. However, the moment the divine's exteriority relative to the human sphere was established in principle, appropriation through identity was linked in "egalitarian" fashion with obligation toward the other, thus gaining the force of an explicit code—though this occurred unevenly, depending on the model adopted. But even where the Reformation was rejected, where the mediating Church maintained its positions, the physical and symbolic factors that hastened the fracturing were present. Modern religious consciousness has without exception been based on a bed of incarnated religiosity—in its social relations, in its political forms, in the practical dynamics of civilization, in the unconscious side of dogma itself—and this religiosity inexorably imposed its direction on this consciousness. A Christianity-influenced reality lay beneath the faith and determined its evolution. French religious history is a model of how the modern dehierarchizing of being was imposed in Counter Reformation lands, through other channels than those claimed by the doctrine. The religion of politics could have imposed this dehierarchization even without a "work ethic" and secular asceticism. Monarchical absolutism provided an effective carrier for the realization of terrestrial autonomy. In Jansenism, we see an extreme example of culturally adapting to the world by rejecting it, of promoting the modern by attempting to maintain tradition. Rarely did the appeal to the primitive Church's example so strongly serve to promote the new relation to God.

We should not focus particularly on this development's theological manifestations. It would probably be more valid to hypothesize that we are dealing with one broad transformation, uneven, fragmented, and differentiated, but ultimately identical. The long-term intercultural and transregional comparison must be guided by the idea of sameness in difference. What occurs somewhere through doctrinal collapse occured elsewhere as a slow reshaping of political authority and the collective bond. The only prerequisite was that the confessional and cultural consequences of tearing the divine away from any hierarchy of being had to be thematized so they could supply the foundations for constructing a new representation of the physical world. In some places this occurred by promoting rational subjectivity and the infinite universe, while in others it took place by unleashing an unrestricted action to achieve terrestrial integrity. Everywhere we see an inevitably increasing conflict between authority and liberty, as inscribed in the Christian premises. The god who had been separated and freed from hierarchy was a god who simultaneously reinforced the established powers' prerogatives and laid the foundation for individual right. The inviolable sovereignty of consciences was set against the divine nature of collective authority's representatives. Since these developments were not purely conceptual, we cannot judge their success in terms of reflection's development. They were established within a symbolic infrastructure—the difference being that this infrastructure was shaped by active religiosity, by the relation to the invisible incarnated in collective dispositions, and by personal modes of being.

This was a general movement because it rested on the invisible religious revolution of the western Middle Ages, and was made possible by the liberation of the original dynamics of transcendence. The modern break-up of the sixteenth and seventeenth centuries was basically a religious one reversing the logic of the structural link between the two orders of reality. Three major transformations characteristic of modernity emerged from this reversal of the bond between the human and the divine: the transformation of the mode of thinking, the transformation of the social bond, and the transformation of the framework of activity. The reversal was itself derived from the primordial core of Christian reality and was totally specific to the Western Middle Ages. The modest bifurcation of political Augustinism, in accordance with the ontology of Christ's two natures, was the starting point for reinstituting the human world in terms of equality. The step into hierarchical thought and practice constituted the beginning of its dissolution.

CHAPTER 6

Figures of the Human Subject

W<small>E HAVE</small> now reached the point, roughly around 1700, where specifically Christian history comes to a halt. By this I mean history whose activity is indistinguishable from the deployment of a central core of structural possibilities ushered in by Christ's founding action. The enormous shift from a religious organization based on a hierarchically organized overlapping of the visible and the invisible to one based on separation had been essentially completed. Whether regarding the principles of collective reality, the understanding of the world, or the relation to nature, we are henceforth confronted with autonomous domains developing according to their own necessities or dynamics. We shift from the gestation of the main ingredients of modernity within the scope of religious evolution, into their maturation by leaving religion, whereby each sector of activity—the political, the intellectual, the economic and the technical—became the crucible for reabsorbing the previous structuring otherness. The chronological parting of the ways occurred when the expansion of the novel phenomena produced by the unfolding of Christian transcendence—the national sovereign State, the subjective founding of knowledge and law, the investment in the world—turned them against their formative mold and made the incorporation of religion's substance their developmental mainspring. Now the generative phenomenon explaining the exceptional character of our world was in place. It was not simply separate from other worlds, but opposed them, since its basic impulse returned to human-social space what previously and everywhere else directed it from outside. Furthermore, the conclusion of Christian history signaled a historical change. To gauge the novelty of our present we must approach it indirectly via religion, which is the key to our past. Somewhere around 1700, the deepest ever fracture in history occurred, namely, the establishment of human becoming in a logic and mode diametrically opposite to what it had been from time immemorial. The metamorphosis of Christian otherness became the process of its reduction, which explains Christianity's exceptional efficacy.

. . .

Two observations on my use of the word "*end.*" First, reducing otherness does not mean restoring a transparent human identity but rather secularly restructuring difference, separation, and human conflict. The departure from religion does not signal the disappearance of every type of religious experience. It does mean freeing up the organization of collective reality from the other's viewpoint, but the subjective experience of the other remains as a possibly irreducible anthropological residue.

I cannot overemphasize that when I say "end of religion" I am referring to a quite specific phenomenon: the end of the principle of dependency structuring social space in all known societies prior to our own. Religion can only historically express itself formally and materially by having a clearly defined function. Not only does this function no longer exist, it has been turned into its opposite through a transformation that has integrated its component parts into the collective operation. Modern society is not a society without religion but one whose major articulations were formed by metabolizing the religious function.

This did not prevent the faith and the Churches from sometimes playing a social role of the utmost importance, even at the forefront of modernity, as in the United States. This is beside the point. Let us look at the American example, the most interesting because apparently the most paradoxical one. Here we have a country founded by European religious dissenters, hence one where the demand for tolerance and the concern for freedom of conscience was placed first both by necessity and by their institution. One where the commonly shared dogma was always, from the viewpoint of the Christian trajectory, the purest and most advanced and the best adapted to the spirit of modernity; where both the individualized and associative forms of religious practice and organization flow naturally into the social-democratic State, not to mention the original, perhaps decisive ingredient, the native congruence in the puritan laboratory between the religious language and the everyday events of worldly life.[45] Furthermore, all this was submerged in a history taken as the direct unfolding of a divine preordained plan, constantly in close contact with its founding Covenant, without any rifts or revolutionary conflicts over the political community's instituting principles, consequently without major mobilizations of secular ideologies in civil conflicts. So when, as at certain points in the history of the American worker's movement, the class struggle became extremely bitter, it still could not firmly establish the socialist idea nor introduce any accompanying radical disagreements over the values and ends of the collective organization. In these conditions we can imagine the deep-rooted vitality of a religious spirit which was not continually exposed to the heat of the secular mind, as it was in the greater part of the Old World, and where the stakes were not raised to the level of civil war, as in France. While in America the order of belief was still connected with the development of the world stemming from Christian premises, in France it was propped-up by the heritage and ideal of a dead past, so that the spirit of freedom, the labor of reason, the will to transform asserted themselves by defeating religious authority, at the end of a long and arduous battle. Moreover, from the viewpoint of Christian reactions to the civilization born from Christianity, both fates were equally conceivable. There is no fundamental incompatibility between the essence of the evangelical message and the main traits of the world of equality, and their mutual adaptation is perfectly logical. But it is equally true that the dynamics of equality meant the formation of a society where faith became an option with no further hold on collective organization—which is why the dissolution of the incarnated bond with the invisible, and hence the divine, led to rejection. Does this mean that where circumstances allowed religion and the spirit of the age to reach a mutual understanding, society was organized by religion to a greater extent than where its prolonged struggle with the Enlightenment greatly weakened its influence? Not at all. The United States shows us how spiritual and cultural influence was preserved by denominational membership within a society whose workings, orientations, and values were just as far removed from the structure of dependency toward the other as the older, superficially more de-Christianized or laicized, European societies.

Two levels must be distinguished. The complete organization of the human-social sphere by religion is one thing: herein lies the historical truth of the religious phenomenon, and it is at this level alone that it makes sense to speak of the "end of religion"; but the role retained by religious beliefs in societies wholly organized outside religion is completely different. There is a "superstructural" religion capable of outliving "infrastructural" religion. This occurs to such an extent that we could plausibly imagine a society whose members would all be driven by a sincere faith and whose material, political, and intellectual axes would still originate from the dynamic reversal of traditional religious subjugation. Furthermore, why exclude the possibility of a regulated renewal of the jaded Old World Churches which would deliver them from their old demons of authority, a conversion that would give them strength and stamina by allowing them to regroup on the basis of the original collusion between Christianity's spirit and the West's destiny? Though the age of religion as a structuring force is over, it would be naive to think we have finished with religion as a culture. But can we imagine that in the long run the disappearance of the "infrastructure" would not have any effect on the "superstructure"? Should not the disappearance of the basic social function of the religious provoke a slow but inexorable fading or erosion of the very possibility of a belief? It is tempting to think so. But here we come up against another problem which clearly complicates the issue: that of the subjective function preserved—or acquired—by religious experience when its social function is obliterated. How far is it capable of taking up the challenge and contributing to our survival? Is it capable of anchoring a shared and socially instituted belief? Will it not rather fragment the remnants of humanity's oldest preoccupation into an anarchic fluid mass of private, erratic, and diffuse religions? For now I can only establish the parameters and indicate the unknown factors.

.   .   .

By "end" I do not mean a clean break producing a radically original world, completely different from earlier ones. The novelty of the present is enormous, but it arose from a reorganization of the data and articulations of the previous world. We have not changed history, but rearranged the order of the unchanged basic factors controlling its direction. Consequently, there was no ultimate recovery of human's conscious power to regulate freely their social behavior. We have not emerged from the shadows of external dictatorship into the full light of deliberate choice and premeditated control regarding the forms of practices and the modalities of the collective bond, as if any obstacle, separation, opaqueness between man and himself could be removed by bringing the previous external ordering principle back inside. Obstacle, separation, opacity will always remain, but within individuals themselves, in the relation between individuals, at the heart of their collective-being—with no external guarantee to protect and maintain them unchallenged. Bringing the social foundation back among humans, placing it within their reach, and making it wholly human, does not mean putting it directly in their possession. It governs them, directs their actions, shapes their relations with themselves, with others, with things. It dramatically imposed its constraints to maintain the stability of the regime where humans govern themselves. The difference is that by obeying its commands and encountering its limits, we are no longer at odds with the gods but with ourselves. The process of reincorporating the instituting transcendence has now progressed a certain distance, the network of organizational constraints it put in place has stabilized, the illusions have disappeared—and we are probably beginning to understand this network and to gauge the stakes involved. All of which means nothing less than confronting the very conditions for the existence and possibility of the human-social phenomenon. The trend away from religion since roughly 1700 means forcibly aligning personal and collective experience, in every register, with what both constitutes and constrains us. In a sense, we are now finally emerging from this departure. This major reorganization has occurred without anyone's knowledge. We have gone through it. Because it has for the main part been accomplished, we are now beginning to be aware that it has occurred. We are reduced to imagining what irrevocable necessities its path has forced on us. As a result, future history will revolve around one question: having recognized these necessities, what can we do about them?

Being-a-Self: Consciousness, the Unconscious

The other is always at the heart of these constituting necessities. This no longer means submitting to something other than human, but discovering humans as other both for themselves and for what is different from them. Reducing otherness does not mean eliminating the dimension of the other in the name of pure presence but transferring the other into immanence. On this point we can fully reassure those who fear the one-dimensional flattening of a world delivered up to the immediacy of the senses. Once we are freed from any external indebtedness, brought back into the circle of identity, and forced to face ourselves, the organizing principle turns out to be the other in ourselves, whether we are dealing with the social relation, the intra-intersubjective relation, or the relationship to reality. So we can identify what would be the central question of transcendental anthroposociology whose project I have already mentioned. The heart of what makes the human-social possible is the enigmatic ability to divide oneself off from both the self and from the nonself, which structurally speaking is always the same, whether the division relates to *power*, *consciousness*, or *work*. I will not go in detail into the internal analysis of this anthropogenous mechanism. For the moment I will keep to the historical and descriptive approach and restrict myself to providing some material for a future validation. I will do this by showing in rough outline how the modern reabsorption of religious otherness may be generally understood as rearticulating individual and collective experience in the order of the other—an other neither exterior nor sacred, an other who is we ourselves. It is an immense problem to establish your identity when it is no longer given by others and, strange though it may sound, an even greater problem to conform to yourself when you are released from your allegiance to the gods.

I have already traced in detail how we reshaped our practices by bringing the other into the relation to nature. The reign of religious otherness implied an identification with nature, being immersed in it, and understanding the self in association with it. The main modern reversal corresponds to the process which, when external determination had ceased, led humans to present themselves as active others with regard to the totality of the given. This included their own reality and took place in accordance with a twofold dynamic reducing all reality in its otherness and constituting it differently. I have tried to establish that this is the basic disposition from which derived the understanding of activity as *labor*, its deployment as *technique* (and the autonomization of its operative extension in the *machine*), and its social horizon as *production*. Here action and knowledge are tightly linked and, as we have already seen, we can use corresponding terms to describe the self-positioning of the rational subject in its reciprocal relation to the constitution of the world's objectivity.

But we must go beyond the organization of the conceptual order and place the formation of the modern self in its entirety back within the general process of reducing otherness, which it strikingly illustrates. In particular, it seems to me that the period of intense religious guilt during the sixteenth and seventeenth centuries, whose history Jean Delumeau has recounted, should generally be interpreted in these terms.[46] Here, the other was the evil, understood as the fatal mark of the shortcomings of this humble world and of the degradation of the creature delivered to itself, all of which justified the call of the other life and the attempt to struggle against oneself and tear oneself away from the misery of the mortal condition. Here again, the (uneasy) stability of what we might call the "traditional" Christian position proceeded by an (unstable) compromise between the individualization of the sinner's conscience in relation to God and integration into a hierarchy of being where terrestrial imperfection is *de jure* impersonal. Christians are much more than guilty people awaiting pardon for their transgressions of the divine law. They are beings inwardly confronting themselves and aiming to go beyond all worldly misfortune, their own faults being the most sensitive focal point of this misfortune. And it was through this tormenting responsibility that they were in their inwardness individuals, and not simply subjugated beings destined to be punished or rewarded by an unrelenting god. But so long as a hierarchically organized understanding of the orders of reality prevailed, this specifically Christian action of making people aware of their responsibilities was counterbalanced by a clear exoneration of individuals. There was a measure of evil in the constitution of the here-below, due to its ontological inferiority. The fault lay with the order of human things. It spread between humans, who endorsed it, although it made little sense to attribute it to them absolutely as subjects. They were its culpable agents without being its source or its cause. The two components coexisted within a system whose internal principle and external causal factors have already been described. Any trend to individualize faith was simultaneously a trend to individualize penitence. Belief and guilt kept pace with one another.

The major break came with the breakdown of the hierarchically structured continuity between the human and divine sphere. It resulted in a radical change in the perception of human fallibility and the world's imperfection, in keeping with the changed relation to God his separation brought about. Evil was no longer primarily a characteristic of reality, and only secondarily a personal action; it tended to be attributed to individual choice. Human moral freedom causes evil, as clearly seen by its

designation as the will to evil. Transgression became the archetypal figure of the creature's power over itself in relation to its creator. The image
of Satan portrayed transgression as a revolt against God's willed order,
and in this revolt the subject's distance from itself, its ability to freely
choose itself, reached its peak. From the religious viewpoint, the arrival
of the modern subject signaled its *inculpation*—and not just figuratively.
Sin, taken to extremes, was the model of subjectivity as freedom. There
could be no philosophy of conscious self-control without a basis in this
fundamental internalization of the origin of evil. Besides, it is not good
enough to attribute the inculpation of the faithful, as happened in the
wake of the two Reformations, to the arbitrary constraint of a perverted
pastoral action. We must judge to what extent this inculpation participated in the founding of modernity, to what extent it was an aspect of
the ontological de-hierarchizing and the accompanying disentangling of
the mind, the world, and God, which liberated being from reason. This
inculpation was a necessary transitional stage for the emergence of subjective autonomy, its translation into the register of moral experience and
of assuming responsibility for the self. But it was only transitional and
destined to be overcome. The indictment of humans was the beginning
of their exoneration.

God's withdrawal, which initially caused the evil objectively present in
the world to be pushed back into the unoccupied inwardness of the sinner, logically led, at a later stage, if not to evil's total expulsion from the
world, at least to a radical relativization of its influence. Evil still existed,
but it said nothing about the ultimate nature of things or of the being of
humans. It no longer originated in ontology but in pathology. Once God
was disconnected from it, deficiency was no longer a determining attribute for this world, which does not mean the world became perfect,
but that privation and deficiency no longer defined it. An outstanding
sign of the world's changed status is that evil reached the point of being
imagined to be in the service of the good: we see here the problematics
of Leibnitzian theodicy (1710) or that of Mandeville's "private vices, public virtues." Let us leave aside questions of intrinsic validity raised by
this incipient schema of the "cunning of reason," so that we can retain
its character as an historical indicator of the process of reducing otherness. Evil was not by itself the truth of the world, it only had meaning
as an element of a totality carrying its global nullification. I must now
show in detail how the new perception of the world's integrity would receive its classic expression by projecting historical thinking into time,
into the framework of the open future. Perhaps evil was not in the service of the good, but even if the task was limitless, evil was always technically surmountable according to the perfectibility and the progress
which realized the human sphere's ontological self-sufficiency in infinite

time. An ontologically closed world is a spatially infinite one (wherever you go, you never get away from it) opening onto the infinite future of human history (it demands an inner fulfillment which can never be completed). I will restrict myself to outlining such a world's viewpoint. What is particularly important is to bring to light the inner logic of this anthropological reversal and the basic continuity linking the "pessimistic" and the "optimistic" moment. The "rehabilitation of human nature"[47] was the logical completion of reassimilating the principle of terrestrial inferiority, which actually began by condemning man's fundamental corruption.

The Churches' divergence from the evolving spirit of the age, a direct result of Christian history, is best seen on this ground. The orthodoxies remained out of step with the trend they initiated. They took the first step but generally refused to take the second (in different ways, I might add). By retaining a bleak picture of human fallibility and malevolence, they clung to a hierarchical vision of reality as the touchstone and guarantor of the religious. At the same time they subjectivized the capacity to sin and therefore opted for dehierarchization and laid the foundations of natural religion and confidence in human moral instinct and sensibility. Understanding the fracture in this way meant admitting that it was not totally irreparable. As I said earlier, let us not exclude a surprising future reconciliation of adversaries united by their original collusion.

So much for the first stage: the two-tiered reduction of otherness in the moral order, which created the classical idea of a subject created by its own will and freedom. A second stage was set in motion around 1800, dissolving this pure self-identity and causing the reemergence of the other at the core of personal action. The subject was no longer in full possession of itself with the ability to choose in full awareness, but was consciously dispossessed and determined by a part of itself it did not know. Whether this occurred within the framework of an inner struggle between the attraction of evil and the desire for good, or in the framework of the individual's pact with itself—of a natural convergence between the inclinations driving it and the code to which it must submit— the truth of the subject's reality was realized in its relation to the self or the act of self-disposition. Now at the opposite extreme, this truth was typically relinquished to busy thoughtlessness, whether spontaneously obeying a law these subjects did not need to think about, since they constituted it (register of the normal); or whether a hidden defect prevented them from conforming to it, since the subjects always contradicted themselves before opposing the reigning norm (register of the pathological). The formation of this anthropology based on dethroning conscious self-control was ultimately seen as part of the exoneration process I have just referred to, whose pursuit deprived people of responsibility. This proceeded along two axes. The first internalized the law: whereas it used to be imposed totally from outside, the very representation of instituting otherness, it now became the pivotal point of internal order, the keystone of subjective instauration. The second pathologized the split: transgression followed from the absolute priority knowingly accorded by individuals to the satisfaction of their egotistical ends, at the expense of the impersonal common norm. Transgression thus represented their failure to coincide with the norm; it ended up representing inner discord and became the archetype of alienation, unconscious self-destruction masquerading as self-affirmation.

It is easy to define the turning point where this challenge to the principle of responsibility began, a challenge whose actions can be followed all through the nineteenth century, especially in the course of the medical-judicial debate.[48] It coincided with the arrival of the political individual. Behind the supposedly self-possessed classic subject stood its subjugation.[49] If the subject gained control over the distance between the master and itself, this occurred through dependence on the God maintaining it and, correlatively, through the links still binding it to its peers. Free inwardness presupposed external subjection. What was thought in terms of presence and self-identity actually resulted from the impression of the viewpoint of the other in itself—resulted from difference imposed by what is owed to God and what is owed to one's fellow humans. Also, the revolutionary desubjugating process, by making humans citizens of a community containing its own grounds within itself, created conditions for a complete renewal of psychological understanding. Every representation we nowadays make about personal action had its origins here. Political emancipation dissolved the basis of the classical idea of a reflexive authority, by withdrawing individuals from the network of obligations which used to make them fully aware of their responsibilities deep within themselves. It simultaneously created a new implicit interpretative framework, a new accord on the relation between the subject and its actions, by replacing the imperative of conscious transparence with that of the similarity of individuals.

Previously, it had been important to establish the free decision uniting the subject to its action, namely the principle guaranteeing the impersonal universality of the subject's conduct. Now it became important to understand the special reasons determining the subject's behavior and causing each individual's action to be attributed only to that individual, with the tacit understanding that all harbor in their concrete individuality the motives capable of driving them, which can only be explained from within their personal traits. It should be quite obvious that dethroning the power of self-consciousness was the logical conclusion of

this process of attributing blame on an individual basis, putting the notion of conscious self-control under very great pressure and completely
subverting it once this process reached a certain stage—that is, once the
introduction of the historical viewpoint into the personal sphere supplied
the lever for a purely internal explanation. It is irrelevant that this
process took place unbeknownst to the subject or despite its wishes; what
matters is that the subject corresponded with itself in every point, that
its truth was found in the totality of its qualities and gestures, its actions
and thoughts, its desires and its dreams. Everything arising from or occurring in the subject revealed it far more truthfully than it could possibly have known for itself. Marginalizing the criterion of choosing the self
was the outcome, or the condition, or the necessary accompaniment for
attributing to subjects all their expressions and making them take stock
of themselves. The conscious control of individuals over themselves was
only disputed so they could more fully be themselves. It is thus advisable
to relativize somewhat the famous "narcissistic wound" inflicted on the
individual by the challenge to its ability to have full control over itself:
reflexive self-possession was only denounced as a fiction in order to guarantee the victory of the pure individual.

Consciousness and unconsciousness were actually two sides of self-
adequation, two symmetrically opposite instances of conforming to the
self by dividing off from the self. Moreover, if we were to analyze in detail the transition from one to the other in terms of transformation, we
would probably see that much more was needed to complete it. Take the
first instance: adequation in terms of controlling the self. I have said it
was mistakenly conceived as self-proximity, self-presence, self-trans-
parence, whereas it originated in the split opened up in the self by
obligation toward the other, and in the necessity/ possibility of seeing
oneself from the other's viewpoint. If we start from there, we must follow the metamorphoses of this force of difference vis-à-vis the self. In
one respect the self vanished with the dissolution of the restricting bond
to both God and the other. This process ended up depriving humans of
responsibility, which would lead to disclosing the reign of the nonreflexive in them. It also led to the second representation of self-adequation,
this time in terms of constitutive dispossession and of the constraint to
yield to an inner logic beyond one's self-control. The subject was never so
much itself as in this self-ignorance. In other words, corresponded to itself through its division. Inverting the sign which transformed the master
into the servant should not obscure the renewal of the subject's function
in every detail. But this is only one side of the matter: we cannot so easily dispense with the question of the structure of subjectivity. Around
1900, when the unconscious replaced consciousness as the emblem of
truth's relation to the self, the problem of reflexive difference and iden-

tity, abandoned since its philosophical culmination in Fichte and Hegel around 1800, suddenly reemerged in phenomenology. This was not simply a chronological coincidence. It involved an actual fundamental interdependence that must be clarified historically and logically. From then on, there could only be a real advance in the question of subjectivity by starting from the complementary nature of its two sides so as to illuminate one through the other. The reflexive faculty and the power of the nonreflexive in us were to be understood as interdependent moments of one and the same operation. Organizing the subject in accordance with the other became a dual process: not only was consciousness to be thought of no less in terms of division than the unconscious, but these dividings off from the self had to be clearly articulated. What separates us from the unknown about ourselves should be seen in conjunction with this other, no less enigmatic gap providing us with knowledge of ourselves. The complete ignorance of reality constraints, namely this paramount ignorance of ourselves could not, structurally speaking, be dissociated from what opens us up to the reality of others and installs us squarely in the middle of their world by perceiving it—that is grasping the same world as the others—or expressing it. Actually, we are still scarcely in a position to know what the fully developed subject-form would be like. What we can clearly discern is that it would be far removed from the traditional idea of subjectivity and its assumed prerequisites. Much ground remains to be explored if we are to understand the operating conditions of a being for itself—endowed with thought—which simultaneously only exists through itself—whose organization contains its own principles wholly within itself. Briefly, what could lay the foundation for the existence of something like an *autonomous self*? Concepts for thinking about post-religious man do not yet exist.

Collective-Being: Governing the Future

I have carefully sketched this history of post-theological individuality because it lets us draw a parallel with the history of collective forms. The evolution of the political bond over the last three centuries corresponds to a path profoundly analogous to the one I have just described. I believe the genesis of the democratic phenomenon, in particular, can only be understood over the long term as the setting up of a subjective form of social functioning. The arrival of democracy meant the transition from the subjugated religious society to the society subject to itself as a society structured outside religion. However, the "subjectivity" in question has absolutely nothing to do with the meaning ordinarily given to this word. I am not suggesting anything like a miraculous transition from an obscure otherness to a crystal-clear identity generated by a unified community, completely self-aware, and capable of unanimity. The laborious installation of the democratic process took place by abandoning the ideal of a social self immediately present to itself, with the help of rules of collective action constituting the conditions for a more authentically subjective collective functioning.

From Subjugated Society to Social-Subject

We find the classic equivalent of the subject's power over itself in contemporaneous doctrines of political sovereignty. They had a common religious origin: the separation of God, which transformed the notion of man, equally altered the representation of political power. The separation gave rise to the cognitive subject and its world-as-object by first reuniting within a single *res cogitans* faculties once hierarchically conceived in terms of degrees of being, and next by reabsorbing in a homogeneous *res extensa* these differences formerly linked to the coparticipation of the visible and the invisible. The separation created the moral subject by giving the inner human being total self-responsibility, but also provoked a new vision of sovereign power and function by entrusting the Prince with the unique responsibility for collective-being. The king ceased to be a privileged rung in the hierarchy of powers, the mediator connecting the visible chain of natural communities to the invisible principle. His will alone maintained the existence of a politically bonded collectivity. He was granted monopoly over a social bond while no longer having anything in common with the spontaneous cohesiveness created by ties of blood, territory, or profession. The sovereign tended ideally to replace the systematic plurality of communities and bodies with the reflexive unity of a collective being constituted from its individual members' social desire. The order governing human communal life was no longer an external given but had to be willed into existence. It presupposed the intentional effort of a power completely dedicated to this aim and completely free of the order's means and actions for self-perpetuation. This was the new face of power in the modern State: the specialized instance through which the community achieved subjectivity, the unifying operation of the sovereign making the community correspond with itself in all details and coincide with its own instituting principle—its founding pact. In this regard, Hobbes's approach was strictly homologous to that of Descartes, and was the theoretical expression—refined and radicalized of course, but historically appropriate—of the effective transformation of power, which took place in the absolutist State.

Though it may fly in the face of conventional wisdom, we can still call this transformation the emergence of representative power without being anachronistic. Indeed, the sovereign ceased to externally incarnate the law in order to become the instrument, "divine by right" but wholly terrestrial in substance, of the human community's relationship to itself. The sovereign no longer "represents" the foundation's effectuating exteriority, he corresponds within the political body to the immanent necessities of its holding-together. This major inversion of the terms relating power and society, top and bottom, justifies us in speaking of our entrance into the age of political representation. Power's actions stopped being placed under the sign of the *de jure* dissimilarity between top and bottom, the obligatory reflection of instituting transcendence. It switched to realizing society's inner adequation to its own principle, based on the coincidence between the bottom which is acted upon and the top which acts. Not only were images of power at stake, so too was the unconscious symbolic substrate of highly effective enterprises, both inspiring the administrative State's dynamics. The sovereign State's establishment initiated a logic of *de jure* necessary identity between the ends of the political instance and the origins of the social body it was responsible for. Of course, this process resulted in an apparent increasing strengthening of previous forms of authority. It adopted the methods of intensified coercion and a philosophy of coercive obedience, which seemed rather to aggravate previous subjugation than to announce the age of citizenship. But we must examine the schemas beneath the inexorable establishment of the will's reign; they ultimately brought about the end of the resources placed in its service. The democratic reversal was inherent in the premises of the absolutist State. As it developed, this reversal opposed the absolutist State and made overtures to a legitimating figure, based on the convergence of power and society, which exposed this figure's own exteriority in regard to the nation. The demand for a complete coextension of the collective will and its sovereign implementation took shape in and through an absolutist State, soon to be shaken by this collective will—this nonseparated, directly acting social self, which Rousseau memorably described as the general will.

The democratic ideal had the monarchy as its formative background. The demand for the total union of power and society was expressed through this archetypal separated power, through the change in the nature of royalty induced by the sixteenth and seventeenth centuries' religious revolution. This demand was imposed to the point where power and society ultimately became indistinguishable, forming the horizon of modern politics. This vision of a social wholly self-present self basically relied on an external support, and here again we can see parallels with the constitution of the individual subject. This vision presupposed a traditional representation of the collective ought-to-be—it owed much to the absolutist voluntarist framework this vision developed in, and would

not have existed without the renewal of some of its basic traits. Let us
begin with the fundamental presupposition that a society must want to
be, in order to be, along with the attendant consequences: the necessary
union of the governing and the governed that created knowledge of the
social self, the clearest version of this union being the amalgamation and
coincidence of individual wills within the sovereign. The most modern
aspect of contract philosophy—individualist artificialism—tacitly derived support from a residue of the previous representation of the social
bond's conditions of existence—the (conscious) coincidence of the atom
with the whole and the (reflexive) conjunction of the incorporated political community with its instituting principle. Put differently, the invention of the social-subject always took place within the framework of the
subjugated society. This invention takes up at least two of its features:
the complete adaptation of the part to the whole; and the total congruence of the collective with its founding law. To summarize drastically,
this occurred simply by bringing back to the present what used to take
place through preexisting law, and correlatively transmuting into adherence what used to originate in the organic bond. This is why the dissolution of the Ancien Regime and the advent of the society of individuals
marks the end of this apprehension of the political in terms of subjective
plenitude. We enter a world where the sovereign's willed unification of
power and society no longer has meaning; where the general coincidence
of the human community with its imperative originating principle lacks
any reason to exist. This is a world, consequently, where the notion of society in accord with its origin, and the definition of the correct political
form as the reiteration of the primordial pact, no longer has legitimacy;
where the idea which previously forced the union of instituting wills in
the collective act no longer has support. Thus the old monarchy took
with it the very philosophy that rose against it and finally brought it
down. Democracy triumphed at the cost of losing its initial inspiration.

   Democracy not only lost this inspiration but developed in opposition
to it. The society subject to itself unfolded counter to the inaugural determination of the ideal social subject. We can summarize two centuries
of democracies' hesitant development by saying that subjectivity was implemented in direct opposition to the representation of an immediately
self-present collective self; it occurred through what the latter excluded.
Democracies did not require an amalgamative coparticipation of the particular actors and the public power, which seemed to be necessary for a
totally self-possessed society; they were actually produced by the exact
opposite, by separating off a specialized administrative instance. Moreover, they did not require explicit conscious agreement as part of a projected return to the foundational conditions of society; on the contrary,
they presupposed both the emancipation of individual viewpoints and

de jure ignorance of how their overall coexistence could be assured. They also presupposed the avowed opposition of minds in *de jure* ignorance of what nevertheless made these minds coexist within a common framework. Finally, they did not demand to be concentrated into the intensity of a present, where the pure conscious joining of the community with itself, its reflexive totalization, would occur through the mutual opening up of the participating citizens. This resulted from projecting into the future and opening up to change. Such is the paradox of social reflexiveness as we are only now beginning to understand: it actively adapted to everyone's ignorance of its functioning. Democracy was supposed to be the regime that knows itself through rules and that expressly claims to be what it is, but here, neither knowledge nor will count for anything, because ultimately the regime established under cover of these rules and this project was in practice wholly different from what its instigators imagined. It was not just any regime, but one wholly coordinated with the operation of an active collective subjectivity. Put simply, the newly arrived subjectivity showed a noticeable difference from the initial labored subjectivity: it did not need to be known in order to exist, nor to be expressly willed in order to function. It was constituted not by presence but by difference. This subjectivity was not articulated by converging with the self, but by diverging from it. This is a typical example of reducing religious otherness by transferring the other into the depths of the interhuman relationship: autonomous society, society regulated and determined purely from within—and therefore subject to itself in this narrow sense—becomes a society organized by the other. The sacred other no longer controlled it from outside; now there was the "lay" or immanent other which it was and became for itself, whether through a definition legitimate for its time, through its members' forms of coexistence, or its modes of government.

THE AGE OF IDEOLOGY

I have already had occasion to suggest that the future is to time what the infinite is to space. An ontologically autonomous world which is also closed on itself is only conceivable as a spatially infinite world: however deeply we penetrate its depths, we can never reach its limit nor leave it. Similarly, a society no longer externally determined is a society which must necessarily turn completely toward the future.[50] The future is the obligatory temporal orientation, legitimacy converted into time, of a society containing its own ordering principle. The age of religion was also the reign of a certain legitimate temporality, basically that of the past where pure primeval religion was mixed up with the indivisible dictatorship of origins. In contrast, the major—and recent—originality of transcendent religions is to have restored the external foundation to the present: the original goal and current resolve coalesce in the divine subject. Here we can dispel a widespread misunderstanding regarding the orientation toward the future, one supposedly prevalent in Christianity. I do not deny its novel understanding of history. By situating the divine plan for salvation in history and, through the fall, the coming of the Saviour, and the end of time, Christianity gave history a depth, dignity, and global meaning that no previous tradition had invested in humanity's collective destiny. And it is equally true that through the space made for the eschatological expectation of the resurrection of the body and the last judgment, Christianity made the future the crucial dimension of terrestrial experience.[51] Put simply, the eschatological future, dependent on the deity's unforeseeable external intervention, bears no relation to the historical future that has been the active horizon of our societies for barely two centuries. However fervent the expectation of the approaching end, it did not involve attributing the slightest productive capacity to the human *duree*—particularly in regard to something liable to precipitate the redemptive apocalypse. There is no relation between what happens in history and the end allotted to it from outside (by contrast, the entire activity of the philosophies of history consists in connecting the two). Eschatological expectation confirmed that everything came from God and nothing from humans, confirmed the existing subjugation to the Almighty, and projecting this into the expectation of the last days served to reinforce this belief here and now. The human temporal world was not produced by social practice straining toward an undetermined future, but by its opposite, the attestation of what humans are, the active affirmation that their creation has its own meaning, determinations and exclusive ends.

The future is the temporality of desubjugation, the indispensable temporal axis for a subjective social functioning. It is precisely the role of this productive projection into an open future to supply the pivot around which collective reflexiveness can revolve. It establishes a referential relation to an *other* of a special type—what will be—through which the human community is installed into a process of permanent global reflection, in its many-sided struggle to understand itself while undergoing change, to open itself up to what is changing it, to recover and reconstitute its identity and to structure its change. Thus, the social self has nothing to do with the outbreak of a collective all-encompassing presence concentrated in a common will. The social self is an effectuated self with no need to be conscious of the process forming it; it is a practical self, resulting from society's endless labor on itself. a labor to which it is committed by its internal split in time. From now on, there is no legitimate obligation to renew what used to be, but rather one to create what does not yet exist and what ought to happen. It is true that we were always concerned with a formative obligation to the invisible elsewhere, a matter of duty and indebtedness toward an other than ourself. But this was an invisible elsewhere which, though as unequivocally inaccessible and as capable of provoking fanaticism and superstition as a hidden god, remained on the same level with an entirely lay, entirely terrestrial, and entirely human content. This other was an extremely special type always destined, despite its continually revived transcendence, to be reunited and achieve selfhood in the endless pursuit of a continually retreating horizon.

Consequently, just as it is indispensable to see the intra-societal relation as the structural equivalent of the previous relation to the mythical past or to the present of divine reason, so is it also necessary to emphasize its differences from a religious relation. Formally, the function remains the same, namely to institute the collective by separating off from an invisible pole of ought-to-be, to interpret the self from outside the self. This does not mean we are simply dealing with another side of the eternal religion which is now a religion of the future. By being outside the self, the future gives it a remarkably ambiguous appearance, in which the other and the same are inextricably joined. The non-self is at the same time the virtual self, permanent transcendence is not separated from potential immanence. The method of relating to the self through what is other than the self, though it may have a similar function, has actually been reversed. Take for example, temporal difference, which used to be the instrument of a prohibitive relation accepted as objective. When the invisible legislator takes the shape of the future, the temporal difference becomes the medium for recognizing the creativity of human activity, and the axis for permanently recapturing the collective by identifying it through its very mutability. This situation is the exact opposite of the official religions' understanding of the world and the human bond. How is it possible to uphold tradition in such conditions without causing major confusion?

The truth is that during the initial period, now drawing to a close, the relation to the future has borrowed forms of religiosity so much that it seems to be a substitute faith. The reasons for speaking of "secular religions" are well-known: eschatological beliefs, the quest for salvation through history, sacrifices for better times on a massive scale. I would prefer to speak of the age of ideologies so as to clearly distinguish legitimation by the extra-social (and correlatively by the past or the present) from legitimation by the intra-social (hence by the future). Yet we must not try to determine the substance of our societies' relation to the future by their discourses and convictions. However great the latter's role may have been, they do not convey the substance of that relation. They are an intermediary moment where the new, namely willingness to change, had to follow a familiar process and compromise with the old, had to fit into the inherited framework of the culture of the unchangeable, and reach agreement with the externally imposed, hence stable and known, religious vision of order. There was history, but history aimed toward the end of history; there was change, becoming and the production of the human-social in time, but in accordance with the eternal laws of becoming and in a perspective of an ultimate summation-reabsorption of change. There was the future, but on condition that its direction be known and controlled. I believe we can consider ideology in its varied historical formations as a discourse which broke with the religious explanation of things through its orientation toward the future, to which it subordinated the intelligibility of human action. At the same time it nevertheless somehow renewed its structure by attempting to assure itself of the future, to clearly chart its direction, and to subordinate its production to works of a fully conscious will. In this case, the doctrine's eschatological or salvatory thrust constitutes an extreme, but in no way obligatory, aspect of its fundamental aim to fit the not-yet into a predetermined plan by various means. Now the deep truth about the relation of our societies to the future does not lie here; indeed, at a certain stage of development—most likely the one we are currently undergoing—it probably means the ruin of representational systems claiming to know and control the future. As far as the relation to the future that will henceforth constitute and co-ordinate our societies is concerned, this unanimous and planned striving toward an already clearly identified global goal is unimportant. What is important is the practical organization of social activity in all its facets by the imperative of its own production, that is, an imperative to create a new maximizing transformative relation to the given. This organization actually involves opening onto a future whose content is completely undetermined, and tacitly accepted as such, even if it is more and more deliberately prepared, even if its probable channels and precipitating factors are ever more clearly identified. The way in which we work to generate it prevents us from knowing it. And we have no doubt reached the critical point where the very accumulation of the means of change marks the futility of the ideological ambition to predict the in principle unknowable future. The more we try to control the future, the more open-ended it becomes.

The Child and the Future

One example of organization toward the future is the development of education as a separate sphere and activity. A society legitimated by its past tended to remain a society of *apprenticeship*. Entering into life meant fitting into the categories of an inviolable order, repeating in every detail one's predecessor's work. There was no need for special preparation, only the need for a gradual and controlled integration into preordained roles, a regulated incorporation of codes, tasks, and practices by identifying with the fully fledged practitioner. This included institutions intended to pass on more specific skills: the methods being determined by the general form of initiation, itself dependent on an ideal logic of perpetuation. The ideal was to gradually internalize and immerse oneself in the knowledge established by one's predecessors so as to honorably step into their shoes and in turn pass on the tradition. On the other hand, once the goal of personally initiating successors no longer existed, it was replaced by one of forming a subject, to prepare it for existence. This was done by withdrawing the subject from its everyday surroundings, by a special reflection on how best to provide and ensure the development of its full potential, which means we have entered into a completely different temporal logic. The foundation for the sense of the child's difference is the implicit foreknowledge of the difference of the future that the child bears. Reorienting the general social perspectives toward the future has given rise to the figure of the child-king, the archetypal incarnator of value and the privileged object of emotional investment, along with the figure of the child-as-target, the major preoccupation of collective responsibility, if not of reasons of State, and the object of a strategic science, of an increasingly concerted undertaking to maximize the hopes the child represents.

If we wish to grasp what is specific to modern education we must read it in terms of investment in the future. For example, this investment elucidates the separation from life that education demands; it establishes itself at a distance from the present because in truth, this investment prepares the way for something which does not yet have any expression. But we could also re-create the history of its methods in light of this source by continually emphasizing the latent forces of the indescribable ("a well-formed mind") at the expense of its current abilities ("a well-stocked mind") threatened by obsolescence. From this perspective, we can no longer imagine the mechanism that presided over this age's population expansion and time elongation; youth has become the object of a social emblematic cult, which is not concerned with its immediate usefulness, but with accumulating youth's potential, of storing up the power of futurity.[52] We can see here how, in its pure form, our relation to the future actually involves little ideology: not only is there no demand to represent this tomorrow in which so many human resources are invested, we assume this tomorrow is nonrepresentable.

Bureaucracy, Democracy

Organization toward the future means, further, the deployment of a profoundly original type of power. Western bureaucracies' distinctive nature and expansion cannot be understood outside their connection with administering change. As society assumes control of its politically instituted power, it seeks to express this through an administrative authority that takes responsibility for regulating collective existence. For this reason, the democratic State is necessarily a bureaucratic one, and the administrative State historically had to develop into a representative one. Its function was to give shape and practical stability to the community's self-formative capacity, a function that only made sense in the long term. From this viewpoint, the democratic State's profound legitimacy is the future, the point of social space where the sovereign capacity for self-institution is assembled and embodied. This occurred in piecemeal fashion over a long period through an open social interaction unaware of the ramifications of considerable social needs and massive organizational and legislative responses. The growth of the bureaucratic apparatus realized the sovereign subjectivity expected from openly reiterating the original contract. However, this subjectivity was unexpectedly projected into the slowly germinating future and the unconscious automatic operation of an enormous administrative mechanism.

Despite fear of despotic consequences, realizing the principle of popular sovereignty *through* time brought it into existence in a most liberal manner and always will. The State's irresistible growth derived from this principle, which justified its penetration, even into families and individuals, unhampered by private relations that liberal thinkers thought could contain it. This penetration occurred because democratic society puts all its trust in the totality of the ordering mechanisms and representations at the service of transformation. But what could not be foreseen was that this irresistible broadening of State powers did not necessarily involve any authoritarianism; it is as if the democratic process meant appointing oracles to shape society in relation to that society's chosen goal. What is remarkable is that the expansion of the social's self-constituting capacity, as incarnated in the State, only occurred through growing doctrinal neutralization and the increasingly pronounced impersonality of its operations. Contrary to all expectation, the liberalization of the political bond was accompanied by an increased strengthening of public authority.

In other words, integrating the viewpoint of the future with that of democracy, seen as society's self-production, is poles removed from the determination to subject the present to a fixed representation of the future. This determination defines totalitarianism and sums up its antinomic alliance of the old and the new: a (modern) legitimation of power through the future, but carried out by bringing the previous subordination of society under an organizing aim defined externally and definitively. Hence the absurdity of deducing an impending totalitarian danger from the State's growth. The bureaucratic order does not necessarily foreshadow servitude, its development in democracies being diametrically opposed to its omnipotence in communist societies.[53] Indeed, far from imposing an ultimate meaning on history, the democratic-bureaucratic State gained ground by rejecting any prescriptive view of the future and emphasizing its representative openness to the shifting aspirations and initiatives of its members. The State was not sustained by authority's requirements, but by its own need to become neutral toward spontaneous social change, which it allows to occur in piecemeal fashion and which it must summons, coordinate, and call to order—in a word, transcribe into politics—to interpret and control it. In other words, the State grew through civil society's increasing separation and autonomization.

Contrary to liberal wisdom, the emancipation of social actors from the restrictive framework of State allegiance and the freeing of their innovative powers did not bring about the State's decline, or even confine it to exercising clearly specified functions. On the contrary, desubjugating its subjects freed up its own expansive dynamics. The more it lets things drift, the more it ultimately has to do. The human capacity to create, invent, and change, though initially won at the State's expense, did not restrict it to bare subsistence level. This capacity immediately evoked and augmented State intervention, though in a completely new manner. The State required the regulating support of its invested forms as a structuring controlling force, due to its highly successful progress, the imbalances it engendered, the deficiencies it highlighted, and the demands it created. The only restriction placed on this process was that it had to promote a differentiated collective diversity. But mobilizing support as it did transformed it. In this situation, the State's needs also meant ever decreasing old-fashioned authority and ever increasing representation. There was a tendency to extend the social body by progressively eliminating previous functions of *imposing meaning* and placing it in a relation of *functional correspondence*, of *reflection in action*, where, instead of propagating an extrinsic ought-to-be, it tried to embody the social body's practical self-possession. Its structural horizon was the *pure relation* of self to self between poles made as fully congruent as possible by representative exchange. In this situation, the purpose of the State's omnipresence was to make a fully autonomized and "liberalized" society's self-generation in time completely apprehensible and representable. *The complete actualization of futurity's extensive power* was at stake.

Two things emerged from this evolution linking the social implementation of sovereignty as freedom to evolve, with its political implementation as a generalization of the State's role. One transformed the image of the future and the other transformed the means by which its concern took shape. Let us begin with the "infrastructure," the internal equilibrium of the political-administrative system, which was profoundly altered by the relative reduction of the political and the relative autonomization of the administrative. The old hierarchical vision of an exclusively legitimate political instance directing a compliant subordinate bureaucratic machine and theoretically articulating State operations—decisions/implementations—clearly corresponded less and less with its reality. First, because the dogmatic voluntarist political conception of society's representative systematically shaping it in the name of an ideological future, was obviously increasingly unsuited to the State's real function and the attendant administrative view of politics. Second, the desacralizing, technocratic trivialization of government's role coincided with a reinforcement of the intrinsic legitimacy of bureaucracy's role—with a rise in the administrative function's political side, in both content and form. The boundary between noble and profane topics virtually disappeared when the social field as a whole became, in principle, the scene for a self-constituting process refracted in the State. The humblest activity tended to acquire the elevated dignity of political responsibility when the sector involved tended to acquire the same legitimacy for social change and collective management as any other. To which I must add the far-reaching formal consequences of the related infiltration of the representative ethos into administrative practice itself. Central to the bureaus' increasing role was the spontaneous informal integration of consultative and arbitrative procedures guaranteed in principle by suffrage. It gave them an importance and legitimating autonomy which raised them, however vaguely, above their theoretical executive function. Consequently, the characteristically political moment of collective life, the appointment of representatives, tended to be reduced to an explanatory ritual for a general and permanent process. Hence the undeniable decline in the parliamentary function, which is gradually restricted solely to the final decision, to formally sanctioning a legislative process externally controlled by the no less representative administrative wing. This is no cause for alarm: emasculating the official source of political delegation does not signal a disturbing decline in democratic institutions but their triumphant spiritual vitality and new methods for implementing it.

The more the State reflects current social circumstances, the more representation and administration tend to merge, and the greater the *nonrepresentability of the future*. The more its affects social life and the more it mobilizes resources and supervises the future's progress, the less it can be confined to a clearly defined representation. Far from guaranteeing increased control, the proliferation and concentration of tools directed toward the future increasingly broadens its horizon. The future's gaping openness and uncertainty increases along with the resources and the attention we give it. The more we are taken with the idea that we create it, the more our feeling of responsibility toward the future asserts itself; and so, consequently, does the concern to understand how we are creating it, by what means, in what direction. And the more the future's name and image are blurred, the less we know its ultimate outcome. The massive institutionalization of the future has inevitably dethroned its representations, predictions, and religions.

There is no more relentlessly corrosive critique of ideologies, taken as infallible interpretations of the past and the future, than our societies' increasing orientation toward the future and the organizational development symbolizing their capacity to create themselves. Barely half a century ago we saw the counter-revolutionary party of the past, which sought to re-establish traditional, hierarchical legitimacy, lose its significance. We are now witnessing the collapse and full-scale retreat of the archetypal party for the future: the revolutionary cause, which promised humanity's ultimate self-reconciliation. But this collapse also extends to the moderate "centrist" representation of historical movement as progress. While this representation postulates the continuity and identity of basic social forms through time, it simultaneously records their improvement. It thus proves unsuited for shaping radical future change. The representational systems which justified social time, the evolving collective ought-to-be, can no longer be defended. We no longer speak of the desire to renew a living bond with the uninterrupted past. The classic ideological discourses of futurity, whether in the progressivist version of continuity, or radical versions of a revolutionary break, have been exhausted and made obsolete by historical change. By destroying the images which allowed us to intelligibly grasp it, the future looms up *unknown* before us.

Can we speak about this as a "crisis of the future", as if it were a temporary failure of representational power which may be restored? Not at all, for the regime with a faceless future that we are entering, is now the norm. The collapse of ideologies means the simultaneous collapse of the vestigial form of the religious—the last possible reconstruction of a lay social order's image in terms of an external order, whether by adapting its content (eschatology) or by borrowing its structure ("bourgeois" eternity of social relations subject to progress, and the "bourgeois" eternity of family authority subject to market laws and political obligation). In other words, the *secularization of history* is completed as the future becomes unrepresentable. The faceless and nameless future, unconstrained and unaffected by occult determinism, is the *pure future*, removed from the theological cocoon which concealed it for two centuries. From now on, no more diviners, mediators, and sacrificers. For herein lies the future's main paradox: the more the order of the invisible comes to light, the more secular it becomes; the more unpredictable it becomes, the less inevitable it is; the more accountable it makes us, the more it teaches us that we create it. The less possible it is for us to consider the future an object of superstition and worship, the more apparent it becomes that

the future will be *other* than we imagine. The more we accept ourselves
as authors of history, the only remaining enigma is we ourselves. The ordeal of otherness has become the reference point forcing freedom on us,
a sure sign that we are governed by a logic opposite to the religious one
of origins.

The Power of the Identical and the Society of the New

We can best grasp the collapse of our societies' temporal axes, which inform and organize their cultures, by returning to the apparatus which instituted the future. And it is important to understand its origins if we
wish to understand a certain number of apparently contradictory features of our development, particularly those regarding society/State relations, and of the perplexing double-sided dynamics of liberalization and
state-control. This mysterious phenomenon only becomes intelligible
when we consider what the autonomization of a civic pole within society
would have meant. It is all the more puzzling when instead of weakening the State, this double-sided dynamics reinforces it to an unprecedented extent. This reinforced State can now be independent from a
purely social viewpoint, a difficult feat since it lacks any political depth.
This strange situation can only be explained by returning to the origin of
a certain temporalized collective experience, itself seen as the movement
by which a society slips out of the age of religion.

When we retrace the origins of the archetypal temporal machine, western bureaucracy, we quickly see two clearly distinct strata. Western bureaucracy is made permanent within this futurist orientation, supplying
its base and context. This switch toward the future would have been unthinkable without enormous preliminary labor, closely related to the deployment of Christian potentialities, through which the collective act is
gradually embedded in perpetuity and redefined from there. The western
bifurcation is gathered up as a whole into this primordial decision regarding the *duree*. Subjectivation of the social, impersonality of power,
opening up to history are three basic innovations in collective-being with
the same temporal source. The temporal sphere's ontological autonomy
is attested and made concrete through its unending continuity, a direct
result of the Christian process of deploying transcendence. God's separation is verified by time. In contrast to celestial eternity, the perpetuity of
immortal bodies constituted from transitory creatures reveals the human
world as self-enclosed. Individuals are born and die, their communities
and institutions remain. This trite commonplace corresponds to a verita-
ble revolution of the mind and means that these perpetual collectives
ought to exist independently of their visible members and have a more
"real" existence than them, even though these collectives may be quite

intangible. This extraordinary reversal of perspective transmutes visible living beings into representatives of immaterial entities—the crown, the realm, the body politic, later, the State, the Nation—whose unchanging identity through time gives them the status of a person. They are certainly very strange persons since they are devoid of personality, being purely "mental" and fictitious. They nonetheless dictate a general redistribution of authority within society. Legitimate power only exists when exercised in the name of a transcendent collective, and this is responsible for the complete originality of modern western society's forms of political power: the definition of power as nonappropriable, the systematic differentiation of the person from the function, the redefinition of public roles in terms of representation or delegation. The basic impersonality of power results from the personified collective—State or Nation—presumed to actually hold it in perpetuity. France is a person because she is eternal, just as her State is endowed with personality because it never dies. The locus of power is humanly unoccupiable only because it is transcendentally occupied, not by gods, but by invisible terrestrial beings arising from the social body.

We are dealing here not with "notions of time" but with long-term practices (administratively and politically organized), which are both extended and articulated by these personifying "fictions." And it is through this postulating of the collective's subjective and transcendent permanence that western culture was able to become a culture of change. In so doing it shifted the social locus of identity, reestablished it elsewhere in another form, and assured the human actors of the inviolable stability of their world by other means, thus freeing the field for concretely existing individuals to exert their initiative. Once again, the innovation was in reality a transformation. The collective person's invisible internal consistency, despite its continually renewed membership, actually reconstructs the imperative of identity which previously used to pass through the unfaltering continuity of tradition. Actors come and go, but the world is fixed in its patterns and destined to be passed on unaltered to the end of time. The remarkable thing about the western subjectivation is that it gave rise to the immutability of change itself. The more the visible agents not only followed one another through time, but also innovated and renewed established forms, the more they confirmed the unchangeable self-identity of the all-encompassing whole supposed to reunite them; the more they sustained invisible individuality, the more they assured transcendent perpetuity. Hence the significance of the notion of progress for describing this manner of collective self-presence in the midst of an otherwise expanding physical universe. Though there are factors tending to discredit the idea of progress, we must recognize its capacity to reflect an unlimited number of significations without impairing their overall identity. A positive revaluation of change was able to take place precisely because we were already embedded in a new kind of immutability and perpetuity, to which we owe our faith in the fruitfulness of the *duree*. Not only do the most radical changes not endanger the collective entity's basic stability, they reinforce and nurture it. When it comes to orienting activities, this mechanism is unparalleled. It gives an assurance about time which clearly played a part in our resolution to face up to the unknown future. It supplied the solid base allowing the behavior required for investing in the future to develop and become an obvious, everyday fact. A political shaping of collective perenniality took place within the structure of the future and constituted the condition for the historical possibility of the future, giving it a symbolic and practical substratum. We continue to rely on an organization of social time, ranging from the State's administrative continuity and impersonality, a guarantee of its inviolability, to exercizing power in the name of the Nation, an acknowledgment of its personal perpetuity. By virtue of the *same* that it instaurates, this organization of time conditions our opening to the *other* of becoming.

My interest in elucidating the modern relation to the *duree* is not simply to make this truly remarkable culture of change intelligible in terms of the human species' millennia-old reactions and passions; we have actually changed less than we might think, because beneath our worship of novelty remains a good deal of faith in the immutable. The real importance of elucidating this relation is that it helps us better understand the separation of civil society from the State. Making civil society autonomous means freeing up a practical pole of change as opposed to a transcendent one of stability. This pole in turn only becomes truly independent once power has been depersonified, disincorporated, and categorically "representativized." As long as the king was considered to visibly incarnate these invisible terrestrial realities—the crown, sovereign dignity, or the realm's body politic—neither State nor Nation was truly thinkable as a *de jure* autonomous entity. The legitimating invisible was indivisibly connected with, and physically present in, the visible, through the sovereign's person. The sovereign was a limiting figure of the reconciliation of opposites, of maintaining the personification of the virtually nonpersonifiable, which sums up the inner fragility of the absolutist monarchy. The system of hierarchical mediation was by necessity responsible for administering and restraining a principle destined to destroy it. The system of human ties was still connected, *via* the graduated network of dependencies, to the royal source of cohesion. There was nothing within such a framework that could be genuinely considered a "civil society": here the social relationship only had meaning and reality as a link in the political chain, up to and including the family or the profession. Democracy's determination of power as humanly nonappro-

priable definitively specified the political and did so as the perpetual all-
encompassing entities implementing power acquired autonomous individuality. This separation of the political was a direct function of the
collective person's temporal transcendence, the sole basis for separation,
whose completion coincided with the emergence of representation. The
latter was by nature duplicitous as it had to represent not only visible
and living beings at a given moment; but also permanently self-consis-
tent invisible being arising from the death of its members and living off
their posterity.

One can imagine the liberating effect of this affirmation-secession of an
autonomous pole of political identity. It released the totality of concrete
activities and individual relations from obligation to social cohesiveness,
now guaranteed by other means. On the one hand, the political function
guaranteed inviolability throughout the *duree* to the collective's all-em-
brasiveness, by incarnating it in the State's anonymous continuity. Opposite this collective sphere defined by the power of perpetuity was the
properly "civil" sphere of the individual, of the freedom of movement
and the right to have access to the future. For the first time in history
there was an order of purely private human relations based wholly on
mutual will, legitimately ignorant of the constraints inherent in the common social bond. The main outcome was the separation of the economy,
along with the dissolution of any corporate determination of functions in
the name of the common weal. It was replaced by the free dynamics of
divided social labor regulated solely by the inner necessities of the pro-
duction-consumption process, necessities individually assumed (freedom
to initiate undertakings) and anonymously controlled (the "invisible
hand" of the market). We can see what a break with traditional legitimation this instauration of an individual's right to economic initiative,
which implied a right to create an independent source of social relations,
represented. This initiative presupposed the unforeseeable nature of social movement and its creative opening. We can also see how much the
idea of combining and balancing interests and needs, of automatically
guaranteed supply and demand, beyond human intervention, represented a break from a social order dependent on the Prince's omnipresent will. Here again we are dealing with different temporal sub-
strata: the reign of what is to come versus control by what has been. On
the one hand, along with the primacy of political sovereignty was the all-
inclusive presence of the social body before a law prior to and greater
than human plans; on the other hand, the market brought a collective
order taken as resulting from individual action, the stability achieved in
the present presupposing the introduction of so many instabilities that no
one could possibly come to grips with them. From this angle, the ano-

nymity of market control clearly appears as the counterpart to the impersonality of democratic power.

Civil society's emancipation is thus a phenomenon to be understood in terms of social time's distribution and articulation. The change institutionalized at the center of democracy internally sustained two antagonistic temporalities. Though this naturally created discontinuity, it also produced continuity. It simultaneously created the visible new and invisible self-identity. Our societies are simultaneously the most mobile yet most stable ever seen; the "hottest," the most susceptible to continual upheaval, and the most grounded in permanence. This ambiguity expresses the division between civil society and the State: on the one hand is the production of change, the age of the radical original; on the other, the integration of change, the temporal sublimation of the new in invisible sameness.

This capacity to create political perpetuity along with social novelty is a key to western historicity. Entering the age of the future brings with it a necessary dissociation of the local from the global, the individual from the collective, the social from the political. Thus it is less appropriate to speak of a simple reversal of the hierarchical primacy of the whole over the parts, than of a mutual transformation of the whole and the parts by integrating the determining factor of the *duree*—a freeing of the action of the parts in time by the temporal transcendence of the whole. The entrepreneur's or the innovator's freedom arose from the contribution that their differentiating actions brought to collective identity, and from being-in-society's right to be unconscious, a right derived from the unalterable self-presence of the separated and all-embracing collective that this enterpreneur's practices simultaneously presuppose and reinforce. This throws light on such paradoxical relations between State and civil society as those where the politico-administrative apparatus's neutrality is reinforced while its functions and influence are broadened. Its expansion corresponded to the growing separation of the political, which it harnessed throughout the social space, drawn as it was to monopolize the social bond. But the separation of the political meant transcendent collective identity, hence accentuating power's functional impersonality and neutralizing the State through the invisible continuity which justified its increased control. The more the State grew, the more it was placed in the service of something else. By extending itself, it extracted whatever relatively autonomous political inscription and stability existed in civil society's institutions, whether in the family, Churches, professions or enterprises. Whatever holds humans together becomes the State's exclusive domain, which is not to say that it revokes the separation of civil society; on the contrary, it widens the gap between itself and civil society inasmuch as the latter is the sphere of individual autonomy. Put simply, civil society appears less as segments of organized, independent, and influential-social blocks such as the Catholic confessional block used to be in France. Social change becomes in a profound sense the movement of individuals.

Nevertheless, we are probably on the verge of a complete reversal here. The State has in recent decades successfully monopolized the political by finally overcoming the deep-seated resistance of economic power, a success responsible for the State's spectacular growth during this time.[54] Once enterprise, property, or wealth were politically neutralized, the State rediscovered their virtues. The emphasis shifted toward the power of initiative and the necessary freedom for the actors in civil society to maneuver. This would not basically diminish the State's prerogatives, even if it might modify its style of intervention. Nor will it revive civil institutions provided with their own political role. If we moved toward something like a new liberalization after a phase of increased state control, this was a result of the latter's success, because the collective identity established by an expanding public power provided the additional security to openly and creatively rejuvenate freely chosen private relations. Civil society's autonomy could no longer reside in the independence of intermediary bodies, as in the Ancien Regime, but in the unpredictable nature of the individual's response and orientation, which continued to grow as the intermediary bodies declined. In this sense there was complete congruity between the wave of liberalization and the shift toward a pure future removed from ideological projections. The orientation of all activities toward the future, the systematic institutionalization of the capacity for self-creation, presupposed the complete autonomization of initiative and of the productive source constituted by civil society's operation. This does not represent the recomposition of social life in competition with the State, but on the contrary the increasingly widespread admission of individuals to the collective world and a more positive evaluation of their state-guaranteed capacity to diverge. The two "invisibles" now came together: the first, the difference from the self, the non-representable nature of the future destined to be fulfilled by the organization of change; and the second, the invisible of self-sameness, the imperceptible identity of the past, present and future, as guaranteed by the anonymous continuity of the mechanism for change.

Living-with-Ourselves: Absorbing the Other

If I have dwelt at length on the new structure of social time resulting from the transition to legitimation by the future, I have done so to emphasize how far we are dealing with a completely restructured system of collective-being, categorically opposed to those articulated by religious time. If there is society outside religion, it can be measured through these inverted logics of the *duree* and their infiltration into areas seemingly remote from collective activity, ranging from childhood, to bureaucracy, to the order of production and exchange. And if it makes sense to speak thus about a society subject to itself, the manner in which it manages permanence and change clearly shows us how little the human community can hope to master its destiny. A society subject to itself points to a very specific type of organization and mode of functioning based on internal difference, and hence is at the opposite remove to both an external religious functioning and the consequent all-inclusive self-presence one might have expected. Thus subjection to the past was replaced not by sovereign freedom conscious of the here and now, but by the relation of self-identity through the other of the future. This is why it is accurate to speak of a transference of the other from outside to inside the human sphere—bearing in mind the metamorphosis of the supernatural other into the actual functional other, the pivot of a structured identity. The common element was in both cases the instituting difference from the self. Except in the first instance, the difference from the self was an affirmation of the non-self and an organization of a prohibitive dependence, so the social mechanism operated on the attestation that it was not man-made. While in the second instance, based on the otherness of the future, the difference from the self recognized the self-production of the social and appealed to individual action. Everything that will happen tomorrow is presently in the hands of the living. They will not necessarily always know what they are doing; but they cannot fail to recognize that they themselves have brought about whatever comes to pass. At the center of the structuring relation between the actual visible and the invisible future, lies the practical certainty that the causes of social progress are to be found within society itself, distributed among its components. Society subject to itself is society articulated by internal divisions—of time, power, interest, thought—so many effectuating forms of living-with-ourselves, whose practical expressions attest this society's exclusive self-determination.

POLITICAL CONFLICT

This transformation did not take place through the actor's consciousness; it passed through the modalities of the social relation and the organization of the collective arena. The formation of contemporary democratic systems comes down to a slow and painstaking substitution of the deed for the mind, of the reality of the subjective mechanism for the ideal of consciousness. This is shown by the transition from reflexive sovereignty, brought about by concentrating on the present, to the unconscious freedom produced by projecting it into the future. But let us take another example, *the institutionalization of conflict*, which is open to precisely the same analysis. Democracy turns its back completely on what had always appeared to constitute the condition of sovereign subjectivity: democracy is more than just a consensus of minds, it is their close association within a fully self-conscious collective will. And yet placing class antagonism and the conflict of interests at the heart of political competition must be understood as the deployment of the social subject in another form—no longer conceptual, but actual. no longer substantial, but relational.

This institutionalization of civil discord destroyed any possibility of the political community's unified self-possession. But by virtue of its radical oppositional nature, this discord brought the entire social organization into public debate. Anything in the collective arena can become the object of regulated conflict—another way of realizing the sovereign grasp on the totality of collective reality. The struggle of social causes and forces is institutionalized, that is to say, goes beyond the totalitarian illusion of final victory, to produce a culture of compromise between antagonists who know they cannot eliminate each other. And to this extent conflict becomes the organizing schema of a *de jure* fragmented public space assuring unresolvable confrontation. Everything holding actors together is subjected to their grasp, everything takes place between them— using *between* in a precise sense which sanctions neither appropriation nor closure. This is why conflict over the organization of political society is the formal equivalent to the market as the structuring principle of civil society, and is also the necessary counterpart, within the political system, of the impersonality of power. There is nothing externally shaping the bond between humans; nothing in this bond beyond the grasp of their will or not the result of their actions. But at the same time no one among them can determine the outcome. Such is the cohesive principle of the collective as subjective form. Hence the political competition organized by the representation of divergent class interests, the opposed versions of the collective's future constitution, and the disagreement on everything other than the principles of confrontation, instaurates a social self transcending the consciousness of the actors through whom it is established and operates. By balancing opposed factions while opening them up to competition, this organized political competition sets a pattern for social change which might be called society's self-productive relationship to itself. The new arises where parties interact, from a continual process of exchanges, transactions, arbitrations and compromises affecting collective experience as a whole. The social as a whole is virtually renewed in this crucible. The entire instituting process takes place between self and self, in a remarkable combination of the actor's complete involvement with their systematic ignorance of the ramifications of their opposition, each one having only a partial view of the broader picture. The strictly social meaning of their struggle eludes them, it exists independently of them, even though only they can give it any reality. This is a typical instance of a *collective self-reflexivity unconscious of itself*, one that conflict causes to operate without its agents' consciousness. The social-subject exists on the impossibility of reconciliation and in ignorance of their actions' disruptive effects. In other words, the subject still exists even where we have "departed" radically from the "metaphysics of pure self-presence." Here, the owl of Minerva has let twilight slip away. One wonders whether this philosophical creature can ever close the gap between itself and historically created reality.

It would seem reasonable to attribute to the mechanism of conflict a structural necessity relatively independent of its initial formative conditions. This mechanism was born from the integration of the social question arising around 1848 with the mechanism of liberal democracy beginning in the 1880s, through the encounter between universal suffrage and the party of the working "class and masses," to put it schematically. But we must not identify this mechanism simply with its conjunctural substratum—one that later developments have changed considerably, from formal class divisions to their varied ideological significance. The integrating mechanism has worked sufficiently well to deeply transform and neutralize the extremely contradictory terms it was responsible for articulating. Social compromise through the welfare State's regulating the economy on the basis of mass consumption (increased productivity, increased income, broader markets) has modified the partition between property owners and proletarians. As antagonisms were increasingly regulated, political compromise was established. The workers movement, in the "historical" meaning of the word, consequently disappeared as a significant social actor. Similarly, ideologies—whether revolutionary or conservative—have been wiped out, particularly in their mythical totalitarian version of vanquishing the adversary. All of which has alleviated tensions and mitigated extreme confrontation. This does not mean that conflict as the axial form of the political relation will decline into an empty ritual. And by conflict, I mean not only the rival forces and factions struggling for power, but also the structured opposition of antinomic visions of the collective future goals against the interpretive background of conflicting interests questioning the social mechanism itself. This mechanism can quite easily be separated from its previous foundations and reconstructed unchanged in principle, on other bases, whether dealing with the identity of the main actors it sets against each other, or that of the ultimate values claimed by both sides. Bringing incompatibles together does not mean eliminating them. The conflict can be systematic without being strictly ideological, and does not promise any final reconciliation of the human adventure with this conflict's outcome. The main thing is the organizing schema. This means that conflict must potentially involve the totality of collective action and be embedded in civil discord, whether it represents a disagreement on the political stage or involves relations formed between individuals and groups. Moreover, it requires nothing more to operate. So nothing could be more mistaken than to confuse the fate of institutionalized conflict at the heart of the political process with the course of social forces and the conceptual ideas that have substantiated it for the last century. The collective material handled and articulated by conflict could, if necessary, be completely renewed. The only constant destined to remain is the subjective form invisibly asserting itself through conflict.

Modern democracy will thus develop in an atmosphere of unpredictability and surprise, not *invention*. Two centuries of historical change have not added a single basic principle, a single fundamental rule, to those we have known since the eighteenth century. The most extreme contemporary political projects—council communism and self-management—only take the possibilities contained in the premises, namely the rights of the individual, to their ultimate conclusions. Democracy has thus arrived fully aware of the facts and in strict accordance with its initial principles. But this doctrinal continuity is realized through means which are generally at odds with the initial requirements—and are, moreover, regularly denounced as ruinous to the republic they helped establish. Democracy has both an accurate idea and a complete misunderstanding of its own operations. Hence the danger of abstraction: describing the democratic regime on the basis of its political norms does not tell us much about its effective social functioning. I am not appealing to some mysterious alchemy and haphazardly injecting the ideal into reality. The system currently operating seems retrospectively to have been a systematic actualization of a schema defined by strict internal constraints—and of a schema that also displays no real divergence from its initial aim. It is the same, only incarnated in a completely different effectuating form: being-a-subject, subjective articulation is not what we might expect. Our inability to perceive the details of the logic imposed by these constraints does not permit us to believe we are dealing with a completely new emanation of an inventive historical indeterminacy. Just as it is important to recognize the historical process's opaqueness to its agents, so is it important to clearly situate it. In the case in point, reason does not retreat before being's mysterious fecundity, nor is there disagreement as to the direction followed; rather, there is ignorance of the conditions under which a democratic society operates, and this occurs as a function of our ignorance as to what it represents compared to previous subjugated societies.

Identifying subjectivity with conscious power might lead us to believe that sovereignty was achieved by obliterating the internal other, and bringing the governing and the governed into the closest possible proximity. Instead, the State developed beyond all expectation. There is good reason to be surprised by the notion of separation, given the enormous broadening of functions guaranteed by political administration in social life. Given this invasion of daily life and the extension of the State's direct role, would it not be more appropriate to speak of the State's internalization? This difference between the old and the new will have to be our starting point.

We need to understand the transition from a system of exteriority to a system of separation. The exteriority of a royal power representing the sacred and holding the social body together through coercion does not involve its separation; it even excludes the leader's autonomization in relation to the political body's members. Collective order only exists through the living communion of the will from above with its subjects; the exteriority of a royal power here goes hand in hand with the consubstantiality of power and society. Conversely, once the foundation's transcendence was abolished, representative identity, far from resulting in a virtual reabsorption of power into society, provoked power's secession from it, creating the conditions for the State's unprecedented expansion. Indeed, the paradox is that the growth of the State's practical duties and services, which changed it from a remote authority into a daily partner, is actually controlled by an administrative separation of the political, bearing no relation to the "most glorious monarch's" display of superiority. The State's concrete infiltration into society depended on an abstract splitting off from society. The organizing viewpoint's radical distance from society laid the foundations for the unlimited expansion of the organizing endeavor. In other words, the greater the State's role in social life, the more it became an integral everyday part of the collective mechanism, and the more it operated invisibly in the name of compete detachment from the common sphere. Its immanence in civil society grew with its ideal transcendence.

This was primarily because its symbolic function of producing cohesiveness began to be carried out through its real activity and to be hidden in it. This is another paradox we have already noted: the former mediating and preserving power, while seen to be the keystone of the natural order and thus intimately united with society, allowed society's hierarchies, bodies, and communities extensive autonomy in principle, since it was itself based on their social substantiality. This allows us to say that if something like a civil society was theoretically unthinkable within the framework of previous monarchies, something like a truly independent civil society actually existed in them. Civil society's autonomy, on the other hand, only became thinkable with the independent existence of the units comprising it. The State's monopoly over instituting the social bond and the inevitable dispossession of previous pockets of sociality from their public dimension is the entrance into political modernity. On the one hand there is the civil tissue individuals privately create between themselves by either explicit or tacit contract; on the other, there is a derivative from the properly collective link and from the political whole, preserved and controlled exclusively by sovereign power. Power appears to lose its symbolic role in this translation, as if its signifying functions and its real privileges were inversely proportional to each other. Its primordial element was symbolic ostentation while its real influence was limited; on the other hand, when its monopoly on collective-being makes it physically all-pervasive, its force as an image and its capacity for ritual expression are limited. This does not mean that its symbolic function disappears: it simply becomes invisible by becoming coextensive with the State's coordinating and controlling tasks. Pure explicit symbolics are replaced by a hidden symbolics, increasingly more assimilated and concealed within the very operation of an increasingly organized and efficient politico-bureaucratic machine. However open this machine is, its role of guaranteeing collective identity is swallowed up in the practical role of administering collective-being, which role becomes its hidden face and its unconscious necessity. Bureaucratic prose replaces the poetry of the Prince. The State, through its intrusive and meddlesome influence, its meticulous organizing activity, and the proliferation of its resources as a social entrepreneur, guarantees humans the stable legibility of their world formerly delivered by devotion to the god's sacred plans. Faith in the mystical bond with the other is replaced by tangible and unconscious security administered by the all-encompassing organizing agency. This substitution is a major axis for the growth of the separated State. This growth corresponds to the need to take responsibility, through a broad encompassing action removed from individual relations, for the cohesiveness which can no longer be provided by immediate social ties like the family nor guaranteed by the interacting shared representations of the instituting imaginary. The desymbolized world calls for the State to administer it.

But this major expansionary factor would have only limited influence unless it operated with a second one further concentrating the political separately from the social. The democratic dissolution of the foundation's otherness cannot be limited to the exclusive guarantee that the whole to which humans belong is subject to a unifying perspective, and its resulting practical obligations. One could say that the dissolution concentrates everything previously defined as exteriority into power. Previously, power represented the Other and pointed beyond itself to the Other's invisible legitimacy, whereas now it begins to completely absorb it. At the same time power diminishes, if not abolishes, the Other's sacredness. But in so doing, power sets itself up in a position of otherness to society—a "lay" otherness with nothing extra-human to support it, not even a human essence; an other on an equal footing, a functional and not an essential other, but an effective one. Power now assumes an active difference, which its earlier role as an external deity's delegate had forbidden it to do.

Instead of achieving the complete transparence of the political body by reintegrating previous externally projected causes and will, we see the State, through its bureaucratic development, become the specific determining factor of the social. Its unassuming tactics disguised its influence for a very long time. Indeed, compared with its earliest ideology, this artificial device promoting routine enquiries, subtle legal distinctions, obsessive recording of all kinds of data, looks like an external parasitic growth, which the establishment of a harmonious authentic human community would eliminate. Nevertheless, routine administration ends up defeating sublime doctrines. This regulating mechanism for obtaining knowledge develops a dynamics of expropriation and secession that spell the end of notions of reconciliation. The other of the State asserts itself against social sameness by restoring sovereignty to the people. And yet we are not talking about an encroachment on sovereignty, but its fulfillment. The other in question does not lie simply in the State but in the relation between the State and society. The State does not take control of the social as if it were methodically depriving the community of self-knowledge and self-control. On the contrary, it hands over the now institutionalized means of knowledge, facilities for storage and retrieval, powers of investment and orientation. Hence, the historical coincidence between bureaucracies' expansion and the decline of authoritarian forms of power. The fruitful crystallization of the democratic system as we know it, at the end of the 19th and beginning of the 20th century, yields a vital illustration: the development of the State in the form of public services accompanied a renunciation of regal political imperatives. We can speak of a law of democratic State development: its functions and its influence appear to expand as it becomes less imposing—another way of saying that it gains in practical difference what it loses in symbolic exteriority. The State's regulatory prerogatives only broaden in conjunction with its concern to serve and its attempt to be suitably close to its subjects' aspirations. The more the State operates in the name of an objective detachment, while simultaneously becoming more open to representation, the more its intellectual neutrality and impersonal style are highlighted.

Hence it is *simultaneously* true that modern power works toward accumulating knowledge and universally promulgating the norm (Foucault) and that its historical specificity is to recognize knowledge's autonomy and the law's independence (Lefort). Both features must be thought together: modern power is the most extraordinary agent of knowledge that has ever existed, but only insofar as it does not seek to promulgate *its own* knowledge; it is the most all-pervasive, most obsessive law maker, but only because it does not seek to impose *its own* law. Dispossession is here the instrument of appropriation: this entire undertaking to extract knowledge and redefine norms is only needed to guarantee the collective body as such its sovereign self-determination. I repeat: to the collective body *as such*, not to any of its members in particular, neither those who hold power nor ordinary citizens, since the process takes place through the action of both, equally unconsciously. The social body's anonymous self-possession produces this paradoxical mechanism that both expropriates and restores, and withdraws its direct control in order to gain for the collective the freedom to arrange its own codes and operations. Such are the implications of the other working within the representative State: it bureaucratically takes from its delegates in order to democratically give to its subjects.

This duality explains the extraordinarily divergent assessments of the State—depending on whether we concentrate on its disappropriating bureaucratic mechanisms or the political rules permitting the agents' participation. We must go beyond one-sided praise or criticism and grasp the logic uniting both sides of this process. The logic is that of a reflexive social functioning which transcends and is unconscious of the individuals it affects. No doubt accumulating the means of knowing and acting in the State corresponds to a substitutive dynamics which tends to split social life from its own principle. But we should further ask what relation might exist between the representative mechanisms involved in the State's formation and the latter's increasingly expropriative administrative apparatus. Unless, of course, we assume that the delegation is a pure sham. This is the opposite, equally narrow-minded view of bureaucracy: as a screen between the people and its full sovereignty, a screen to be dispelled. It cannot be dispelled because it is through this dispossessive mechanism that the people become sovereign. Nor need we fear the state moloch escaping collective control to enforce its own domination, for it is one of those giants whose benevolence and gentleness increase with its size. Its very capacity to abstract brings it closer to the citizens. In this mutual development of administrative difference and representative coincidence, we attain the pure form of a society subject to itself. Everything takes place between humans—and the State's all-pervasive-ness is there to substantiate the complete repossession of collective-being. But everything also occurs through it in such a way that the social actors cannot possibly appropriate the ultimate meaning of collective-being—whether in individual, dictatorial, collective, or self-managed form—because meaning would then no longer be *among* them, but *in* them. Both representative impersonality and the open exchange it calls for exclude this very appropriation.

. . .

It still remains to establish the structural link between the diverse figures of social subjectivity—forms of power, modalities of the social relation, structures of legitimate time—occurring between society's self-expression and action on it, and to explain their apparent systematization and complementarity. I will limit myself simply to listing them and the lesson to be drawn: namely, that the interhuman bond is thinkable and workable without gods. And further, that we are the inhabitants of a world that at a certain point completely turned its back on the reign of the gods. Certainly, nothing can make that leap irreversible. But even if there were a return to the religious tomorrow, the fact remains that the global social organization that has developed in the West for the past two centuries has shown that a society structured wholly outside religion is not only thinkable, but viable. From now on, we will acknowledge the forms of this society.

They do not correspond to full and clear consciousness. They simply attest that even if our finitude remorselessly destines us to misunderstanding and illusion, it does not inevitably condemn us to place this destiny in the hands of others. We cannot infer an endless perpetuation of alienation from the absence of reconciliation. The space between totally denying the self and fully possessing it can be seen to constitute an exceptional breach in the long history of blindness about the self, or a definitive break away from a founding rejection. This space provided, and will continue to provide, room for humans to *be-among-themselves*, remarkably combining collective reflexivity and individual ignorance, the veracity of the principles and the opaqueness of the mechanism. The opposite of self-otherness would in practice not have been self-identity, but a relation to the self, blending coincidence and difference, causing the conjunction of the whole by dividing the parts or assuring the whole's subjective autonomy by dispossessing the specific actors. The death of God does not mean that man becomes God by reappropriating the conscious absolute self-disposition once attributed to god; on the contrary, it means that man is categorically obliged to renounce the dream of his own divinity. Only when the gods have disappeared does it become obvious that men are not gods.

The Religious after Religion

A complete departure from religion is thus possible, which does not mean that religion has nothing more to say to individuals. There is even good reason to believe in an ineliminable subjective stratum underlying the religious phenomenon, namely personal experience free from fixed dogmatic content. Notions that make religion depend on the inviolable necessities of the symbolic function are still relevant. These notions are based on a sound intuition that the last bastion for collective belief resides in individuals, however those holding such notions rashly and unjustifiably deduce from them the inevitable need for religion. The subjective experience to which constituted religious systems actually refer can operate perfectly well by itself, on idle, as it were. It does not have to be projected into systematic doctrinal representations and socially apportioned out for its implementation. It can also emerge in nontraditional practices and discourses. Even if we assume that the age of religions has been definitively closed, we should not doubt that, between private religious practices and substitutes for religious experience, we will probably never completely finish with the religious. There are two errors to be avoided: one consists of inferring the permanence of the religious function from the existence of this subjective nucleus; the other consists of seeing in the indisputable decline of religion's role in our societies the sure sign of its final disappearance. The discontinuity in religion's social function has already occurred. On the other hand, its continuity in inner experience still has some surprises in store. There can be no doubt that religion's aftereffects will not be limited to maintaining a residual presence, but will range from the bona fide perpetuation of established Churches (now based on personal adherence, not on their original content), to widespread adherence to privately practiced beliefs, including syncretic reconstructions and constantly changing sectarian variants. This is surely a future major source of cultural invention, distinct from endlessly organizing the heritage, and far-removed from classical spiritual expressions. We can already measure it by tracing the creative after-effects of what used to be religious experience in the order of aesthetic feeling or the order of moral codes. I do not intend to explore systematically the anthropological substratum of the invisible's ordeal as exposed by the instituted invisible's withdrawal. I will restrict myself to sketching its outlines and its locations, in the form of a prolegomenon to a science of man *after* religious man, in the sense that religion reveals him as he is once its course has been run, and in the sense that it leaves him to himself. There are three aspects to this brief cartography of the Other's imprint. The schema which previously structured religious man's experience, and which continues to structure our own, can be discerned mainly on three levels: one inhabiting our thought processes; one dominating the organization of the imagination; and one controlling the forms of the problem of the self.

. . .

The primary "residue of religion," the first point of contact between the order of our inner experience and what used to be the explicit experience of the Other, is a thought content. The archetypal seminal schema of the world of belief, namely the *partitioning* of reality, continues to sustain our ways of thinking. It continues to provide us with a religious type of intellectual object, nonthematized hence extremely difficult to pinpoint, used in a supportive manner as a secret decisive source of philosophical discourse in particular. Let us call it the *nondifferentiated*.

Reality as it appears to us, as an inexhaustible multiplicity of sensible qualities, an infinite network of distinct objects and concrete differences, involves another reality: the one that suddenly appears before the mind when we go beyond the visible to examine its nondifferentiated unity and continuity. We encounter this basic process of dividing the real, of splitting the visible and the invisible into two, as a possibility in our most banal thought processes. This process is neutral, it does not in itself involve any interpretation. We next graft onto it an understanding specified by the orders of reality that it merely splits up: appearance and truth, sensible and intelligible, immanence and transcendence, etc. But we are not obliged to do this since we can simply remain with the feeling of the real's apparent duality. This does not mark a return to an external principle; we are dealing with a division of things themselves, of the world as it is presented, grasped from within itself. Part of the world is given to immediate perception, and then something else is presented when we take into account its nondifferentiated global nature, about which the only legitimate statement we can make is *that it is*. When I speak about "a religious type of object" I mean a constitutive mode of apprehending the real, one that bestows a primordial splitting without which no official religious belief would have been possible, but which does not intrinsically produce faith, does not involve any particular conviction, and does not wish to be extended in sacral terms. This apprehension may function autonomously within the most thoroughgoing atheistic framework, which probably explains the current temptation to turn to the language of eastern spiritualities, particularly Buddhists and Taoists. These spiritualities contain no theistic implications, no reference to a separate subjectivity: the *void* or the *nothing* they conjure up is thus better placed than Christianity's customary theological categories to express the pure experience of thought.

The void or nothing: these are extreme figures of the unlimited-undifferentiated, of the borderless uncentered whole, completely continuous and indeterminate, emerging with the insubstantial substance where phenomena converge and dissolve—we escape from appearances and the related belief in plural phenomena, as well as the illusion of our own separate existence. This is a mystical pole which, if we want to establish one outcome of this seminal trial of duplicated reality, is far from exhausted. There is also, however, an operative, positive pole. Indeed, we see it at work again in modern science, which clearly postulates the objectivity of phenomena, but simultaneously disqualifies any direct sensory observation of them, in favor of investigating the object's real properties, which it locates in the invisible.[55] If on the one hand science expels the invisible from the visible (occult causal agencies), on the other it accommodates the invisible in the visible in a profoundly original manner, by installing an invisible certainty about its order at the very heart of the world, more certain than the world's appearances. We are dealing here with a displacement and application of the formative division to the physical reality of things, where the categories of the non-differentiated (reduction to unity, continuity of being, the essential shared nature of phenomena, etc) play the role of regulative ideas, in the Kantian sense, at once unattainable, structuring and motivating. But this same schema is also at the basis of criticisms of science. Science will be justifiably charged with getting bogged down in the world's diversity, vainly pursuing determinations of what is and thus diverting us from the true task of thought, which is to grasp being as being—not being as it exhibits such-and-such a characteristic, but where all its components and determinations are reabsorbed and abolished, leaving only one basic mystery to be understood: namely, why there is something rather than nothing.

The basic philosophical notions arising from and sustained by this source are innumerable. Let us take as a passing example, the notion of *flesh* as used by Merleau-Ponty, which is merely another name for this sustaining nondifferentiation guaranteeing, behind the apparent differences and distinctions between things, the continuous living tissue of the world. This obviously does not disqualify them: they correspond to an authentic and ineliminable requirement of thought. However we would do better to recognize this requirement for what it is—a structural characteristic of our understanding—rather than continue to naively conform to it by monotonously reiterating this age-old concern of the human race. The real question is not that of being, but that of the internal constraints forcing us to present the question in this way. Why is there this structural division presenting all reality in two antagonistic aspects?

                                                                ·   ·   ·

The aesthetic experience seems to me amenable to a similar analysis, insofar as it can be related to a primordial source, which in turn attests the continuing existence of a relation to the world, a relation previously the basis of religious sentiment. Our capacity for emotion at the sight of things arises from a basic mode of inscription in being, which connects us with what used to be the meaning of the sacred for thousands of years. Here we are no longer dealing with our manner of thinking the profound nature of things, but of the way we receive their appearance, of the imaginary organization of our grasp of the world—of our imaginative rather than our intellective faculty.

There is no neutral relation to the real that would be a simple perceptual recording of data. Our engagement with things is pervaded and articulated by the imagination, and is for this reason occupied consubstantially by the imminent possibility of an aesthetic experience—that is, an experience of difference making this involvement irresistibly meaningful for us by showing it to us in an unfamiliar light, by presenting it as other, as opening onto an unknown mystery. This is an experience of difference which during the entire religious era does not appear as such, being completely absorbed in and encoded by the religious experience. It is the experience of the sacred, that is, of the divine presence in the world, of the fracturing closeness of the invisible in the middle of the visible. A *wholly other*, to use Rudolf Otto's expression, suddenly irrupts in the familiarity of things.[56] But beside this ordeal of breaking off, there is socialized ritualized otherness: the locus branded as other by divine law, the presence of god in the temple, the mystery of his presence in the sacrament, etc. The sacred is specifically the presence of absence, one could say, the sensory and palpable manifestation of what is normally hidden from the senses and protected from human grasp. And art, in the specific sense that we moderns understand it, is the continuation of the sacred by other means.

When the gods abandon the world, when they stop coming to notify us of their otherness to it, the world itself begins to appear other, to disclose an imaginary depth that becomes the object of a special quest, containing its purpose and referring only to itself. This is simply because the imaginary apprehension of the real, which previously constituted the anthropological support for religious activity, begins to operate for itself, independently of its previous contents. What was only a means in the general framework of understanding becomes a goal in itself. There thus appears an autonomous activity for exploring the sensory in all its registers and diverse modulations. At the center of its deployment lies an obsessive investigation of the fracturing of everyday life, of the internal transcendence of appearances, of the world being expressed as other to itself. I suspect this could account for western art's changing expressions and proliferating consumption, especially during its radicalization over the last two centuries. There is a wrenching away from routine everyday life: the vertigo of the musical abyss, the poignant heights of poetry, the frantic passion of novelistic intrigue, a dreamlike absorption into the image. But there is also the open-ended attempt to evoke the other deep inside the familiar: the increasingly amazing novelty of sounds, along with their fluctuating empty evocations, the unfathomable "hidden world" uncovered in the midst of a landscape seen a hundred times before, the impressionists' magic revelation of the deeply hidden truth of an inhabited landscape. And further along we encounter the extremely disconcerting obligation to see ourselves in a surreal landscape, where radical strangeness itself surprises us and reminds us of something that we shall never know and yet are sure of. Finally, there is representation that does not represent anything, but whose abstract interplay of lines and marks still manages to tell us about the world we live in, from outside it, and in its absence. From Balzac to Kafka, the revelation of the strange depths of a secret world lying beneath the surface of history and cities, right down to the pure evocation of an indecipherable speech and Proust's revival of the past—all these identify those moments we traverse without experiencing in the mirror of otherness, thus bringing them to life again for us.

This listing has no other purpose than to highlight the common inspiration and dynamics that reunite otherwise very different approaches. These approaches gravitate around our efforts to establish the world's dissimilarity and thus create an exclusive aspect through which the world addresses our imagination. This persistent heritage stems from the time when the world was populated by invisible forces. In order to properly orient ourselves, we must, at the cost of being rigidly methodical, manage to see the world as other, however spontaneously it is given to us. Therefore, alongside the constraint that makes us think that the world yields its truth by being grasped as a nondifferentiated unity, we must recognize the part played by another constraint which structures our imagination and condemns us to seek the world's beauty in the difference which ruptures the identity of its appearances. The world is to be reduced to sameness in the intelligible sphere, but revealed as other in the sensory sphere.

· · ·

The third and final form of experience establishing our continuity with religious man is the experience of the problem that we are for ourselves. Our apprehension of external reality is no longer structured by constraint, but the modalities of the question of being-a-subject. Indeed, if there is a general lesson to be drawn from this enormous body of devotions to something higher than oneself, and of speculations about the intangible reality we have put behind us, it is how difficult it is for humans to accept themselves. It is as if they can only be successfully apprehended somewhere between self-negation and self-affirmation, only by incessantly wavering between the search for their own self-effacement and the quest for a full and necessary self-identity.

We are not: we simultaneously, and in a contradictory manner, want both to be and not to be. So much so that the successive totality of religious techniques may be legitimately understood as having shaped the question opened at our very center by this partition which means taking responsibility for the self—and also *responding* to the question. Hence we see what separates us from the world of religions: we ourselves are uncomfortably experiencing as *problematic* what spiritual systems had presented to us as *resolved*. Hence the endless fascination that the tirelessly recapitulated memory of the worlds of faith holds for us. This encyclopedia of wisdoms holds an ambiguous mirror before us, because we see there our most obscure and pressing concerns, but in a well-regulated and clearly defined form. They therefore entice us, even though it is impossible for us to follow them. For although we desire the soothing effects of a resolution, we are not ready to renounce the freedom to question. Hence these syncretic ever-changing collages to which post-modern individuals are led by their peculiar concern with the sacred. The greater the degree of individualization, the greater the problem of the self, and hence the greater the potential interest in an age when one knew how to deal with this dreadful uncertainty that fills us. At the same time we are unable to subscribe wholeheartedly to any of these earlier belief systems, which would require losing our memory of what brought us to them. There are very good reasons for humans to convert to religion, left, right, and center, after its demise. But there are even better reasons for these conversions not to be profound or long-lasting, since humans cannot abandon the reasons that caused them to convert, which is what must happen if a conversion is to be properly effective. This to-ing and fro-ing and unstable compromise between belonging and withdrawal, between worshipping the problematic and choosing the solution, defines our age's specific religiosity—and is perhaps the best way for the religious to survive in a world without religion.

The entire history that I have presented as a process of reducing otherness can be reread from the viewpoint of a correlative loss of effective response to the divided subject. There is indeed no doubt that the savage mind's system of the origin's radical otherness and the institution of the unchangeable is at the same time the most thorough method possible for neutralizing the self. On the one hand, all are calmly assured of their *necessity* due to their strictly allocated role, their place, age, and sex, which place them in a preordained social framework. In other words, nothing in the system could lead them to ask the question: why me? What am I doing here? Personal contingency is thus neutralized. On the other hand, subjective difference is equally eliminated through the repetitive immobility of "works and days." In an order considered totally sacrosanct, nothing forces you to accept divergence from your own position, the separation of the self involved in innovation. The order of things does not come from you; all you have to do is piously renew the order without raising the issue of your difference from it. Birth and death also prove to have been incomparably easier through this order. You do not have to jump onto the bandwagon of a world where change harshly reminds you of the contingency of the moment you have just entered—why me *now*? Within a world that constantly remains the same, the moment of birth is immaterial: what we would otherwise have experienced remains unchanged. Similarly, the moment of death is not a passage where your undertakings are clearly gratuitous with regard to the world's order, which will be experienced differently by others. Things will continue to be done in a similar way by your peers, as fully as you were able to do it during your shift among the living. We need not look further for the sources of humans' extraordinary attraction to immobility, conformity, and routine: it is the subjective position they allow which makes them so extremely attractive. It is no coincidence that we can recognize something reminiscent of the age-old passion for the immutable, but taken to its extremes, in so-called "autistic" children where the course of subjective impoverishment of the self reaches its ultimate form. If we add to primitive organization of the inviolable this ultimate means of neutralizing personal contingency, a means that supplies the magical understanding of events and of evil, then we are confronted with a perfect system for both "necessitating" and "desubjectivating" the self. A manner of being-a-self beyond the question of the subject. This perhaps goes some way to explaining the enormous *duree* of this mode of social institution, the depth of its ties and its amazing ability to endure.

On the other hand, as soon as we depart from the system of the foundation's absolute otherness, the problem of assuming responsibility for the self appears in two forms: there is both the need to justify the self, and the temptation to dissolve it. There is the will of the gods, which justifies your being, and the mystical appeal to fuse with and disappear into God. There is the promise of eternal life, but also the imperative of renunciation, of self-sacrifice, of forgetting the self. We must pay attention to the successive responses made to the constituting contradiction of being-a-subject and show how the subject's activity becomes more intense as religious exteriority declines. Religion's decline is paid for by the difficulty of being-a-self. Post-religious society is also society where the question of madness and everyone's inner unease experiences unprecedented growth. This society is psychologically draining for individuals, since it no longer protects or supports them when they are constantly faced with the questions: why me? Why was I born now when nobody expected me? What is expected of me? What am I to do with my life, when I alone am to make the decision? Will I ever be like the others? Why has this illness, accident, rejection happened to me? What is the use of having lived if you must disappear without a trace? From now on we are destined to live openly and in the anguish from which the gods had spared us since the beginning of the human venture. Each of us must work out our own responses. For example, in psychosis there is the flight between exaltation and depression, between the paranoid certainty of being the sole center and the schizophrenic effort to obliterate the self as self. But there are also collective responses, and odds are they will increase. For instance, in the form of techniques of relating to the self, the most typical example being psychoanalytic practice with its remarkable inner oscillation and hesitation between restoring the subject and dethroning it (Lacan), which is scarcely imaginable outside our clearly defined cultural moment. Similarly, we have had twenty years of avowed hatred of the subject, producing a cult of its disappearance, only to find ourselves participating in its unrestrained reappearance and narcissistic rehabilitation. Perhaps we will never find a true balance between self-love that wishes to exclude all else and the desire to abolish the self, between absolute being and being-as-nothingness. Such is the daily throbbing pain that no sacral opiate can blot out: the merciless contradictory desire inherent in the very reality of being a subject.

1. I have developed my here schematically presented views on "primeval religion" in: "Politique et societe: La lecon des sauvages," *Textures*, nos. 10–11 (1975): 57–86, nos. 12–13 (1975): 67–105; "La dette du sens et les racines de l'Etat: Politique de la religion primitive," *Libre*, no. 2 (1977): 5–43.

2. For a useful presentation of the classic problematic, cf. Robert N. Bellah, "Religious Evolution," in *Beyond Belief: Essays on Religion in a Post-Traditional World* (New York: Harper & Row, 1970), pp. 20–50.

3. This occurs by impersonally incarnating in the flesh of every member, through initiation marks, the unavoidable submission to the law of ancestors and of the whole. Cf. Pierre Clastres, "Torture in Primitive Societies," in *Society Against the State*, trans. R. Hurley and A. Stein (New York: Zone Books, 1987).

4. Karl Jaspers, *The Origin and Goal of History*, trans. Michael Bulock (New Haven: Yale University Press, 1953). For further clarification cf. Shmuel N. Eisenstadt, "The Axial Age: The Emergence of Transcendental Visions and the Rise of the Clerics," *Archives europeennes de sociologie*, 23, no. 2 (1982): 294–314.

5. This puts me at odds with any defense of the "Genius of paganism" such as Marc Auge's. Cf. Marc Auge, *Genie du Paganisme* (Paris: Gallimard, 1982).

6. Since I am dealing here with two religious figures that specifically raise the problem, namely dualism and the separated gnostic god, it seems opportune to emphasize the gap between the level of explicit discourse and the structure implied here. We are dealing with belief systems that appeared en masse under the name of dualism or otherness: a cosmic struggle of Good and Evil or the true God's complete strangeness to our world of shadows (I am treating these as pure opposites though in reality they are usually combined). From the viewpoint of the ultimate organization of being they postulate, these belief-systems still depend on a unitarian ontology.

This is obvious in the case of a strict dualism. The merciless war waged between darkness and light presupposes their appearance within the same world; their division into two is a version of ontological unity. It is less obvious in the case of gnosticism, whose infinitely remote God seems at first glance to be much more other than orthodox Christianity's absolute subject. Yet true duality comes about through the latter, as the human world gains autonomy, while gnosticism continues to find its origins in a hierarchical understanding which, metaphysically speaking, is ultimately based on the continuity of the orders of reality. The entire hierarchy of realities becomes *one* when seen from the viewpoint of the supreme principle and its suprapersonal absolute, both of which can be accessed by returning through their emanations. The discourse of the other, of cosmic division, of the beyond of being and the divine unknown, have an ontologically identical structure. The flourishing spiritual tradition emerging here is of some interest, in that it both builds a bridge with Eastern spiritualities and allows us to pinpoint Western divergences from them. This tradition, ranging from Manicheism to mystical hermeticism, including the millenarian heresy or Catharism, will shadow this divergence from its birth up to its most modern expression and continually renews itself in response to each significant advance in separating the visible from the invisible. The history of the long hesitation between these two paths most clearly displays the uniqueness of our history and should be reconstructed.

7. To be precise: a *metaphysically closed* world is a physically infinite one. The ontological closing of the human sphere goes hand in hand with its physical opening up. The infinite is both the instrument and the milieu of closure: wherever we go, however far thought may take us, we will always be within the physical universe. In other words, the infinite is our prison, which is the surest testimony to the impossibility of overcoming the limits of the here-below. The infinite is needed to put its seal on the closing of this order on itself.

8. In line with my general approach I have consciously avoided the rationalist philosophical aporias (from Descartes to Hegel) relating to the problematic of the divine subject's accessibility in the objective scheme of things. I will explain why the process I am presenting in a linear fashion has, for those wanting to give it a theoretical expression, shown itself historically as a contradictory oscillation between immanence and transcendence. It seems a choice must be made between perfectly understanding the world, which eliminates divine separation, or making god different, which reintroduces a vestige of unintelligibility (the creation of eternal truths in Descartes). I believe this difficulty is related to the theological heritage of the participation of the visible and the invisible, which continues to inform the classical theory of knowledge, particularly in the form of an intellectual intuition (or in its reconstructed equivalent: the self-apprehension of the spirit). This tension constitutes the true background of the Kantian solution and shows the extent of its scope and meaning. Kant is the first to think rigorously and thoroughly in terms of ontological dualism while others neutralize the most productive trends in their thought by ultimately reintroducing the viewpoint of the One.

9. For a recent example see the penetrating analyses by Augustin Berque concerning the "japanese model." Cf. *Le Japon, gestion de l'espace et changement social* (Paris: Flammarion, 1976), and *Vivre l'espace au Japon* (Paris: P.U.F., 1982).

10. Despotism is not only the "archetype" of the modern machine, as Lewis Mumford maintains, but also its complete opposite. The inversion is as important as the relationship. Cf. Lewis Mumford, *The Myth of the Machine* (N.Y: Harcourt, Brace, Jovanovich, 1973), particularly Vol. 1, Chapter 9, "The Model of the Megamachine."

11. Here I agree with the conclusions of Jean Baechler: "La nourriture des hommes. Essai sur le neolithique," *Archives europeennes de sociologie*, 23 (1982): 241–93. For a critical analysis of the notion of subsistence economy I refer the reader to the work of Marshall Sahlins, *Stone Age Economics* (Chicago: Aldine-

Atherton, 1972) and to the study by Jacques Lizot, "Economie primitive et sub-sistance. Essai sur le travail et l'alienation chez les Yanomani," *Libre*, no. 4 (1978).

12. I am here considering the Reformation more in light of its original inspiration than its ultimate doctrinal expression. I am deliberately focussing on its main impulse, namely its challenge to mediation within a world organized by spiritual union. Far from reaching its logical conclusion, this impulse compromised itself on every major issue affecting the structural link between the two realms and did so in full compliance with the Reformers' intentions. Whether it concerned the doctrine of the Incarnation itself, the conception of the ecclesial bond, or the idea of the Eucharist, the balances established by Luther, Zwingli, or Calvin were far from identical and even varied within each of their doctrines according to the theme. Rejecting transubstantiation led to consubstantiation in Luther, substantiation in Calvin, and symbol in Zwingli—and even here there was a great gap between denying Christ's full presence and completely abolishing it. Similarly, affirming the capacity to be an individual was inseparable from affirming God's power over humans. On the one hand was the rock of pure faith and subjective certainty, but on the other there was no free will; the believer's internal autonomy was won at the price of subservience reinforced by the doctrine of predestination and grace. Humans were alone before God, but depended on him more than ever. Speaking more generally, the Reformation should be conceived as renewing and redefining the compromise running through Christian history. It marked a decisive change by making the logic of otherness explicit, which would in turn make the compromise increasingly difficult, and eventually impossible, to maintain. But it still continued to operate along the same lines and perpetuated the same framework.

13. This, of course, does not mean there was philosophical unanimity and single-mindedness in Islamic society. Once the Koran's message had been properly received, a variety of schools and interpretations flourished—and we can correctly speak of Islamic pluralism. Put simply, agreement had to be reached on the meaning and object of interpretation. It was not concerned with the substance of revelation itself, and the real content of God's will. In Islam, there was no doubting that "The Koran is God's eternal word"; the disputes were about how we should adapt ourselves to this indivisible block of law and meaning. Christianity was the reverse of this. In Islam we indisputably had God's direct expression, whereas Christ's mediation (in turn mediated by the gospels) created uncertainty about ultimate truth. For the same reason this also meant that Islam had no orthodox authority whereas Christianity required an apparatus for imposing dogma.

The case of Shiism inside Islam shows the effects of reintroducing even restricted hermeneutic mediation. Henry Corbin speaks of an "equidistance" between "the legalism of a purely external legalitarian religion, and the implications contained within the Christian idea of divine incarnation," that is, the Church and its doctrinal authority. The extension of the Prophet's revelation into the system of Imams, the idea of the Koran's hidden meaning, and the demand for an esoteric interpretation, introduced operational and recruitment norms distinctly different from Sunni orthodoxy, as well as conditions for a religious life marked by turmoil and sectarian differences. By differences, I mean not only philosophical or ritualistic variation, or even the internal deviation of the mystical path (Sufism) but secession relating to the very understanding of the divine. Unlike Christian heterodoxy, Islamic heterodoxy respects the literal meaning of God's word and debates its esoteric significance, rather than believing it contains a hidden wisdom. See for example, Henry Corbin, *En Islam iranien*, Vol. 1, *Le shi'isme duodecimain* (Paris: Gallimard, 1971); Henri Laoust, *Les Schismes de l'Islam* (Paris: Payot, 1975).

14. The internal history of monasticism should be reexamined in this light, particularly the interpretations of St. Benedict's code concerning the proper way to link the active and contemplative life. In this context, the example of the Cistercian reform at the beginning of the twelfth century comes to mind. We might say that in the two major rivals, Cluny and Citeaux, were embodied the two options for the coexistence of the two realms, either hierarchical intermeshing or egalitarian duality. The re-hierarchization at Cluny between heaven and earth freed the monks from material tasks to do what was essential, namely, to pray. But this was done, even if by servile hands, to enhance our terrestrial abode. On the other hand, the Cistercians tried to reunite the different levels of the community's work so that the hiatus between heaven and earth and the accompanying constraint to attain the beyond by actively enhancing the value of the here-below, was taken into account. This was disguised as a return to natural purity when it was really a major advance in exploiting the potential de-hierarchization inscribed in the Christian nucleus. On the opposition of the two models, cf., for example, Georges Duby, "Le monachisme et l'economie rurale," in his *Homme et structures du Moyen Age* (Paris: Mouton, 1973).

15. The content of this transition is neatly summarized by Herbert Luthy:

> The edifice of the Catholic Church rests on separating the functions of "those who pray" from "those who suffer." In the hierarchy of values embodied in its own hierarchy, sanctity, meditation and charity are placed much higher than utilitarian work, which is necessary for the needs of the body, but not for the salvation of the soul. Like the other Reformers, but exceeding them in radicalism, Calvin destroyed this hierarchy of functions and virtues in order to bring them all together into the indissolubly unified Christian life required of every individual: the duty of all Christians is to pray, read, and meditate on the word of God, to gain his support, to cater for the needs of their families, to live a holy, that is, an austere and industrious life, and further, if God bestows this distinction, to fight and be a martyr for the faith. In short, it means placing the meditative and active life side by side, and fighting in accordance with their current strength and state of grace. One can never do without the other, and each is on the same level as the other: "To work is to pray." There can be no compromise with this absolute requirement. (*Le Passe present* [Monaco: Editions du Rocher, 1965], p. 63.)

16. Pierre Chaunu, *Histoire, science sociale: La duree, l'espace et l'homme a l'epoque moderne* (Paris: S.E.D.E.S., 1974); and *Le Temps des Reformes: La crise de la chretiente* (Paris: Fayard, 1975).

17. I have borrowed this expression from Robert Fossier, *Enfance de l'Europe, X–XII siecle*, Vol. 1, *L'homme et son espace* (Paris: P.U.F, 1982).

18. Cf., for example, Guy Fourquin, "Le temps de croissance," in *Histoire de la France rurale*, Vol. 1, *La formation des campagnes francaises des origines au XIV siecle* (Paris: Editions du Seuil, 1975); Robert Fossier, *Enfance de l'Europe*, Vol. 2, *La revolution de l'economie*. On the basic issues, see the suggestive remarks by Pierre Chaunu in *La Memoire et le sacre* (Paris: Calmann-Levy, 1978), pp. 128–33.

19. I am using the expression of E. Le Roy Ladurie, which is the title of the opening essay in his book *Le Territoire de l'historien*, Vol. 2 (Paris: Gallimard, 1978).

20. At this point I would refer the reader to the second part of my article "Des deux corps du roi au pouvoir sans corps. Christianisme et politique," *Le Debat*, no. 15 (Sept.–Oct. 1981).

21. Benjamin Constant, *De la religion consideree dans sa source, ses formes et ses developpements* (Paris, 1824–31), 5 vols., Vol. 1, Chap. 1, "Du sentiment religieux." One of the best books on the subject and undeservedly forgotten.

22. Without listing either the classic or recent discussions of writers such as A. Lods, E. Dhorme, H. Ringgren, R. de Vaux, or A. Caquot, I will mention, from a vast bibliography, only a few works that specifically deal with my basic concern, the invention and development of monotheism: Yehezkel Kaufmann, *Connaitre la Bible*, French trans. (Paris: P.U.F., 1970); William F. Albright, *From the Stone Age to Christianity* (Baltimore: Johns Hopkins University Press, 1957); Theophile J. Meek, *Hebrew Origins* (New York: Peter Smith, 1960). Special mention should be made of the study of Jean Bottero, "Le message universel de la Bible," in *Verite et poesie de la bible* (Paris: Hatier, 1969), pp. 15–73. It offers in a concise form the most perceptive, reliable, and appropriate analysis one could hope for.

23. Recently, for example, by H.W.F. Saggs, *The Encounter with the Divine in Mesopotamia and Israel* (London: The Athlone Press, 1978).

24. I am referring in particular to the discussion about the propositions put forward at the beginning of the century by J. H. Breasted, *A History of Egypt* (London: Hodder and Stoughton, 1909), and *The Dawn of Conscience* (New York: Charles Scribners' Sons, 1933), and taken up by Freud in *Moses and Monotheism*, trans. K. Jones (New York: Vintage Books, 1939).

25. This is what happens in a consistent dualism. But there are all sorts of possible intermediate positions that blend relative dualism with a version of monotheism, which seems to have been what Zarathustra himself did (Paul Du Breuil, *Zarathoustra et la transfiguration du monde* (Paris: Payot, 1978). There is a struggle between the two principles in space-time, but the universal sovereign reigns above them in his uncontested superiority. Every gnosis begins with this division. I raise this point because recent research has reopened the problem of relations between Persian spiritual notions and the monotheistic formulations of post-exilic Judaism. So I will reiterate both the legitimacy and limitations of the comparison. The divine's separation from creation and his consequent direct all-powerful involvement at every stage was structurally quite different from the ultimately superior nature of Ahura Mazda at the top of a hierarchy of realities

and entities united by their very oppositions within a single all-inclusive ultimate
reality. Both approaches have parallel causes but one of them (Zoroastrianism)
remained at the level of an internal reform of the previous overlap of the visible
and the invisible, while the other (Yahvism) was from the outset established in a
sphere outside the previous overlap (even if only to restore it later to some extent).

26. We can recognize, from another angle, the features elicited by Max Weber
to define Israelite prophecy in *Ancient Judaism*, ed. and trans. H. H. Gerth and
D. Martindale (New York: The Free Press, 1952), pp. 267–335. Regarding the
character of prophets: Weber says they were "political demagogues" and not pro-
fessional oracles. They were independent men who addressed the people on their
own initiative based on a strictly individual experience, in an atmosphere of solitude and incomprehension. Although he was inspired, the prophet was still an
ordinary man; he did not place himself above the common ethical norm by his
asceticism, he did not sketch out a path of withdrawal from this world and mystical participation in the divine. Nor did he present himself as a saint or as a saviour called on to guide a community of followers gathered around him. This is
because, from the perspective of preserving the prophetic message, this withdrawal only made sense in a context of addressing the people as a whole and
with a purely ethical aim in mind: collective obedience to Yahveh's commandments in this world. "The prophets stood in the midst of their people and were
interested in the fate of its political community" (p. 299). They did not give any
answers to the metaphysical enigma of the universe; they did not claim to bring
a new idea of God and his wishes. Instead, they appealed exclusively to Israel's
faith in its God and generally to the fulfillment of the law he had given, ignorance of which was fatal to Israel. They were neither wise men, nor salvation specialists nor religious reformers, but rather conformist dissidents. To my mind
these are all unique characteristics, which can only be explained by the mechanism of Mosaic creativity, the prophets' intervention being a tightly controlled
use of this mechanism.

27. Helene Clastres, *The Land-Without-Evil: Tupi-Guarini Prophetism*, trans.
J. G. Brovender (Chicago: University of Illinois Press, 1995).

28. The question of Jesus' self-consciousness and self- presentation as Messiah, and the accompanying ambiguities, would require a detailed exposition in
itself. We would have to reconstruct the complex interaction caused by: his self-
identification with and differentiation from the book of David and esoteric Judaism's use of the term "The Son of Man"; the ambiguity between being proclaimed God's son and claiming the immediate status of a Messiah; his inscription
in a context marked by the struggle of the zealots (from whom he distinguished
himself while not disavowing them). On all these matters, cf., for example, Oscar
Cullmann, *Christology of the New Testament*, trans. Shirley C. Guthrie and
Charles A. Hall (Westminster: John Knox, 1980). It could be said that Jesus was
a deferred Messiah. As P. Lamarche aptly remarks in his historical introduction
to the book by J. Liebaert, *L'Incarnation* (Paris: Editions du Cerf, 1966), he had
recourse to the notion, while temporally distancing himself from it. His time had
not yet come. "While not repudiating the title, he did not want it for now." The
fulfillment of his messianic status was put off until after his death and resurrection. He truly became the Messiah by being the complete opposite of a Messiah.

All these ambiguities and discrepancies only make sense within a general logic of inversion making Jesus a Messiah diametrically opposite the Messiah.

29. I would like to quote more fully the declaration of Chalcedon (451): "We all with one voice confess our Lord Jesus Christ, one and the same Son, the same perfect in Godhead, the same perfect in manhood, truly God and truly man, the same consisting of a reasonable soul and body, of one substance with the Father as touching the Godhead, the same of one substance with us as touching the manhood; like us in all things apart from sin; begotten of the Father before the ages as touching the Godhead, the same in the last days, for us and for our salvation, born from the Virgin Mary, the *Theotokos*, as touching the manhood, one and the same Christ, Son, Lord, Only-begotten, to be acknowledged in two natures without confusion, without change, without division, without separation; the distinction of natures being in no way abolished because of the union, but rather the characteristic property of each nature being preserved, and concurring into one Person and one subsistence." *Creeds, Councils and Controversies: Documents Illustrating the History of the Church, AD* 337–461, ed. J. Stevenson, revised by W.H.C. Frend (London: SPCK, 1989), pp. 352–53.

30. This new twofold requirement of interiority and universality did not lead to an imposed rejection of habits and customs. On the contrary, outward respect for tribal customs was the first sign of wisdom, the important thing being to know what to retain of them given their relativity. But a thus conceived, ostensible adherence to traditional customs ruined them by basing these customs on what was most contrary to them, an inner distance from them. Such conformism destroyed the base to which it conformed. We must keep this in mind if we wish to appreciate the precise role of successive revivals of Stoicism in the European tradition. This sort of submission was more relentlessly corrosive than any rebellion.

31. Louis Dumont, "The Christian Beginnings: From the Outworldly Individual to the Individual-in-the-world," *Essays on Individualism* (Chicago: University of Chicago Press, 1986), pp. 23–59. Ernst Troeltsch, *The Social Teaching of the Churches* (Westminster: John Knox, 1992). On Troeltsch cf. the recent book by Jean Seguy, *Christianisme et societe* (Paris: Editions du Cerf, 1980).

32. This is no doubt why the problem of the future life acquired such importance in Christianity. The idea of, and hope for, the other life was not only valued as a paradigm of the separation of the two natures. It took the form of a solution to the constituting aporia, namely, how to tear yourself away from a world you cannot leave.

33. This brings to mind Pope Gelasius' version, in 494, of Church-State relations. Its ambiguity posed the question of knowing how far a hierarchically coherent and stable vision of the relations between the authority of the beyond and that of the here-below was possible within a Christian framework. On the one hand it undoubtedly arose from the idea of making such an attempt. "There are mainly two things by which this world is governed: the sacred authority of the pontiffs' and the royal power. . ." Quoted in F. Dvornik, "Pope Gelasius and Emperor Anastasius I," *Byzantinische Zeitschrift* 44, Munich, 1951, p. 112. The man of God is higher in higher (spiritual) matters, but lower in lower (temporal) matters: the formula appears to be that of the strictest hierarchical partition and in-

terlocking, and Dumont does not hesitate to draw a parallel with Vedic India (see his remarks in *Essays on individualism*, pp. 45–52). On the other hand the fact remains that in the type of superiority claimed by Gelasius for the pope lay the germ of something other than this balanced complementarity—"priests carry a weight all the greater as they must render an account to the Lord even for kings before the divine Judgment," in Dvornik, op. cit., pp. 112–113. Not without reason was the discourse later referred to by proponents of theocracy. It is perhaps true that this is not done as a function of its direct import but rather as a function of the Christian way of really understanding the structural link between the spiritual and the temporal, where unequivocal absorption and subordination, along with the huge contradictions they open up, tended to basically supersede their well-ordered coexistence. Any "hierarchical complementarity" at the heart of a Christian order could only exist in opposition to the long-term tendencies of the latter's professed principles. If we assume that Gelasius correctly interpreted the hierarchical spirit, his successors' "misinterpretation," amounting to its inversion, was equally correct.

34. ". . . before the advent of Christ there existed men who were kings and priests all in one, in a pre-figurative sense, yet in actual reality. Sacred history (Gen. XIV) records that such was Saint Melchisedech. But as the Devil, who always tyrannically arrogates to himself what is proper to divine worship, has copied this, the pagan Emperors had themselves called Supreme Pontiffs. But when the One had come who was truly king and Pontiff, then no Emperor adopted the name of Pontiff and no Pontiff claimed the supreme dignity of the king, although as His members, that is of the true King and Pontiff, they are said to have, in participation of His nature, obtained in a splendid way both, thanks to His sacred generosity, so that they are called a kingly and priestly race. But he has remembered human frailty and by a marvellous dispensation has regulated what would serve the salvation of His own by keeping the offices of the two powers by distinctive functions and dignity." In Dvornik, op. cit. p. 114. On these texts, see in particular the studies of F. Dvornik, *Early Christian and Byzantine Political Philosophy: Origins and Background* (Washington, DC: N.p., 1966).

35. A good example of this is given by Caspary's study on Origen's political theology and his exegetical method, based around the theme of the "two swords." Cf. G. E. Caspary, *Politics and Exegesis, Origen and the Two Swords* (Berkeley: University of California Press, 1979).

36. At the moment I am only considering the case of Christianity, but the analysis applies equally to Judaism. The example of Philo of Alexandria attests that this was a general trait of the monotheistic faith.

37. Thanks to a fascinating book by Jacques Gernet, *China and the Christian Impact: A Conflict of Cultures*, trans. Janet Lloyd (Cambridge: Cambridge University Press, 1986), we can broaden the comparison I have made between Greek and Christian thought to include Chinese thought. This is of crucial importance to my thesis. When talking about Chinese thought, are we, as Gernet claims, dealing with "another type of thought which has its own articulations and is radically original," one which is therefore completely foreign to our own and has no point of contact with it inasmuch as it rejects oppositions "which have played a fundamental role in Western thought ever since the Greeks: being and becoming,

the intelligible and the sensible, the spiritual and the corporeal . . ."(p. 208)? I do not think so, and I believe it would be possible to show that the characteristics Gernet has isolated as constituting Chinese thought originate from a different use of the same fundamental potentialities to which Christian thought entrusted itself. The break with mythical thought was similar: Chinese thought, like Greek thought, gathered together and reassembled the source of all things into one unique principle. But Greek thought tended (without pushing it to its ultimate conclusion) to separate this ordering principle and reunite it separately from sensory reality. Chinese thought did not do this. It placed the principle in the midst of things. And as a result it considered it to be a vacuum. In the first case, we are led to the representation of a finite cosmos, closed in on itself. In the second case, we are led, by similar logical constraints, to the opposite representation of a central "enormous vacuum" of unspecified dimensions and duration. What we should establish is how the "impersonal heavens," the finite cosmos along with the intelligible heavens and the creator god, are thought to be conceptual schemas with a common root, whose correspondence with socially and historically defined organizations can be specified, along with precise rules of transformation allowing us to pass from one to the other.

38. Here J.-P. Vernant remains quite convincing. Cf. *The Origins of Greek Thought* (New York: Cornell University Press, 1982).

39. In another sense, a dogma like the Trinity was a typical outcome of combining the Christian faith's fundamental elements with the general framework of Greek thought. The Trinity completely offsets the duality acknowledged in the Incarnation. I should not have to point out that the Trinity only gained its significance through its implicit goal of overcoming the yawning gap between the Father and the Son. A third term was indispensable for permanently reinstating them, along with heaven and earth, into a unique scale of being.

40. This union of opposites provided room for "popular beliefs" such as miracles, magical influences and correspondences, the cult of intercession, devotions to every supposed materialization of the invisible in the visible, with scarcely any of orthodoxy's boundaries. It was not doctrinal relaxation or tolerance, but a feature of the system. When the paramount doctrine was the overlapping of heaven and earth's hierarchies, there could be no clear separation of good beliefs and "pagan superstitions." Whether they were accepted or not, the latter could only be seen as continuous with the most secure articles of dogma.

41. I have made particular use of the following: Y. Congar, *L'Ecclesiologie du haut Moyen Age* (Paris: Editions du Cerf, 1968), and *L'Eglise de Saint Augustin a l'epoque moderne* (Paris: Editions du Cerf, 1970); R. W. Southern, *Western Society and the Church in the Middle Ages* (London: Penguin, 1970); W. Ullmann, *The Growth of Papal Government in the Middle Ages* (London: Methuen, 1955), and *Principles of Government and Politics in the Middle Ages* (London: Methuen, 1961). The definitive perspective on the basic issues is still that provided by H.-X. Arquilliere, *L'Augustinisme politique: Essai sur la formation des theories politiques du Moyen Age* (Paris: Vrin, 1972), and *Saint Gregory VII: Essai sur sa conception du pouvoir pontificale* (Paris: Vrin, 1934).

42. I am using the term proposed by H.-X. Arquilliere, *L'Augustinisme politique*. The term has been disputed by Yves Congar, *L'Ecclesiologie du haut*

Moyen Age, pp. 273–74. He similarly rejects those of "theocracy" and "hierocracy" in concluding: "So I will renounce the search for a meaningful label and simply speak of a unifying ideal, of a unique and basically religious, even soteriological and supernatural, aim."

43. Cf. supra, Chapter 4, subsection entitled "The Structure of Terrestrial Integrity." One cannot fail to be struck by the coincidence of this expansionary phase at the end of the tenth and beginning of the eleventh centuries, with orthodox and heterodox trends in religious consciousness. Spirituality which, since the Carolingians, was strongly centered on God the Father and the political models of the Old Testament, shifted to a spirituality situated within the framework of monastic fervor, whose axis was the Son of the New Testament. This spirituality, essential to the revival of pacifistic values, was a legitimate interpretation of faith. It should not surprise us that activating the religion of Incarnation went hand in hand with enhancing the world's value, even if ambiguously, by fleeing it. If we admit the correlation, we can understand why this shift took place in opposition to the sudden appearance of a heresy systematically denying the Incarnation and, through it, the flesh. I am tempted to add that it is usually precisely when a religion teaching terrestrial difference takes shape, that we see the return of a radical salvation religion, where the extreme devaluation of the herebelow sanctions the prospect of withdrawing from its futility and reuniting with God. On the one hand, Christ's kingdom shakes the harmony between heaven and earth promised by the imperial (and biblical) model of the conquering god and the sovereign-priest; on the other, the affirmation of the One reemerges in a mystical and gnostic form. On the millenarian heresy, see the studies of Huguette Taviani, "Naissance d'une heresie en Italie du Nord au XIe siecle," *Annales E.S.C.*, no. 5 (1974); "Le mariage dans l'heresie de l'an Mil," *Annales E.S.C.*, no. 6 (1977); "Du refus au defi: Essai sur la psychologie heretique au debut du XIe siecle en Occident," *Etudes sur la sensibilite au Moyen Age*, Actes du 102E Congres national des societes savantes (1977), (Paris, 1979); Georges Duby's introduction to his *The Three Orders: Feudal Society Imagined* (Chicago: University of Chicago Press, 1980), which is put into perspective by Jean-Pierre Poly and Eric Bournazel in *The Feudal Transformation*, 900–1200, trans. Caroline Higgitt (New York: Holmes and Meier, 1991).

44. Ernst Kantorowicz, *Frederick the Second*, trans. E. O. Lorimer (New York: Richard R. Smith, 1931); *The King's Two Bodies: A Study in Medieval Political Theology* (Princeton: Princeton University Press, 1957), pp. 97–143, and my commentary, "Des deux corps du roi au pouvoir sans corps. Christianisme et politique," *Le Debat*, nos. 14 and 15 (July–Sept. 1981).

45. Here I am following an observation made by Alain Clement, to which I will add this remark: due to the specific features of their history and geography, Americans have avoided what is probably one of the most deeply destabilizing experiences for religious consciousness, one that was quite familiar to Europeans along with the effects of subsequent decentering due to the polycentrism of their space. I refer to the experience of conflict involving a religious legitimacy which at one extreme means religious wars, as well as patriotic mobilizations glorified by the Church, versus the simple obligation to coexist with an enemy who has been chosen by God just as much as you have. We must also consider American

"isolationism" as an important precondition for the vitality of religious sentiment there—the fact of not having had to come repeatedly to terms with the shock of an equal and symmetrical claim to divine election. Their isolationism was all the more secure given that it was pluralist and contained its own dose of relativism. And once it became an integral part of the international scene, the global enemy proved to profess atheism . . .

46. Jean Delumeau, *Sin and Fear: The Emergence of a Western Guilt Culture*, 13th–18th Century, trans. Eric Nicholson (New York: St. Martin's, 1990). I am focusing on the epicenter of what Jean Delumeau looked at over a long period.

47. I am using the title of the outstanding book by Roger Mercier, *La Rehabilitation de la nature humaine* (1700–1750) (Villemomble: Editions "La Balance," 1960).

48. In relation to crime and madness, crime alone, suicide and then sexual perversions. For a starting point for these discussions, cf. Gladys Swain, "D'une rupture dans l'abord de la folie," *Libre*, no. 2 (1977), and "L'aliene entre le medecin et la philosophie," *Perspectives psychiatriques*, 1, no. 65 (1978).

49. On this point I take the liberty of referring to the analysis I and Gladys Swain proposed in *La Pratique de l'esprit humaine* (Paris: Gallimard, 1980), in particular pp. 384–412, "La societe des individus et l'institution de la parole."

50. For a particularly suggestive historical sketch of this major switch of organizing temporality in the modern West, see Krzysztof Pomian, "La crise de l'avenir," *Le Debat*, no. 7 (1980), as well as *L'Ordre du temps* (Paris: Gallimard, 1984), pp. 291–308, "Orientation vers l'avenir et dilation du temps."

51. On all this, cf. the classic exposition by Oscar Cullmann, *Christ and Time: The Primitive Christian Conception of Time and History*, trans. F. U. Filson (New York: Gordon Press, 1977).

52. Today the long-term trend is inconsistent with the reality of the moment. Hence the genuine nature of the "crisis of the future" that present uncertainty about the means and ends of the School. It is due to the perception of the relative antinomy discovered between two sets of requirements: individuals' concern for self-fulfillment in the present, which has become the short-term determining factor; and the imperative to prepare them for the future, which constitutes the most influential long-term factor determining the educational question in our societies. The crisis is not about our representation of the future but our obligation toward it.

53. I have deliberately maintained a view of democratic development that excludes it from logically extending into totalitarianism. My analysis actually challenges the idea of an omnipresent structural possibility of totalitarianism within contemporary societies while allowing us to specify the circumstantial nature of totalitarianism and reexamine it from three angles: (1) from the viewpoint of its precise historic moment: the phase represented by the *age of ideology* intermediate between extrinsic determination (by religious legitimation) and intrinsic determination (by projection into the future); (2) from the viewpoint of the internal articulation of its constituents and its contradictory alliance between the old and the new, between archaic aims (the desire for total awareness and ultimate coincidence with the collective order's true principle) and modern resources (the very bearers of the democratic unconscious); (3) from the viewpoint of its location: the

type of societies where it asserts itself, the historical basis of its deep-rootedness (in relation to the democracies' deep-rootedness) and the specific combination of circumstances behind it (the transition from empire to nation). This will be the subject of a forthcoming work.

54. Generally speaking, the history of relations between society and State since the seventeenth century should be rewritten in terms of cycles, where a phase in which the State shaped and set limits was followed by one where the civil sphere was liberated and autonomized. This was made possible by the social space's stability, homogeneity, and legibility created by the political machine's voluntarist influence: we cannot overestimate the territorial monarchies' role in the appearance of the self-regulated market. But liberating the social initiatives created the space and the demand for the State to intervene and reconstruct at a higher level. We should not let the process's cyclical nature and conflictual appearance conceal the deep interdependence and cooperation of its two poles. This point clearly emerged in regard to the transition from seventeenth-century Statism to eighteenth-century Liberalism in Western Europe, as seen in the comparative study by Marc Raeff, *The Well-Ordered State: Social and Institutional Change Through Law in the Germanies and Russia,* 1600–1800 (New Haven: Yale University Press, 1983).

55. On this fundamental transition from direct to indirect knowledge, along with the transfer of the invisible that it involved, cf. Krzysztof Pomian, "Natura, storia, conoscenza," *Enciclopedia Einaudi,* Vol. 15 (Turin, 1982).

56. Rudolf Otto, *The Idea of the Holy* (London: Oxford University Press, 1923).

Bibliography

Albright, William F. *From the Stone Age to Christianity*. Baltimore: Johns Hopkins University Press, 1957.

Arquilliere, H.-X. *L'Augustinisme politique: Essai sur la formation des theories politiques du Moyen Age*. Paris: Vrin, 1972.

———. *Saint Gregory VII: Essai sur sa conception du pouvoir pontificale*. Paris: Vrin, 1934.

Auge, Marc. *Genie du Paganisme*. Paris: Gallimard, 1982.

Baechler, Jean. "La nourriture des hommes. Essai sur le neolithique." *Archives europeennes de sociologie*, 23 (1982): 241–93.

Bellah, Robert N. "Religious Evolution." In *Beyond Belief: Essays on Religion in a Post-Traditional World*. New York: Harper & Row, 1970, pp. 20–50.

Berque, Augustin. *Le Japon, gestion de l'espace et changement social*. Paris: Flammarion, 1976.

———. *Vivre l'espace au Japon*. Paris: P.U.F., 1982.

Bottero, Jean. "Le message universel de la Bible." In *Verite et poesie de la bible*. Paris: Hatier, 1969, pp. 15–73.

Breasted, J. H. *A History of Egypt*. London: Hodder and Stoughton, 1909.

———. *The Dawn of Conscience*. New York: Charles Scribners' Sons, 1933.

Caspary, G. E. *Politics and Exegesis, Origen and the Two Swords*. Berkeley: University of California Press, 1979.

Chaunu, Pierre. *Histoire, science sociale: La duree, l'espace et l'homme a l'epoque moderne*. Paris: S.E.D.E.S., 1974.

———. *Le Temps des Reformes. La crise de la chretiente*. Paris: Fayard, 1975.

———. *La Memoire et le sacre*. Paris: Calmann-Levy, 1978.

Clastres, Helene. *The Land-Without-Evil: Tupi-Guarini Prophetism*. Trans. J. G. Brovender. Chicago: University of Illinois Press, 1995.

Clastres, Pierre. *Society Against the State*. Trans. R. Hurley and A. Stein. New York: Zone Books, 1987.

Congar, Y. *L'Ecclesiologie du haut Moyen Age*. Paris: Editions du Cerf, 1968.

———. *L'Eglise de Saint Augustin a l'epoque moderne*. Paris: Editions du Cerf, 1970.

Constant, Benjamin. *De la religion consideree dans sa source, ses formes et ses developpements*. Paris, 1824–31.

Corbin, Henry. *En Islam iranien*, Vol. 1, *Le shi'isme duodecimain*. Paris: Gallimard, 1971.

Creeds, Councils and Controversies: Documents Illustrating the History of the Church, AD 337–461. Ed. J. Stevenson, revised by W.H.C. Frend. London: SPCK, 1989.

Cullmann, Oscar. *Christ and Time: The Primitive Christian Conception of Time and History*. Trans. F. U. Filson. New York: Gordon Press, 1977.

————. *Christology of the New Testament*. Trans. Shirley C. Guthrie and Charles A. Hall. Westminster: John Knox, 1980. Delumeau, Jean. *Sin and Fear: The Emergence of a Western Guilt Culture*, 13th–18th Century. Trans. Eric Nicholson. New York: St. Martin's, 1990.

Du Breuil, Paul. *Zarathoustra et la transfiguration du monde*. Paris: Payot, 1978.

Duby, Georges. *The Three Orders: Feudal Society Imagined*. Chicago: University of Chicago Press, 1980.

————. "Le monachisme et l'economie rurale." In Duby, *Homme et structures du Moyen Age*. Paris: Mouton, 1973.

Dumont, Louis. *Essays on Individualism*. Chicago: University of Chicago Press, 1986.

Dvornik, F. "Pope Gelasius and Emperor Anastasius I." *Byzantinische Zeitschrift* 44 (Munich, 1951): 111–16.

————. *Early Christian and Byzantine Political Philosophy: Origins and Background*. Washington, D.C.: N.p., 1966.

Eisenstadt, Shmuel N. "The Axial Age: The Emergence of Transcendental Visions and the Rise of the Rlerics." *Archives europeennes de sociologie*, 23, no. 2 (1982): 294–314.

Fossier, Robert. *Enfance de l'Europe, X–XII siecle*, Vol. 1, *L'homme et son espace*; Vol. 2, *La revolution de l'economie*. Paris: P.U.F, 1982.

Fourquin, Guy. "Le temps de croissance." In Fourquin, *Histoire de la France rurale*, Vol. 1, *La formation des campagnes francaises des origines au XIV siecle*. Paris: Editions du Seuil, 1975.

Freud, S. *Moses and Monotheism*. Trans. K. Jones. New York: Vintage Books, 1939.

Gauchet, M. "Politique et societe: La lecon des sauvages." *Textures*, nos. 10–11 (1975): 57–86, nos. 12–13 (1975): 67–105.

————. "La dette du sens et les racines de l'Etat: Politique de la religion primitive." *Libre*, no. 2 (1977): 5–43.

————. "Des deux corps du roi au pouvoir sans corps: Christianisme et politique." *Le Debat*, nos. 14 and 15 (July–Sept. 1981).

————., and Gladys Swain. *La Pratique de l'esprit humaine*. Paris: Gallimard, 1980.

Gernet, Jacques. *China and the Christian Impact: A Conflict of Cultures*. Trans. Janet LLoyd. Cambridge: Cambridge University Press, 1986.

Jaspers, Karl. *The Origin and Goal of History*. Trans. Michael Bulock. New Haven: Yale University Press, 1953.

Kantorowicz, Ernst. *Frederick the Second*. Trans. E. O. Lorimer New York: Richard R. Smith, 1931.

————. *The King's Two Bodies: A Study in Medieval Political Theology*. Princeton: Princeton University Press, 1957.

Kaufmann, Yehezkel. *Connaitre la Bible*. French trans. Paris: P.U.F., 1970.

Ladurie, E. Le Roy. *Le Territoire de l'historien*, Vol. 2. Paris: Gallimard, 1978.

Laoust, Henri. *Les Schismes de l'Islam*. Paris: Payot, 1975.

Liebaert, J. *L'Incarnation*. Paris: Editions du Cerf, 1966.

Lizot, Jacques. "Economie primitive et subsistance: Essai sur le travail et l'alienation chez les Yanomani." *Libre*, no. 4 (1978).

Luthy, Herbert. *Le Passe present*. Monaco: Editions du Rocher, 1965.

Meek, Theophile J. *Hebrew Origins*. New York: Peter Smith, 1960.

Mercier, Roger. *La Rehabilitation de la nature humaine* (1700–1750). Villemomble: Editions "La Balance," 1960.

Mumford, Lewis. *The Myth of the Machine*. New York: Harcourt, Brace, Jovanovich, 1973.

Otto, Rudolf. *The Idea of the Holy*. London: Oxford University Press, 1923.

Poly, Jean-Pierre, and Eric Bournazel. *The Feudal Transformation*, 900–1200. Trans. Caroline Higgitt New York: Holmes and Meier, 1991.

Pomian, Krzysztof. "La crise de l'avenir." *Le Debat*, no. 7 (1980).

———. "Natura, storia, conoscenza." *Enciclopedia Einaudi*, Vol. 15. Turin: 1982.

———. *L'Ordre du temps*. Paris: Gallimard, 1984.

Raeff, Marc. *The Well-Ordered State: Social and Institutional Change Through Law in the Germanies and Russia*, 1600–1800. New Haven: Yale University Press, 1983.

Saggs, H.W.F. *The Encounter with the Divine in Mesopotamia and Israel*. London: The Athlone Press, 1978.

Sahlins, Marshall. *Stone Age Economics*. Chicago: Aldine-Atherton, 1972.

Seguy, Jean. *Christianisme et societe*. Paris: Editions du Cerf, 1980.

Southern, R. W. *Western Society and the Church in the Middle Ages*. London: Penguin, 1970.

Swain, Gladys. "L'aliene entre le medecin et la philosophie." *Perspectives psychiatriques*, 1, no. 65 (1978).

———. "D'une rupture dans l'abord de la folie." *Libre*, no. 2 (1977).

Taviani, Huguette. "Naissance d'une heresie en Italie du Nord au XIe siecle." *Annales E.S.C.*, no. 5 (1974).

———. "Le mariage dans l'heresie de l'an Mil." *Annales E.S.C.*, no. 6 (1977).

———. "Du refus au defi: Essai sur la psychologie heretique au debut du XIe siecle en Occident." *Etudes sur la sensibilite au Moyen Age*, Actes du 102E Congres national des societies savantes (1977). Paris: 1979.

Troeltsch, Ernst. *The Social Teaching of the Churches*. Westminster: John Knox, 1992.

Ullmann, W. *The Growth of Papal Government in the Middle Ages*. London: Methuen, 1955.

———. *Principles of Government and Politics in the Middle Ages*. London: Methuen, 1961.

Vernant, J.-P. *The Origins of Greek Thought*. Ithaca, N.Y.: Cornell University Press, 1982.

Weber, Max. *Ancient Judaism*. Ed. and trans. H. H. Gerth and D. Martindale. New York: The Free Press, 1952.

Index

aesthetic experience, 203
aesthetic feeling, 200
Africa, 10
African history, 106
African monarchs, 140
Age of Ideology, 176ff, n.53
agriculture, 24, 71
Alexander the Great, 106, 129
America, 4, 163, n.45
autonomous self, 172
autonomy, 64ff; of conscience, 83, 132, 135, 138; human, 64ff; inner, 137, 138; individual, 189; political, 59; spiritual, 131; terrestrial, 86, 89, 155, 159
axial age, 34, 43ff, 150

Balzac, H. de, 204
being: collective being, 12, 15, 16, 21, 27, 34, 57, 58, 90, 120, 127, 132, 165, 172ff, 185, 191, 196, 199; hierarchy of being, 150, 160, 167; unity of being, 60, 63, 108, 141; ways of being, 12, 15
being-a-self, 16, 132, 166ff, 206
being-a-subject, 102, 194, 204, 207
being-for-the-other-world, 159
being-in-the-world, 72, 87ff, 123, 129, 130, 132, 143, 158
being-in-this-world, 62, 74, 159
being-in-time, 89
belief system, 24, 51, 77, 205, n.6
Bloc, M., 140
Buddhism, 14, 75
bureaucracy, 80, 135, 157, 180ff, 191, 198

Calvin, J., 65, n.12, n.15
catharism, n.6
Catholicism, 4, 61
Chalcedon, 126, n.29
Chaunu, P., 87
child, 179ff
China, 14, 44, 48, 109, n.37
Chinese thought, n.37

Christ, 77, 78, 81, 82, 84, 118–43, 151, 153, 158, 161, 162, n.13
Christianity, 3, 4, 15, 16, 23, 34, 76–105, 114, 124, 131–36, 145–46, 150–52, 160, 162–63, 177, 201, n.6, n.13, n.32, n.36
Christology, 81, 125ff
Citeaux, 159, n.14
city, 81, 129, 147, 148ff
City-Church, 65
City-State, 4
civil society, 182, 187, 189, 192, 195, 196
Clastres, H., 111
Clastres, P., 26, n.1
Clement, A., n.45
closure, 84, 192, n.7; terrestrial, 78, 84
Cluny, 14
collective belief, 5, 200
Confucianism, 14
conquest, 14, 37, 41ff, 92, 106, 120, 129, 157
Constant, B., 102, 148
Corbin, H., n.13
council communism, 194
covenant, 109ff, 113, 116, 117, 118, 163
crowded world, 87ff, 155

Delumeau, J., 167, n.46
democracy, 4, 92, 147, 172, 174, 180, 187–89, 192–94
democratic state, 163, 181, 197
Descartes, R., 173, n.8
dispossession, 7, 12, 23ff, 33, 171, 196, 198
divine oneness, 62, 72, 74, 108, 114
domination, 14, 26, 35–37, 39ff, 70, 88, 92, 93–94, 116, 117, 126, 128, 134, 139, 141, 153, 198
dualism, n.6, n.9, n.25
duality, 47, 62, 69, 94, 105, 142, 144, 146, 198, 201, n.6, n.39; of being, 75; onto-logical, 59, 73, 109, 132; religion of, 107, 115; system of, 60
Dumont, L., 27, 131, n.31, n.33

12/04